THE CRAFT OF THINKING

LOGIC, SCIENTIFIC METHOD, AND THE PURSUIT OF TRUTH

THE CRAFT OF THINKING

LOGIC, SCIENTIFIC METHOD, AND THE PURSUIT OF TRUTH

SECOND EDITION

ANÍBAL BUENO
MOREHOUSE COLLEGE

RALPH D. ELLIS
CLARK ATLANTA UNIVERSITY

KENDALL/HUNT PUBLISHING COMPANY
4050 Westmark Drive   Dubuque, Iowa 52002

CONTENTS

ACKNOWLEDGMENTS

The authors wish to express their sincere thanks for the significant help and support they received in the production of this revision of *The Craft of Thinking*. Lynda Ellis produced our cover design. Towanda Esquilin provided typing and other secretarial support. Nick Georgalis, Randy Auxier, and Barry Hallen offered helpful comments on early drafts of the text. Norman Fisher provided a number of exercises and suggestions on the revision of the text. And Lana Bueno helped with final text preparation.

PREFACE FOR TEACHERS

Work on this text began in 1980 at Morehouse College. Both authors felt the need for a more rapid and effective way to introduce students to the basic techniques of formal logic without getting them too bogged down in the cumbersome, calculus-like technicalities in many introductory philosophy and critical thinking texts of the past twenty-five years. We have used these materials in the classroom, continually revising and expanding the teaching strategies based on student performance.

This text seeks a compromise between two opposing trends in the teaching of critical thinking. At one extreme are the more traditional, formal logic methods, such as the standard text by Copi, *Logic* (first printed in 1953).[1] The advantage of this approach is that it develops precision in deductive reasoning, so that, at least in principle, after mastering the techniques, students can evaluate the validity or invalidity of arguments. This is an important goal. Students insecure in their ability to determine validity in arguments also feel insecure in their ability to evaluate others' reasoning. Consequently, they shy away from intellectual controversy, remain susceptible to authoritarian manipulation of their beliefs in all domains, and lack creativity and competence in problem solving. Learning the traditional methods of formal logic can go a long way toward alleviating this problem, but only if the student masters the complicated techniques. Although math, philosophy, and some natural science majors may do well in courses based on these techniques, others flounder and become utterly lost.

At the other extreme are more recent attempts to avoid formal techniques altogether, or to give them lip service without requiring students to actually solve deductive problems using the techniques. Within this second category are numerous texts. Some try to help students with personal psychological problems; others advise students on how to use "case study" methods developed by education specialists; and still others encourage students to articulate the assumptions they make in forming opinions, without teaching any precise way to determine confidently whether a given argument is deductively valid. Students in these courses fail to achieve the confidence to evaluate the validity of an argument—a skill needed in any intellectual forum, and crucial for becoming a creative and accurate problem solver.

---

[1] Irving Copi, *Introduction to Logic,* 9th ed. (New York: MacMillan, 1982).

The present text incorporates the advantages without the disadvantages of both approaches. Our teaching experience with the materials convinces us that we have accomplished this goal, not merely by changing the way the materials are packaged and presented, but by developing new content. We have developed ways of streamlining formal logical techniques to achieve a system that requires minimum technical apparatus but retains the precision of the more complicated systems. In some cases, this has required developing simpler notations. In other cases, it has required developing ways of communicating the techniques to students without using many of the traditional, even archaic, technical terms of formal logic, such as "figure," "mood," "fallacy of the undistributed middle," and so forth.

In some instances, we have empirically validated the improvement in our students' performances. In the summer of 1987, one of the authors used a UNCF summer grant to develop a new method of teaching logical fallacies. The strategy was based on the observation that students grasp an abstract concept best when the concept is expressed in behavioral terms, i.e., in such a way as to state what the student can *do* with the principle. For example, the principle of *modus tollens* tells us that we can negate both terms and reverse their order; the fallacy of denying the antecedent tells us that we should not merely negate the two terms. After applying this technique the following semester, the seventy students' grades on the test on fallacies averaged fifteen points higher than the sixty-five students who were taught using the more traditional method the previous semester.

Several other advantages of our approach are not reflected in most recent textbooks. One major service to students is the extensive treatment of scientific reasoning in Chapters 8 and 9. Of the numerous logic and critical thinking texts available, few if any provide more than a cursory treatment of this topic. The reason is to be found probably in the traditional contrast in the agendas of two separate courses: Logic, which deals with deductive reasoning techniques thoroughly; and Philosophy of Science, which deals with inductive and scientific reasoning. The problem of separating these topics into separate courses is that students who are not philosophy majors—including math, natural science, and social science majors—seldom take more than one of them. Consequently, science majors are deprived of basic training in scientific reasoning, one of the main benefits they would expect from a critical thinking course. Moreover, in an age of increasing technology, when more and more social and political issues revolve around the assessment of cause and effect relationships, it is no longer acceptable for students not to be familiar with the basic uses and typical abuses of scientific reasoning.

For analogous reasons, we have included "Thinking Logically about Value Issues" in Chapter 7. Critical thinking texts seldom include such a unit, and when they do, they do not show how precise deductive reasoning can actually be used to evaluate the reasoning behind philosophical value assumptions; instead, they merely take philosophical positions as unquestioned premises, and discuss the ways that concrete, real life conclusions could be reached from those premises—if they were to be accepted in the first place. The problem with such an approach is that students cannot evaluate the premises themselves, which is by far the most important challenge of thinking logically about value issues. For example, what reasons are there for preferring a theory of distributive justice over a utilitarian theory as a premise for making political decisions? Our text provides tools and techniques for addressing these kinds of questions.

This text develops a system of syllogistic logic dealing with combinations of universal and nonuniversal statements that makes it continuous with *sentential* logic (which treats only universal statements). In this way, both types of logic are combined into one system, so that both can be learned easily and quickly. Most introductory logic courses cover only sentential logic, leaving syllogistic logic for a separate and more advanced course, which covers the most advanced contemporary way of treating syllogistic logic, or "predicate logic," as developed by Frege.[2] Thus, without taking the more advanced course, students still cannot handle such a simple example as 'No snakes are flying creatures; some flying creatures are mammals; therefore, some mammals are not snakes.' The way we handle this problem is to introduce a few simple syllogistic principles that can be *added on* to what the students already know about sentential logic, resulting in a short Chapter 5 on the logic of syllogisms.[3]

Teachers should be aware that we have defined the relation of '*implication*' more broadly than most texts to combine both sentential and syllogistic logic into one system. We define the relationship of implication as including three types of situations: we say that '**p** implies **q**' whenever one of the following relationships obtains:

1. If **p** then **q**   (where **p** and **q** are propositions)
2. All **p**'s are **q**'s   (where **p** and **q** designate properties)
3. **p** is a **q**   (where **p** is an individual and **q** designates a property)

Some systems of logic do not define the second and third types of relationships as implications, but instead deal with them by means of a completely separate system of syllogistic logic. We define all three types of relationships as implications to simplify and clarify logical analysis, without sacrifice of precision or problem-solving power. Logic texts usually treat implication as obtaining only when one *proposition* implies another *proposition*. But sometimes it is useful to think of a term *within* a proposition as implying another term within that proposition. For example, we can think of the statement 'All Spelman students are women,' as asserting that the property of 'being a Spelman student' *implies* the property of 'being a woman.' That is, *if* someone is a Spelman student, *then* that person is a woman. Because of the 'if-then' relationship here, we can think of this statement as expressing an implication. Similarly, with 'Mary is a Spelman student,' it is convenient to think of the statement as expressing an implication, because it asserts that the property of 'being Mary' implies the

---

[2]Peter Geach and Max Black, eds., *Translations from the Philosophical Writings of Gottlob Frege* (Cambridge: Cambridge University Press, 1952).

[3]The method of syllogistic logic we are using is similar to the "term logic" developed by Fred Sommers in *The Logic of Natural Language* (Oxford University Press, 1982).

property of 'being a Spelman student.' That is, *if* someone is Mary, *then* that person is a Spelman student. Or, if we know that the individual who stole a briefcase is a Spelman student, we can let **p** stand for 'the individual who stole the briefcase,' and **q** for 'Spelman student,' and thus write this statement simply as '**p** → **q.**' The advantages of defining implication in this broadened way will become increasingly obvious as we proceed.

No text should neglect the importance of using examples whose content is *interesting* to most students. For example, Chapter 9, "The Use and Abuse of Scientific Reasoning," focuses heavily on scientific issues that are interconnected with sociopolitical controversies, such as cause and effect theories about poverty, crime, Third World development, and other social problems. This pragmatic focus motivates students from a variety of backgrounds to be interested in logic, and to learn it more readily.

The explanations in the text make every effort to be simple, concise, and easily understandable. Teachers should be able to spend a minimum of classroom time explaining principles and techniques, and more time applying and illustrating them with actual examples.

INTRODUCTION

Human beings as a species possess one main advantage for survival—our ability to think. Other animal species are much faster or stronger than we are, and most have more discriminating senses. Humans survive by means of adaptability, complex processing of information, careful, long-range planning, and the ability to critically question our hypotheses about the realities facing us. One of the most important applications of these skills is in the development of strategies for socially cooperative activity in solving the problems we confront. As social, political, and technological realities become more complicated, the ability to think logically, critically, and independently becomes increasingly important.

It is crucial to distinguish between critical thinking, which is an active, questioning process, and the mere accumulation of information. Unfortunately, the more our educational systems emphasize the assimilation of ever-mounting masses of accumulated information, the less time is left for students to develop the critical, questioning functions necessary for logical analysis.

In recent years neuroscientists have become increasingly aware of the severe limitations of the learning that takes place through the passive absorbing of information. The brain is structured to operate by means of active searching for information and understanding, not passive absorption. We now realize that the human frontal lobe, whose comparatively huge size distinguishes our brains from those of other animals, is designed to facilitate formulating questions about the array of information with which we are presented—the focusing of attention, questioning of logical validity, and forming of hypotheses.[1] Moreover, because of the electro-chemical pathways in the brain, the entire cortex, with all its thinking and memory functions, works more efficiently when activated by this questioning activity of the frontal lobe.

The "Learning to Learn" program, developed at the Harvard School of Education, used this new knowledge about the active, question-directed nature of the brain to help improve students' grades.[2] The main strategy was a very simple one: In the margin next to each paragraph

---

[1]For further discussion of this aspect of brain functioning, see Alexander Luria, *Higher Cortical Functions in Man* (New York: Basic Books, 1980); Michael Posner and Mary Rothbart, "Attentional mechanisms and conscious experience," in A. D. Milner and M. D. Rugg, eds., *The Neuropsychology of Consciousness* (London: Academic Press, 1992); Antonio Damasio, *Descartes' Error* (New York: Putnam, 1994); Ralph Ellis, *Questioning Consciousness* (Amsterdam: John Benjamins, 1995); Natika Newton, *Foundations of Understanding* (Amsterdam: John Benjamins, 1996).

[2]Joshua Slomianko, "Learning to Learn," seminar presented at Atlanta University, August 1987.

in a textbook, the student is asked to write the question to which the information contained in that paragraph could constitute a possible answer. Within one semester, the grade point average of these students increased by an average of 1.5 on a 4.0 scale—a much greater increase than among students using other tutoring methods. And the improvement was just as dramatic in courses involving rote memorization as for those that stressed critical thinking.

Why would such a simple method work so well? Because students had to adopt an actively questioning frame of mind rather than a passive, receptive one. And we now know from the neurological work mentioned above that the frontal cortex is active when we ask ourselves a question—especially when we formulate a question for ourselves (as opposed to merely responding to someone else's questions); this is when the frontal cortex increases its level of electrical and chemical activity. And when the frontal lobe is activated, the rest of the brain quickly follows suit. We remember information more effectively when we ask ourselves questions about it during the learning process, and this formulation of questions is a primary aspect of making sense out of the information. The Harvard experiment dramatically emphasizes the usefulness of developing habits of critical thinking and questioning in any learning process.

Can logical ability be developed and improved, or are we simply stuck with the luck of a hereditary draw that determines our IQ? Increasing evidence suggests that intellectual skills are not just hereditary, but that we can develop them. In fact, it has now been demonstrated empirically that a course in logic or critical thinking, if it emphasizes the kinds of formal logical analysis covered in this textbook, dramatically increases a student's IQ. David and Linda Annis[3] have documented that a logic course structured in this way increased their students' IQ scores by an average of ten points (after compensating for the normal test-retest increase, which is about one to two points). To appreciate what a dramatic increase this represents, consider that, on most measures of IQ, the average college student falls within the upper 15 percent of the population. After the improvement reported by Annis and Annis, this same average student would fall within the upper 4 percent.

Still other empirical studies have shown that, by practicing our logical thinking skills, we improve the functioning of our brains. Kretch and his associates[4] have found that rats that participate in learning experiments throughout their lifetimes, and therefore must use their brains to actively solve problems, show alteration not only in the structure, but also in the chemical composition of their brains. Dissecting the brains of the rats at death, Kretch finds that they contain significantly more acetylcholine and a larger number of glial cells—factors known to be associated with enhanced learning and problem solving. Kretch also finds a significant increase in the sheer *mass* of the brains of the rats that must use their brains to solve problems.

The method used in this book is similar to the one Annis and Annis used. The backbone of the strategy is to begin by consciously reflecting on the inference rules that we rely on in everyday reasoning; to abstract the patterns we normally follow so as to formulate rules of inference; to make sure that invalid rules are not followed (by considering examples that show

---

[3]"Does Philosophy Improve Critical Thinking?" *Teaching Philosophy*, 3, 1979, 2ff.

[4]David Kretch, Mark Rosenzweig and Edward Bennett, "Effects of Environmental Complexity and Training on Brain Chemistry," *Journal of Comparative and Physiological Psychology* 53, 1966, 509–519.

that these invalid patterns of logic cannot be trusted to guarantee true conclusions from true premises); and then to consciously apply the rules to various examples to increase our skill at making reliably valid inferences.

In this way, we develop confidence in relying on certain rules of inference. We then feel confident enough of our own logical thinking that, when someone else's logic seems wrong to us, we can compare their arguments to the patterns of reasoning we have learned to rely on; if the other person's logic is found wanting by these criteria, we can then feel sure that it is the other person's logic that is faulty, not our own. Only by developing a reliable set of criteria for correct reasoning can we feel confident enough to evaluate arguments by applying those criteria, even in situations that may be unfamiliar to us or emotionally charged.

Many important questions in life depend more on the use of logical reasoning than on any other kind of knowledge. For this reason, logic is considered to be a branch of philosophy, whose purpose is to address questions that cannot be answered by means of empirical knowledge, that is, knowledge based on physical observation. Fields of empirical knowledge, such as physics, chemistry, and psychology, have become so important in modern cultures that we tend to forget that not all knowledge *is* empirical.

It is fairly obvious that many things are learned empirically, beginning with sense perception. Through the senses we become aware of the existence and qualities of individual things. We can also generalize from the characteristics of individual perceptions and build general knowledge based on our experience as well as that of others. In this way, we learn that crows are black, that canaries sing, that water quenches our thirst, and a host of other things. More complex than these generalizations is our theoretical scientific knowledge, such as Newton's gravitational theory, or the quantum theory. Scientific knowledge is derived from experience with the help of theoretical constructions called models or theories. We shall discuss the kind of reasoning involved in developing reliable scientific models and theories later in this book. The relationship of scientific knowledge to individual perceptions is no simple matter, but we know that the main function and importance of this kind of knowledge is directly related to the fact that it can be used to predict and often control events.

Empirical knowledge, then, is based on sense experience. My knowledge of the existence of the color yellow is a bit of empirical knowledge based on sense perception. My knowledge that canaries are yellow follows as an empirical generalization.

But certain kinds of knowledge are acquired by examining concepts in the mind. We learn, for example, that two things equal to a third are equal to each other by examining in our minds what is involved in the idea of equality. To acquire that bit of knowledge, we do not need to make a large number of observations, or to experiment; we need to understand the meaning of "equality." That two things equal to a third must be equal to each other seems to follow from the very nature of the idea of equality. Further, once we have seen this, we know that this statement applies to any objects whatsoever; there can be no exceptions.

Examples of the kind of knowledge acquired by analyzing ideas are:

"237 + 2 = 239."

"A whole is greater than any of its parts."

"If the definition of a term in a proposition is substituted in place of the term, the meaning of the proposition will be preserved."

"Let **a**, **b**, and **c** be three whole numbers: If **a** is greater than **b**, and **b** is greater than **c**, then **a** is greater than **c**."

These propositions are seen to be true simply by examining in one's mind the relationship between the concepts used in them. Knowledge of this type is not empirical. In philosophy, any knowledge acquired through the analysis of concepts in the mind is called "*a priori*" or "conceptual" knowledge.

A priori knowledge has two main advantages that enable us to rely on it with a great deal of certainty. The first is *necessity*. If we grasp the concept of equality, we know that two things equal to a third *must* be equal to each other, no matter what particular things we may be considering. This is not something that happens to be true of some objects. It is a universal and necessary truth about equality. *We cannot conceive of it being otherwise.* This characteristic of *a priori* propositions, that it is absurd or contradictory to think that they might be otherwise, is called *necessity*. *A priori* truths are *necessarily* true, not just frequently or in a number of observed specific cases.

The second characteristic of conceptual knowledge is *universality*. A conceptual proposition applies to all relevant cases without exception because conceptual truths are based not on particular examples, but on general concepts. We know that the above statement about equality applies to any objects whatsoever. Any two objects that are equal to a third must be equal to each other. There can be no exception, because this truth follows from the very concept of equality. An exception would be absurd. This quality of *a priori* propositions—that they apply to all cases without exception—is called *universality*.

It is important to notice that empirical knowledge does not have these two properties. For example, we know from overwhelming empirical evidence that crows are black and that cats meow. However, exceptions to these generalizations are not at all absurd or contradictory. It is possible that a white crow may exist. We cannot say that it is impossible. Empirical knowledge is not necessary or universal. Exceptions are always possible.

Logic and mathematics are *a priori* sciences. They study relationships between concepts, not aspects of empirically observable nature, as the natural sciences do. That is why the propositions of logic and mathematics have necessity and universality. We shall see in the next several chapters that the basic principles of logical reasoning can be discovered by examining the meaning of concepts such as implication, negation, and validity. For this reason, principles of logic can be relied upon as absolutely trustworthy instruments, and we can use them with utmost self-confidence as criteria for evaluating the logical validity of inferences and arguments.

In brief, conceptual knowledge provides knowledge of certain necessary relations between concepts. By means of conceptual knowledge we can learn that certain structures are not possible in the world. We also learn that certain structures necessarily imply the existence of other structures. But conceptual knowledge does not give us knowledge of *actual things*. Conceptual knowledge can be used to yield knowledge of actual things when it is supplemented by empirical knowledge. For example, we can prove that the area of a rectangle is given by the product of its two sides. This is conceptual knowledge. It is necessary and universal, but it does not of itself give us any particular knowledge about empirical reality. However, if I happen to be dealing with floor tiles, I can use that formula to find out the area of a tile. I have, on the one hand, the conceptual knowledge that the area of *any* rectangle is given by the formula just mentioned. On the other hand, I have the empirical knowledge that I am dealing with a tile that is approximately rectangular in shape, and that its sides measure 10 and 12 inches. Putting together the conceptual and the empirical knowledge that I have, I can figure out that the area of my tile is 10 X 12 = 120 square inches. *The combination of the two kinds of knowledge* produces the concrete knowledge of the area of the tile I am dealing with.

This book deals with the most basic principles of conceptual knowledge—the principles used in making logical inferences in all kinds of contexts. Our assumption is that, by becoming clear and precise in understanding these principles, we can develop them into reliable criteria for evaluating reasoning and confidently deducing our own conclusions from the information given. Only by being clear and precise in our understanding of the way these principles work can we feel confident enough to use them as criteria in evaluating the reasoning of others, and in drawing creative inferences from given information, even when these inferences lead us into uncharted territory.

CHAPTER 1

Fundamental Concepts

I. The Uses of Language

Human languages are extremely complex and marvelously efficient tools that perform many different functions. It is the purpose of this chapter to examine the most important ones. Let us begin by examining the usual type of situation in which people communicate through language. It is very simple. Person *A* has something that he wishes to communicate to another, *B*. *A* makes an utterance, and *B* hears it and understands it. We see then, that the use of language in communication normally involves a situation in which there are four different elements: the *speaker* or *addresser*, the *hearer* or *addressee*, the *utterance itself* (a series of sounds), and the *subject-matter* or *referent* of the utterance. (i.e., the meaning it conveys).

Let us now introduce a useful technical term. Any utterance that is capable of communicating a complete meaning we shall call a *verbal message*. We are now prepared to begin our analysis. If we examine how verbal messages relate to the four elements in the act of communication, we shall be able to discern four different functions that language can perform.

1. The Informative Function

There are verbal messages that make an assertion about a subject matter. In everyday language they are called statements or assertions; they convey something that can be either true or false. Messages of this kind are said to perform the informative or referential function of language. This is the function of language through which we express and communicate beliefs. The essential characteristic of informative messages is that they are capable of being true or false. Thus, the message "The book is on the table" performs the informative function, because it is capable of being true or false. In contrast, the messages

1.   Ouch!
2.   Please, close the door.
and
3.   What time is it?

are neither true or false. It simply does not make any sense to ask whether they are true or false. This distinction does not apply to them. They do not perform the informative function; they perform other functions we shall presently consider.

2.   The Expressive Function

There are messages that reveal feelings of the addresser. A person who says "Ouch!" or "Hurrah!" conveys a feeling. These expressions, however, are not statements. They do not make assertions capable of being true or false. Messages that convey feelings and attitudes of the addresser are said to perform the *expressive function*.

An expressive message may be said to act as a symptom. A person who says "Wow!" expresses an attitude of admiration or perhaps a feeling of excitement. Saying "Wow!" is one of the things English-speaking people usually do when they feel admiration or excitement. We can say that the message "Wow!" is a symptom of the presence of such feelings. It is an *expression* of them, rather than a *statement* about them. The expressive function is found in its purest form in interjections. Purely expressive messages do not make assertions; hence they are neither true nor false.

The expressive and the informative functions are often found together in one and the same message. Frequently expressive meaning is added to an informative message by means of features of speech such as emphasis, changes of intonation, distortion of sounds, etc. The following examples are both informative and expressive.

1.   I have a TERRIBLE headache. (The word "terrible" is emphasized by making it louder).
2.   There was a hu-u-u-u-ge crowd in the park yesterday. (The u-sound is lengthened to make the sentence expressive.)

3.   The Directive Function

There are messages whose meaning is not related to a subject-matter or to the feelings of the addresser, but to the addressee. They have the purpose of influencing the addressee's behavior. Consider, for example, the message "Please, close the door." It is clearly not informative, because it is not capable of being true or false. Nor is it expressive. It is a command. It has the purpose of causing the addressee to perform a certain action. *Messages that attempt to influence the addressee's behavior are said to perform the directive function.* This function is found in its purest form in commands. Many languages have special verb forms that are used to convey the directive function (the imperative mood). Questions also perform the directive function. A question is a request for an answer, hence an attempt to influence the addressee's behavior.

The directive function is frequently found combined with one or both of the preceding functions in one single message. Consider, for example, the following statement, made by a mother to her unruly six-year old son:

The neighbors' children are so well-behaved.

The statement is informative. It is also expressive, because it conveys admiration. Moreover, it contains a directive component, for the neighbors' children are being held up as an example to imitate.

4.   The Aesthetic or Poetic Function

The message itself is one of the components of the act of verbal communication. The message is a physical event, a succession of sounds. Often we encounter messages whose meaning is partially conveyed by their sound-structure. Consider the following pairs of expressions.

1.	plain Jane	plain Susan
2.	silly Sally	silly Elizabeth
3.	horrible Harry	horrible David
4.	Haste makes waste	Hurrying causes waste.
5.	Waste not, want not.	If you don't waste, you will not want.

There is something about the expressions on the left that makes them quite different from those on the right. The former have a certain "expressiveness"; they are considered "witty" or "clever." The latter are, so to speak, "flat" or neutral. "Silly Sally" might be used to make fun of a girl named Sally. But, "Silly Elizabeth" would not have the same effect if it were used to make fun of a girl named Elizabeth. The latter expression is not "witty." "Haste makes waste" is an often-repeated proverb. "Hurrying causes waste," although it conveys the same idea, does not have the same expressive force.

The reason for the particular expressive force of the first group of phrases is not hard to find. They all contain particularly striking sound-patterns. The words "plain" and "Jane" rhyme. The words "silly" and "Sally" have exactly the same sounds, except for the first vowel. Likewise, "horrible" and "Harry" have very similar sound patterns. "Haste makes waste" contains a striking pattern of three stressed syllables. The first and the fourth rhyme (they both end in /aste/). The second shares with the other two the vowels and the /s/ sound. "Waste not, want not" has a strong sound parallelism between its two parts.

These expressions contain a peculiar kind of meaning. The words seem to enact or dramatize the meaning they convey. In our first example, the resemblance between the words "plain" and "Jane" seems to "rub off" on the things the words refer to. It is as if the hearer were tempted by the words to engage in a sort of bastard reasoning, and said to himself: "Since the words are sort of the same, then being Jane and being plain are sort of the same too." The other examples produce similar effects. We shall call this peculiar form of a meaning *enacted meaning*.

Let us consider another example, this time in a foreign language. There is a well-known Italian proverb about translators: "Traduttore, traditore." It means literally "Translator, traitor." Even if you don't know Italian, as soon as you learn the meaning of the two words you realize the meaning of the proverb. The strong resemblance between the two words suggests a meaning that can be rendered into words roughly as follows: "A translator, by the very nature of what he does, is a traitor. Translating something means betraying or distorting it." All this, or something like this, is compactly expressed by the resemblance. But the rather long verbal translation we have given of that enacted meaning does not have the force, brevity, and directness of the original expression. It is no doubt because of this concentrated enacted meaning that the expression has become a proverbial saying in Italian. The idea of the inadequacy of translation is embedded in the structure of the expression in a way that is more forceful and direct than any paraphrase can be. The meaning is powerfully conveyed, although the proverb is not a statement. It does not have a verb; it consists of two nouns separated by a pause. It should also be noticed that, since the English equivalents of the Italian words do not have the same kind of resemblance, the English translation of the proverb is "flat"; it does not have enacted meaning.

Many of the devices through which enacted meaning can be created by sound-patterns are studied in rhetoric and literary criticism and have traditional names. The main ones are *rhyme, assonance, alliteration* and *rhythm. These figures of speech create enacted meaning through relationships of similarity and contrast between sound-patterns.* We shall call them *phonological figures of speech* (i.e., figures of speech that depend on sound). Enacted meaning can also be created through juxtaposition and comparison of ideas. Let us consider the following expressions:

1. Oh, my love's like a red, red rose, that's newly sprung in June (Robert Burns)

2. My son is a chip off the old block.

3. Loyalty is the flame of the lamp of friendship.

4. He is a snake in the grass.

5. Love is a sickness full of woes

    All remedies refusing;

    A plant that with most cutting grows,

    Most barren with most using

    Why so?

    More we enjoy, more it dies;

    If not enjoyed, it sighing cries

    Hey ho.

    (Samuel Daniel, Hymen's Triumph, I, V)

6. A stitch in time saves nine.

7. Too many cooks spoil the broth.

8. All that glitters is not gold.

9. Only still waters reflect the stars. (Chinese proverb)

10. Back to the farm! Green meadows, the smell of flowers, warm fresh milk, roosters crowing at sunrise. . . .

In example (1), the meaning is conveyed by an explicit comparison. Comparisons are a common way of creating vivid, concrete meanings. In literary criticism comparisons are traditionally called similes.

In example (3), the meaning is conveyed by equating loyalty to a flame. A sort of proportion is set forth: Loyalty is to friendship as a flame burning in a lamp is to the lamp. There is no explicit comparison here. Loyalty is said to be a flame. What we have is an implicit comparison. It is a familiar literary device—*a metaphor*. A metaphor may be defined as a figure of speech in which an object is likened to another by speaking of it as if it were that other. Examples (2) and (4) are also metaphors. Example (5) describes love by means of a series of metaphors. The well-known proverb "A stitch in time saves nine" conveys enacted meaning in yet another way. It is neither a simile nor a metaphor. There is no comparison of two dissimilar things, either explicit or implied. But we know that the proverb is not a statement about the art of sewing. It really refers to any situation in which timely, disciplined work is needed. The statement about the timely stitching becomes a *symbol* of a great many situations that are similar to it. A symbol (in this sense) is simply an object that, in a given context, stands for many different things, and thus sums up many ideas and feelings.

Example (7) also functions as a symbol. It is not about cooks and broth. It refers to any situation in which many people try to give orders. Example (8) is also a symbol. It warns us against things that are superficially attractive (things that "glitter"), but are not valuable (they are not "gold"). The Chinese proverb in example (9) also functions symbolically; it is left for the reader to interpret as an exercise.

Example (10) evokes the experience of farm life by suggesting visual pictures and other sensations that are characteristic of it. Such sensory pictures are usually called *images.*

The most common devices through which enacted meaning is created *by juxtaposition of ideas* are the simile, the metaphor, the image, and the symbol. We shall call the figures of speech that depend on the juxtaposition and comparison of ideas the *semantic figures of speech.*

Let us summarize. We have seen that enacted meaning can be created by similarity and contrast between sound-patterns and by the juxtaposition and comparison of ideas. A fundamental characteristic of enacted meaning is that *it arises from the form of the message itself.* If we attempt to express a given message with different words, its enacted meaning is usually diluted or destroyed. Furthermore, discourse that contains enacted meanings is usually rich and suggestive. It often conveys several levels of meaning. We shall call this characteristic *compactness.* Because of this compactness, discourse that is rich in enacted meaning can express human experiences in their full concreteness and complexity. It is the kind of discourse most adequate to convey concrete experiences and can for this reason be moving and persuasive. Enacted meaning constitutes the *aesthetic* or *poetic* function of language.

Messages that function aesthetically are very common. *The aesthetic function is found whenever the sound-structure of a message contributes an important part of the meaning, or when part of the meaning is conveyed by juxtaposition and comparison of ideas.* The existence of aesthetic meaning in a particular message can usually be recognized by the fact that, if the message is expressed in different words, an important part of the meaning is lost. Verbal messages that function at least partially aesthetically are extremely common. They can be found in witticisms, puns, jokes, proverbs, advertising jingles, slogans, mottoes, aphorisms, and of course, in poetry and other works of literature. Also, the aesthetic function pervades discourse whose function is to persuade or to influence beliefs, as in court proceedings, sermons, ceremonial statements, political advocacy speeches, etc. We shall conclude this chapter with a summary of the functions of language in the form of a table.

THE FUNCTIONS OF LANGUAGE

The Informative Function

The message makes an assertion about a subject-matter.
The message is capable of being true or false.

The Expressive Function

The message conveys feelings or attitudes of the addresser.
The message is not capable of being true or false.
Interjections are the purest kind of expressive messages.

The Directive Function

The message attempts to influence the behavior of the addressee.
Directive messages are neither true nor false.
The purest form of directive message is the command.

The Aesthetic or Poetic Function

The message contains enacted meaning.

Enacted meaning is conveyed by similarity and contrast relations between sound-patterns (phonological figures of speech), or by juxtaposition and comparison of ideas (semantical figures of speech).

The enacted meaning of aesthetic messages tends to be destroyed by translation into other words. Enacted meaning tends to be rich, suggestive, and compact. Thus, it can adequately express human experiences in their full concreteness, complexity, and depth. Typical forms are puns, jokes, proverbs, mottoes, aphorisms, jingles, slogans, poetry, and all speech whose aim is to convey concrete experiences.

Enacted meaning arises from a creative use of language.

II. Reasoning

1. The Nature of Reasoning

Logic is the branch of philosophy that deals with the principles of correct reasoning. As a first rough approximation, we may describe reasoning, or making an inference, as a process through which a person obtains new knowledge from old knowledge. Let us consider some examples.

(1)   Mr. Smith is either at home or at the office.
      Mr. Smith is not at home.
      Therefore, Mr. Smith is at the office.

(2)   There is a party tonight.
      I have an exam tomorrow.
      If I go to the party tonight, I will not be able to study for the exam.
      If I do not study for the exam, I will flunk it.
      I will not flunk the exam.
      Hence, I cannot go to the party tonight.

(3)   If the weather is good, Mary will go to the concert.
      The weather is good.
      Therefore, Mary will go to the concert.

(4)   Out of 300 people polled in Chicago, 288 (96 percent) reported that they drink coffee with their breakfast. Hence, we can infer that approximately 96 percent of the people in Chicago drink coffee with their breakfast.

(5)   Most canaries sing.
      So, the canary I just bought will probably sing.

(6)   This car has about the same weight and power as mine.
      Hence, it probably gets about the same mileage as mine.

(7)   All men are mammals.
      All mammals are animals.
      Therefore, all men are animals.

(8)   All thrushes are birds.
      All birds are vertebrates.
      Therefore, all thrushes are vertebrates.

All the above examples have a common pattern. One or more statements that are assumed to be true are used as evidence to obtain a new statement. In logic, the statements that constitute the evidence are called *premises*. The new statement is termed the *conclusion,* while the process of inferring the conclusion from the premises is called an *argument.*

Statements are utterances that make an assertion about a subject matter. Their essential characteristic is that they are capable of being true or false. In logic, statements are called *propositions*. A proposition is defined as an utterance that is capable of being true or false. This definition, furthermore, implies that exclamations, commands, and questions are not propositions.

An utterance is a proposition if it is capable of being true or false. It is irrelevant whether we actually know it to be true or false. Thus, the statement 'There are living beings on Jupiter'[1] is a proposition because it is capable of being true or false, although we do not know at present which.

One more clarification is necessary. A proposition is the *meaning* of a verbal message, not its sound or its graphic pattern. Thus, the English sentence, 'Two plus two equals four,' and the statement '2 + 2 = 4,' written in arithmetic language, both convey one and the same proposition, although they are expressed in two different symbolic systems. Likewise, the English sentence, 'The book is on the table,' and the German sentence with the same meaning, '*Das Buch liegt auf dem Tisch*' both express the same proposition.

To summarize: Reasoning consists in constructing *arguments*. An argument or inference is a process through which one or more propositions, believed or assumed to be true (the *premises* of the argument) are used as evidence to show that a new proposition (called the *conclusion*) is also true, or at least probable.

2.   Deductive and Inductive Arguments

The most fundamental distinction in logic is that between deductive and inductive arguments. All arguments by their very nature make the implied claim that they give evidence for the truth of the conclusion. But some arguments claim that their evidence *conclusively* establishes the truth of the conclusion. Examples (1), (2), (3), (7), and (8) above are of this type. They make the claim that the conclusion is conclusively established by the premises: If the premises are true, then the conclusion is *definitely* true. In contrast, arguments (4), (5), and (6) claim only a degree of probability for the conclusion.

Arguments which claim that *the premises constitute conclusive evidence for the conclusion* are called *deductive* or *necessary.* This claim is usually indicated by the word 'therefore.' Often it is also expressed by saying that *the conclusion follows logically from the premises.*

If, in a given argument, the conclusion is established beyond doubt by the premises, the argument is said to be *valid.* If the claim that the conclusion follows logically from the premises is incorrect, the argument is termed *invalid.* Arguments (1) and (3) above are valid as shown by

---

[1]In standard American philosophical usage, and especially in logic, single quotation marks are generally used to highlight the *meaning of a proposition or concept,* whereas double quotation marks are used to indicate that the material quoted is taken from *what some specific person or document actually said.* For example, a philosopher might refer to the concept 'inalienable rights' (indicated with single quotation marks) in discussing theoretical questions about the concept of 'rights,' and then might state that the Declaration of Independence refers to certain "inalienable rights" (using double quotation marks to indicate that this phrase is a direct quotation from a passage in the document). In logic, by contrast to other disciplines, single rather than double quotation marks are often used in referring to concepts or symbols that occur in statements or arguments.

a simple analysis of each. The first premise of (1) states that there are two possibilities: either Mr. Smith is at home, or at the office. But the second premise eliminates the first possibility. Thus, only the second is left. Hence, if the two premises are true, the conclusion must also be true, and the argument is therefore valid. The first premise of (3) states that good weather is enough to get Mary to go to the concert. The second premise asserts that there is good weather, thus it follows that Mary will go to the concert. Again, the argument is valid.

It is important to note that *validity is not a matter of degree.* Either the conclusion of an argument follows from the premises, or it does not. If an argument is valid, then nothing can be done or need be done to improve it. There is no such thing as a more or less valid argument.

Inductive arguments are very different from deductive ones. Arguments that claim that the premises constitute only *probable* evidence for the conclusion are called *inductive* or *probable.* In these arguments, the conclusion does *not* follow deductively from the premises. Hence, it is possible for the premises to be true and the conclusion to be false. All that is claimed for the conclusion is a certain degree of probability.

In inductive arguments, there is an evidentiary leap from the premises to the conclusion. Therefore, the conclusion may be said to be a more or less well-founded guess based on the evidence of the premises.

Inductive arguments are classified as more or less weak or strong. Various degrees of strength or weakness are possible. Hence, *the concept of validity does not apply to inductive arguments.*

Many factors may influence the strength of an inductive argument. One such factor is the size of the sample used. Argument (4), for instance, would be stronger if the number of people polled had been three thousand instead of three hundred, and even stronger had the number been one million. Another factor is what is called the 'fairness' of the sample. If the people polled in argument (4) all belonged to one single ethnic group or lived in one neighborhood, the argument would be weaker than it would be if the polling had been done with individuals of different ethnic groups and from different sections of the city.

In arguments based on analogy, the degree of similarity between the object about which we already have knowledge and the object to which that knowledge is analogically extended in the conclusion is an important factor. Consider the following argument: "The human mind is very similar to a precision instrument. Precision instruments are very delicate and tend to break down very easily. Therefore, the human mind tends to break down easily." This argument is weak because the analogy is vague: In what sense is the human mind similar to a precision instrument? In contrast, argument (6) above presents a fairly good analogy because the weight and the horsepower of a car are factors known to affect gas consumption.

An informed, adequate evaluation of inductive arguments involves the study of scientific method. The branch of logic that studies inductive arguments is called *inductive logic* or *philosophy of the scientific method.* The study of *deductive* arguments is the subject matter of deductive or *formal logic,* and this is our concern in the first part of this book. In later chapters, we shall return to the subject of inductive logic and scientific method.

3. Old Definitions of Deductive and Inductive Arguments Are Inadequate

Certain old and familiar, but now discredited, definitions of deductive and inductive arguments state that deductive arguments start with general premises and lead to a particular conclusion, and that inductive arguments start with particular premises and lead to a general conclusion. (Or, in brief, deductive arguments "go" from the general to the particular and inductive arguments "go" from the particular to the general.) These definitions have considerable merit, but have been shown to be inadequate, because they do not account for all possible cases.

Consider argument (1) above. Both its premises and its conclusion are particular statements. Thus, it goes neither from the particular to the general nor from the general to the particular. Arguments (3) and (8) present similar cases. Argument (7) has general premises and a general conclusion. Thus, none of these arguments can be classified as either inductive or deductive according to the old definitions. Yet, we have seen that (1), (3), and (7) are deductive arguments, and (6) is inductive.

4. Validity and Form

Consider argument (7) above. It is easy to show, by an analysis of the premises, that this is a valid deductive argument. The first premise states that men are a subgroup of mammals, and the second asserts that mammals are a subgroup of animals. These relationships can be easily visualized by a simple diagram. Imagine that we place all men inside a circle. The statement that men are a subgroup of mammals can be graphically shown by placing one circle inside another. The smaller contains all men, the larger all mammals:

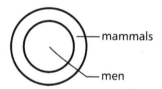

This diagram expresses that the group 'men' is contained in the group 'mammals.' We can now add to the diagram the second premise by adding another, still larger circle representing the group 'animals.'

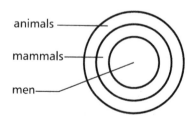

If we now inspect the diagram, we can see that the group 'men' *is* contained in the group 'animals.' And this is the conclusion of the argument. Thus, by drawing the conditions stated in the premises, we have also depicted the conclusion in our drawing. Hence, if the premises are true, the conclusion must also be true. The argument is valid.

Now consider argument (8). It is immediately obvious that we can analyze this argument in the same way we analyzed the preceding one. The diagram will be as follows:

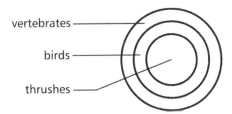

This argument is, of course, valid because it has the same pattern or form as the preceding one: Since the first one is valid, so is the second. And it is clear that we could construct an indefinite number of other arguments on the same pattern, and they would all be valid. Thus, in general, if **a**, **b**, and **c** are terms that stand for kinds of things, we can assert that *any argument that has the form*

(9)   All a's are b's.
       All b's are c's.
       Therefore, all a's are c's.

must be valid. This pattern or form, in which the letters **a**, **b**, and **c** take the place of the terms, shows the logical form that the two preceding arguments have in common. We have abstracted from the content or subject matter of the argument and found a common form. And we can assert that any argument that has that form must be valid.

This analysis leads us to an important conclusion: *The validity or invalidity of a deductive argument depends on its form, and not on its content.* It is for this reason that deductive logic is also called *formal* logic. It deals with argument forms, rather than particular arguments. Or, put another way, it concerns itself with the *form* of thinking and not with the *content of knowledge.*

In this respect, logic resembles mathematics. The latter also deals with abstract formal patterns. Logic and mathematics are said to be *formal* sciences, because they deal with abstract concepts in opposition to the *empirical* sciences, which study nature.

To summarize: The problem of determining the validity or invalidity of a deductive argument is to be approached by determining the *form* of the argument. The task of deductive logic is to analyze argument forms to determine their validity or invalidity.

5.   Valid Arguments and Sound Arguments

We have seen that argument (1) above is a valid deductive argument. This means that if the *premises* are true, then the *conclusion* is also true. But we do not know whether or not the premises are true. We do not even know who Mr. Smith is. This, however, does not matter. *The validity of the argument is a relationship between the premises and the conclusion, and the actual truth or falsity of the premises is irrelevant to this.* The point is that *if* the premises *were* to be true under certain circumstances, *then* the conclusion would also be true. This conditional or hypothetical relationship is all that 'validity' implies—no more, and no less.

Thus, if we have an argument that is valid, but one or more of whose premises are false, then *we cannot be sure of the truth of the conclusion.* It may be true, but it may be false.

Consider the following:

(10)   All snakes are birds.
All birds are round.
Therefore, all snakes are round.

(11)   All snakes are birds.
All birds are reptiles.
Therefore, all snakes are reptiles.

(12)   All snakes are reptiles.
All reptiles are birds.
Therefore, all snakes are birds.

All of these arguments are *valid,* because they all have the same form as argument (7) above. In argument (10), the two premises are false and the conclusion is false also. In argument (11), the premises are both false, but the conclusion is true. *This is simply a coincidence; we have not proved the conclusion is true, because we have not started with true premises.* In argument (12), we have both a true premise and a false one, and the conclusion happens to be false.

We can conclude, then, that if we have a valid argument and all its premises are true, the conclusion must also be true. Under any other conditions, we can say nothing about the truth or falsity of the conclusion.

Let us now introduce another useful concept. A valid argument with true premises is said to be *sound.* Arguments (7) and (8) are sound; arguments (10), (11), and (12) are *valid but not sound.* Obviously, it follows that if an argument is sound, then its conclusion must be true.

The following table summarizes our classification of arguments.

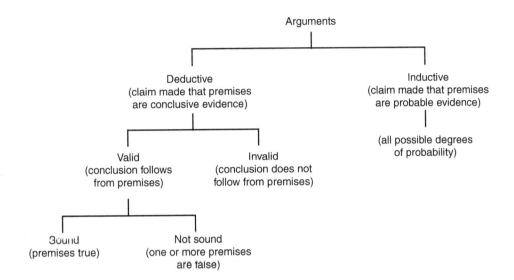

The following verbal equation states the relationship between the premises and the conclusion for valid arguments:

Knowledge about the premises:	*Knowledge about the conclusion:*
If all premises are true . . .	**The conclusion is true.**
If one or more premises are false . . .	**The conclusion is not determinable by logical means.**

6. How Deductive Reasoning Is Used

We have seen that the conclusion of a deductive argument is proven true if two conditions are satisfied: The argument must be formally correct or valid, *and* the premises must be true. The first condition is a matter to be settled by the rules of logic. We have also seen that the primary function of this process is to determine the validity or invalidity of arguments. The second condition, however, lies outside the field of logic. The truth of the premises may often be settled by experience or observation, or by reference to accepted scientific theories. Sometimes, however, we merely assume a premise to be true in order to find out what follows from that assumption. In that case, we use the premise as a *hypothesis.*

When we construct a valid argument, what we can know for certain is only that *if* the premises are true, then the conclusion is also true. But the actual *truth* of the premises, and therefore of the conclusion, cannot be determined by the rules of logic alone. Deduction is not an independent means of reaching truth; it is a tool that allows us to find out how various propositions are related to other propositions.

Deduction is essentially used in two different ways. The first is when we know (or assume) one or more propositions to be true. If we then draw a conclusion by means of a valid argument, we know that the conclusion must be true. It will be true *in fact,* if we started with factually true premises; it will be only *hypothetically* true if we started with merely assumed premises. This very important relation can be expressed by saying that *in a valid argument the property of truth is transmitted from the premises to the conclusion.* In other words, the conclusion we reach can be no more reliable than the premises with which we begin.

The second way that deduction can be used is by deducing a false proposition from a set of premises. If a false proposition follows deductively from a set of premises, then we can infer that at least one of the premises must be false. In other words, *in a valid argument, the property of falsity is transmitted from the conclusion to the premises.* If we can validly deduce a false conclusion from a set of premises, then we know that at least one of the premises is false.

Let's consider an example of the second way. Suppose a detective, investigating a murder, reasons as follows: "It was raining and it was muddy around the house on the night of the murder. If the murderer had come in through the window, he would have left mud tracks. But there are no mud tracks. Therefore, the murderer did not come in through the window." The detective realizes that the murderer could not have come in through the window, because if the murderer had come in through the window, there would have been mud tracks; but there are none. In this inference, the assumption (premise) that the murderer came in through the window (in conjunction with the other premises) leads to the conclusion that there must be mud tracks. But this conclusion is known to be false. From this the detective infers that the property of falsity must be transmitted from the conclusion to the only premise that he thinks could be false. If it is false that there were mud tracks, then it is false that the murderer came in through the window.

This second technique of deductive reasoning is extremely important because it allows us to prove that a proposition is false. *It is the technique used to eliminate incorrect assumptions.* Hence, it is the method used to test the assumptions we make in all sorts of situations, and the theories we create to explain all kinds of things.

To summarize: There are two fundamental uses of deductive reasoning. (1) From a set of true premises, we can obtain a true conclusion by using a valid form of inference. This allows us to prove a conclusion to be true. (2) We can prove a proposition false if we can show that a false proposition follows logically from it. This allows us to prove an assumption to be false.

7. The Principle of Contradiction

The most fundamental law of rational thought is the *Principle of Contradiction*. It can be stated in two ways:

1. An object cannot both have an not have a property at the same time and in the same respect.

2. A proposition cannot be true and false at the same time.

In the first statement of the principle we have to specify *in the same respect* because many properties have degrees. Suppose, for example, that Tom is taller than Dick and Dick is taller than Harry. Then we can say that Dick is tall, in relation to Harry, but not tall in relation to Tom. There is no contradiction here. This kind of relationship can happen with any quality that admits degrees.

The principle of contradiction applies to rational thinking and statement, but not to all thinking and all assertions. It does not apply, for example, to the aesthetic function of language. But *rational speech is subject to the principle of contradiction*. Why? Let us see. First of all, the Principle cannot be "proved" in the sense that *it cannot be derived from a more fundamental principle by deduction*. There is no principle that is more fundamental. But we can show that a person who does not abide by this principle cannot engage in rational speech. The first argument is this: Suppose my friend Fred says, "I don't see why I should accept this limitation imposed on me by the principle. I am prepared to accept that statements that are true are also false, and vice versa." Fred has a problem, for he cannot make any assertions. If he says, "Today is Tuesday," or "The sun is shining," and he accepts these statements as being true, then he has to say in accordance with his premise that *they are also false*. So he cannot make any statements of fact.

A second reason the principle of contradiction must apply to rational speech is the following: If the statement, "A table is not a horse," is true, then by Fred's premise it is also false. Hence, a table *is* a horse. And since the same argument can be applied to any statement that asserts that an *A* is not a *B*, then anything is anything else you want. This makes nonsense of the concepts we use to identify and classify any objects.

When a person affirms and also denies a proposition, he or she makes a statement that has the form "**p and not-p**," where **p** stands for a proposition. Such a statement is called an *explicit contradiction*. Additionally, a set of propositions is said to be *inconsistent* if an explicit contradiction can be deduced from them. We shall study some important uses of these concepts in Chapter 6.

CHAPTER 2

Arguments Based on Implication

1. Conditional Propositions and Implication

In this chapter, we begin our study of the fundamental techniques of deductive logic, with the logical relation called *implication*. Consider the following argument:

(1) If Tom invites Mary to the party, then she will go.
Tom will invite Mary to the party.
Therefore, Mary will go to the party.

The first premise of this argument consists of two parts joined by the words 'if' and 'then.' Each of these parts is a complete sentence, i.e., a proposition. It is fairly obvious that the sentence means that if the first part ('Tom invites Mary to the party') is true, then the second part ('Mary will go to the party') will also be true. Sentences of this type are called in logic *conditional propositions* or *implications*. We say that the first part of the proposition *implies* the second.

A proposition may imply another for a variety of reasons. Let us examine the following implications:

(2) **a.** If it rains, the ground gets wet.
b. If he is French, then he is European.
c. If you help Mr. Smith carry his packages, he will give you a dollar.
d. If one drops some sugar in water, it will dissolve.
e. If Texas loses the game, I will eat my hat.

The implication in statement **a** is based on a cause-and-effect connection; water causes the ground to get wet. In **b**, the implication is grounded on the relationship between the terms "French" and "European." Anyone who is French must also be European, because the French are a subgroup of the Europeans. The basis for the implication in **c** is the presumed fact that Mr. Smith has decided to give a dollar to anyone who will help him. In **d**, the implication is based on a physical property of sugar; it is soluble in water. In **e**, the implication is created by a promise made by the speaker.

We see, then, that different kinds of reasons lead people to assert implications. However, there is a common core of meaning in all the sentences considered. In each, the assertion is made that *if the first part is true, then the second is also true.* In other words, the first part of an implication is a *sufficient condition* for the second. In logic, the first part of an implication is called the *antecedent,* and the second the *consequent.*

The preceding analysis will enable us to evaluate some fundamental types of argument. We have seen that the content of propositions is irrelevant to the validity or invalidity of arguments. Thus, in dealing with implications, we can disregard the grounds upon which they are asserted. We are concerned solely with their form. The form of an implication is simply the assertion that one proposition implies another. It can be rendered in schematic form as:

Something or other   **Something else**
(a proposition)   ***implies***   *(another proposition)*

Thus, the implication in example (1) above actually asserts:

The proposition 'Tom invites Mary to the party'
implies the proposition 'Mary goes to the party.'

The implication consists of two separate statements plus the assertion that they are related by implication. To emphasize this fact, we shall use boxes to enclose the antecedent and the consequent. Our example becomes:

| Tom invites Mary to the party | implies | Mary will go to the party |

2.   *Modus Ponens* and the Fallacy of Asserting the Consequent

Let us return to argument (1). We know from the preceding analysis that the first premise means that if the proposition 'Tom invites Mary to the party' is true, then the proposition 'Mary goes to the party' is also true. We rewrite our implication using boxes, as explained above, and enclose the second premise and the conclusion in boxes. This allows us to see the units of which the argument is composed and obtain the following pattern:

1. | Tom invites Mary to the party | implies | Mary goes to the party |

2. | Tom invites Mary to the party |

Therefore, | Mary goes to the party |

We have eliminated the future tenses in these statements because they are logically irrelevant: that is, they do not change the truth or falsity of the propositions in which they occur.

It is easy to see that the argument is valid. The conclusion follows from the very meaning of the first premise, since it states that if 'Tom invites Mary to the party' is true, then 'Mary goes to the party' is also true. But the second premise states that 'Tom invites Mary to the party' is true. Hence, 'Mary goes to the party' must also be true. The argument is valid because we know from our discussion of validity that *any* argument that has this form must be valid.

Now, to further clarify the form of the argument, let us replace the propositions by arbitrary designations. It is customary in many logic texts to use letters in alphabetical sequence, beginning with **p,** although the use of these particular letters is arbitrary. However, for the time being, we shall use them. Let us designate the proposition 'Tom invites Mary to the party' **p** and 'Mary goes to the party' **q.** The result is the following schema:

1. **p** implies **q**
2. **p**

Therefore, **q**

This is the *form* of the argument, abstracted from the content. We know that any argument that exemplifies this form must be valid. This form is traditionally called *modus ponens*. It can be easily memorized and used to evaluate arguments.

Two other shorthand symbols commonly used in logic are the symbol '→' to stand for '*implies*,' and '∴' as an abbreviation for '*therefore.*' The form *modus ponens* can then be written as follows:

1. **p** → **q**
2.   **p**

∴   **q**

Consider another common type of argument that appears similar to the preceding one.

1.   If Tom invites Mary to the party, she will go.
2.   Mary will go to the party.
Therefore, Tom invited Mary to the party.

Can we determine whether this argument is valid? Yes; in fact, it is an easy task. The first premise states that Tom's invitation is sufficient to get Mary to go to the party, but it does *not* state that it is *necessary* for him to invite her in order for her to go. From the information given, there is no reason why Mary could not go to the party without Tom's inviting her. It is entirely possible that she will go without his invitation. Since we cannot infer, from Mary's presence at the party, that Tom invited her, the argument is invalid. Let's use the letters **p** and **q** again to convey the form of the argument. We get the following schema:

1. **p** → **q**
2. **q**

∴ **p**

On the basis of our knowledge of validity, we can say that *any argument that has this form must be **invalid**.*

This argument form is a source of confusion because it is so similar to *modus ponens* that people often think it is valid. An argument form that, although invalid, often misleads people into regarding it as valid, is called a *fallacy*. This particular form is called the *fallacy of asserting the consequent* (or *fallacy of the consequent*). The schema can be memorized and used in the analysis of arguments by noting that if any argument follows this pattern, it is invalid.

Our knowledge of these two forms can help evaluate arguments. Consider two examples.

(3)   **a.** If an acid is added to the solution, then a gas will form.
An acid was added to the solution.
Therefore, a gas will form.

b. If it froze last night, then my flowers are dead.
My flowers are dead.
Hence, it froze last night.

We want to know whether the arguments are cases of *modus ponens* or of the fallacy of asserting the consequent. The procedure is very simple. First, we put the implication in the simple form we have learned:

Then we use the letters **p** and **q** to name the antecedent (on the left) and the consequent (on the right), and place the same letters where they belong in the rest of the argument. Place the letters under the corresponding propositions and inspect the resulting form.

Analyzing example (3)a, we can restate the implication and rewrite the rest of the argument as follows:

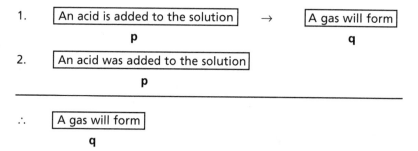

Note that the words 'if' and 'then' are not part of the propositions. Also, the future tense in the second premise is logically irrelevant. It is clear that the form of the argument is:

$$1.\ p \rightarrow q$$
$$2.\quad p$$
$$\therefore\quad q$$

This argument is clearly a case of *modus ponens,* and hence valid. Repeating the same procedure with argument (3)b, we obtain the following:

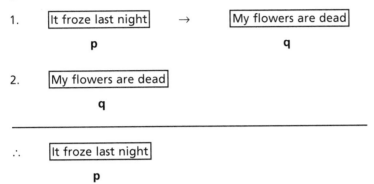

The form of this argument is:

$$
\begin{array}{ll}
1. & p \to q \\
2. & q \\
\hline
\therefore & p
\end{array}
$$

Notice the difference. It reveals the fallacy of asserting the consequent, and thus is invalid.

3.   *Modus Tollens,* Transposition, and the Fallacy of Denying the Antecedent

Consider still another pattern of reasoning in which the fundamental premise is an implication:

(4)   If Tom invites Mary to the party, she will go.
Mary will not go to the party.
Therefore, Tom did not invite Mary to the party.

Using a similar procedure we can find out whether this argument is valid. First, we notice that a negative sentence is simply a way of stating that a certain proposition is not true. Thus, the second premise of the argument can be restated as:

'It is not true that Mary will go to the party.'
or,
'The sentence "Mary will go to the party" is not true.'

Some careful reflection will show that the argument is valid. The first premise says that Tom's invitation is a sufficient condition to get Mary to go to the party. However, the second premise states that Mary will *not* go to the party. Hence, Tom could not have invited her, because then she would have gone to the party. We can infer that Tom did not invite her. The argument is valid. Let's now use the letters **p** and **q** in the usual manner to bring out the logical form of the argument. The negative propositions we shall call **Not-p** and **Not-q**. We obtain:

1. **p** implies **q**
2. **Not-q**

Therefore, **Not-p**

This valid form of argument is traditionally called *modus tollens.*

It is convenient to have an abbreviation for the term 'not.' Customarily, the symbol '~,' the *tilde,* is used. We can now write the form *modus tollens* as:

1. $p \rightarrow q$
2. $\quad \sim q$

$\therefore \quad \sim p$

Any argument that follows the form of *modus tollens* is a valid argument.

A slight variation on this same pattern is to reason that '$p \rightarrow q$' entails the conclusion '$\sim q \rightarrow \sim p$' and *vice versa.* We shall call this principle the principle of *transposition.* It can be stated as follows:

$$p \rightarrow q \qquad \text{and} \qquad \sim p \rightarrow \sim q$$
$$\therefore \sim q \rightarrow \sim p \qquad\qquad \therefore q \rightarrow p$$

Notice that in this situation each proposition entails the other. This relationship between propositions is called *logical equivalence.* The customary symbol for logical equivalence is '≡.' '$x \equiv y$' means that **x** and **y** both imply each other, or are logically equivalent. In section 8 of this chapter, we shall discuss the concept of logical equivalence in more detail. For now, we can use the concept of logical equivalence to write the principle of transposition more simply as follows:

$$(p \rightarrow q) \equiv (\sim q \rightarrow \sim p)$$

In behavioral terms, we can simply say that the terms of any implication can be negated and reversed to yield an equivalent statement.

We have now studied three argument forms in which the fundamental premise is an implication. It is not difficult to see that there is a fourth possibility: the situation in which we know that an implication is true and its antecedent (the *if* clause) is false. The following argument is an example of this pattern:

(5)   If Tom invites Mary to the party, she will go.
Tom did not invite Mary to the party.
Therefore, Mary will not go to the party.

Let's analyze this argument. The first premise states that Tom's invitation is a sufficient condition for Mary's going to the party, but not a *necessary* one. That is, the given information in the first premise does *not* assert that if he does not invite her, then she will not go. It is possible, for example, that she may decide to go *alone*. Thus, the argument is *invalid.* The form of this invalid argument is:

$$1. \quad p \rightarrow q$$
$$2. \quad \sim p$$
$$\therefore \quad \sim q$$

This invalid form is called *the fallacy of denying the antecedent.* It is important because, since it seems very similar to *modus tollens,* it is often confused with it. *Modens tollens,* however, is valid, whereas *denying the antecedent* is always invalid.

We will now analyze two arguments that exemplify the last two forms we have studied.

(6) a. If this is a bird, then it is a vertebrate.
         This is not a bird.
         Hence, this is not a vertebrate.

     b. If the solution turns the blue litmus paper red, then it is acid.
         The solution is not acid.
         Therefore, the solution will not turn the blue litmus paper red.

We evaluate the arguments, as before, by determining their form. Again, we shall use the letters **p** and **q** for the antecedent and the consequent of the first premise. (Again, there is nothing special about the letters '**p**' and '**q**'; other letters would do as well.) We then place the same letters and the word 'not' where they fit in the rest of the argument. Example (6)a has the following form:

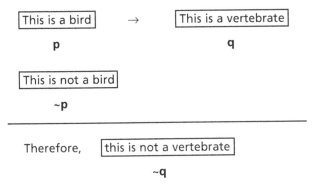

The form of the argument, then, is:

$$1. \quad p \rightarrow q$$
$$2. \quad \sim p$$
$$\therefore \quad \sim q$$

The argument is a case of the *fallacy of denying the antecedent.* It is therefore invalid.

Proceeding in the same manner with the second example, 6(b) above, we can let **p** stand for 'The solution turns litmus paper red' and let **q** stand for 'The solution is acid.' We then obtain the form:

$$1. \quad p \rightarrow q$$
$$2. \quad \sim p$$
$$\therefore \quad \sim q$$

The argument is a case of *modus tollens.* It is therefore valid.

4.   Summary of Argument Forms Based on Implication

In this chapter, we have studied two fundamental forms of valid reasoning based on a premise having the form of an implication. We have also studied two *invalid* patterns of reasoning that are a source of confusion. The *valid* forms are the following:

$$1. \quad p \rightarrow q \qquad \textit{Modus Ponens}$$
$$2. \quad p$$
$$\therefore \quad q$$

$$1. \quad p \rightarrow q \qquad \textit{Modus Tollens}$$
$$2. \quad \sim q$$
$$\therefore \quad \sim p$$

$$(p \rightarrow q) \equiv (\sim q \rightarrow \sim p) \qquad \textit{Transposition}$$

The *invalid* forms are:

$$1. \quad p \rightarrow q \qquad \textit{Fallacy of Asserting}$$
$$2. \quad q \qquad\qquad \textit{the Consequent}$$
$$\therefore \quad p$$

$$1. \quad p \rightarrow q \qquad \textit{Fallacy of Denying}$$
$$2. \quad \sim p \qquad\qquad \textit{the Antecedent}$$
$$\therefore \quad \sim q$$

5.   Three Types of Implications

So far, we have discussed only those logical relationships in which one *proposition* implies another *proposition*. But it is also useful, in analyzing the logic of certain types of arguments, to think of a term *within* a proposition as implying another term within that same proposition. For example, in the statement 'All Spelman students are women,' we can think of the statement as asserting that the property of 'being a Spelman student' *implies* the property of 'being a woman.' That is, *if* someone is a Spelman student, *then* that person is a woman. Because of the 'if-then' relationship here, it is useful to think of this statement as expressing an implication. If **p** stands for 'Spelman student' and **q** stands for 'woman,' then the implication can be represented diagrammatically as:

$$p \rightarrow q$$

A similar situation occurs with a statement such as 'Mary is a Spelman student.' It is convenient to think of this type of statement as expressing an implication because it asserts that the property of 'being Mary' implies the property of 'being a Spelman student.' Although it might sound awkward in English, it would be true to say that *if* someone is Mary, *then* that person is a Spelman student. Thus, if **p** stands for 'Mary' and **q** stands for 'Spelman student,' then this statement also can be represented diagrammatically as:

$$p \rightarrow q$$

Similarly, if we know, for example, that the individual who stole a briefcase is a Spelman student, we can let **p** stand for 'the individual who stole the briefcase,' and **q** for 'Spelman student,' and write this statement also as:

$$p \rightarrow q$$

Reasoning as before, we know that the property of 'being the person who stole the briefcase' implies the property of 'being a Spelman student.' A useful example of this situation might occur when we are trying to solve a mystery: Suppose we know that the individual who stole a briefcase was a Spelman student, and we know that all Spelman students are women. We could then infer that the individual who stole the briefcase was a woman. (The formal pattern of this inference will be discussed in the next chapter. For now, the important point is simply to realize that such statements can be interpreted as implications.)

It is therefore convenient to define the relationship of implication as including three types of situations in which a relationship is asserted between two propositions or between two concepts; we say that '**p** implies **q**' whenever one of the following three relationships obtains:

1.   If **p** then **q**   (where **p** and **q** are propositions)
2.   All **p**'s are **q**'s   (where **p** and **q** designate properties)
3.   **p** is a **q**   (where **p** is an individual and **q** designates a property)

Some technical systems of logic do not define the second and third types of relationships as *implications*, but instead deal with them by means of 'syllogistic logic' (which we shall discuss in a later chapter). We are defining all three types of relationships as implications here because doing so makes the process of logical analysis easier and simpler, without sacrificing any precision or ability to deal with various types of logical problems. The ease and simplicity of treating implications in this way will become increasingly obvious as we proceed.

6.   Different Ways of Expressing Implication

The relationship of implication can be expressed in everyday language in many different ways. Let's examine the most important ones.

One of the most frequent forms is 'If **p**, then **q**,' as in 'If it froze last night, then my plants are dead.' Often the word 'then' is omitted.

Another common way of expressing implication is by the use of expressions such as 'This *implies* that . . . ,' or 'This *means* that . . . ,' as in 'I was late to work; this means that I am going to get into trouble.'

Implications are also often conveyed by sentences with the pattern 'Whenever **p**, **q**,' as in 'Whenever some lead is put in nitric acid, a gas will form.'

Implications can also be expressed in terms of *sufficient conditions*. We have already learned that the antecedent of an implication is a sufficient condition for the consequent. Hence, a statement of the form '**p** is a *sufficient condition* for **q**' means the same as '**p** *implies* **q**.' Thus the sentence 'Tom's invitation is a sufficient condition for Mary to go to the party' means the same as

| Tom invites Mary to the party | $\rightarrow$ | Mary goes to the party |

Implications are also expressed in terms of *necessary conditions*. Consider the following statement: 'In order for John to be admitted to the party, it is necessary that he have an invitation.' This proposition does not mean that if John has an invitation, then he will be admitted to the party, for there may be other requirements. (In other words, having an invitation is not a *sufficient* condition for admittance.) However, if John is in fact admitted to the party (that is, if the proposition 'John is admitted to the party' turns out to be true), then we can infer that John has an invitation, since otherwise he would not have been admitted. Hence we have an implication:

| John is admitted to the party | $\rightarrow$ | John has an invitation |

From this diagram, we see that the *necessary condition* is the *right* side—the consequent—of the implication. This analysis is clearly applicable to all similar cases, and its results can be expressed in a simple mechanical rule: *A necessary condition always goes on the right.*

Implications are also often expressed by means of the phrase 'only if,' as in 'Mary will go to the movie only if her boyfriend goes with her.' It is clear from the meaning of the sentence that *the expression 'only if' introduces a necessary condition.* Since the necessary condition goes on the right, the logical form of the proposition is:

| Mary goes to the movie | → | Her boyfriend goes to the movie |

This proposition may appear paradoxical. It must be remembered, however, that implication has nothing to do with causality. The proposition does not assert that Mary's going to the movie somehow *causes* her boyfriend to go. It asserts that there are reasons to believe that the truth of the first proposition is a sufficient condition for the truth of the second. Thus, if we know that Mary in fact *has gone* to the movie, we can infer from the above initial premise that her boyfriend must have gone too, *precisely because his going was a necessary condition for her going;* if *he* had not gone, then *she* would not have gone. Therefore, if we know that she went, then we also know that he too must have gone.

The expression 'provided that' is a synonym for 'if.' It introduces a sufficient condition, as in 'Mary will go to the party provided that Tom invites her.' (*If* Tom invites her, *then* she will go. His inviting her is thus a sufficient condition for her going.)

Sometimes implications are expressed in the grammatical form of *subjunctives,* as in sentences such as the following:

> If I *were* rich, I *would* buy a yacht.

Sentences of this type are called 'subjunctive conditionals.' They are used to convey conditions whose realization is regarded as contrary to what has actually occurred. In the example just given, it is clear that I am not rich, yet the sentence asserts that if I *were* rich, then some other consequence would follow. From the standpoint of logic, it is irrelevant whether the condition expressed is impossible, improbable, or contrary to fact. Subjunctive conditionals express implications, just as do conditionals involving factually true propositions. In fact, the use of logic to infer what *would* happen in subjunctive situations is one of its most important and useful applications.

The preceding analysis provides us with a rapid and simple technique to reduce conditional propositions to the simple form '$p \rightarrow q$,' which we shall call the 'standard form' of implication. This reduction is necessary in order to bring out the logical form of the arguments we wish to evaluate.

Aside from minor verbal differences, there are only two different ways to express an implication. The first is *by asserting that something is sufficient for something else;* the second is *by asserting that something is necessary for something else.* In the first case, we know that the sufficient condition goes on the left and the other proposition on the right. In the second case, the necessary condition goes on the right, and the other proposition on the left. Thus, we arrive at a mechanical rule that always works: First, we determine whether the statement we are considering talks about a sufficient condition or a necessary one. If it talks about a sufficient condition, then we put that condition on the left, and the other proposition on the right, and we have the actual implication asserted in the statement. If the statement talks about a necessary condition, we place the necessary condition on the right, and the other proposition on the left. It is often necessary to make grammatical changes in the statements.

Consider some examples:

(7)   **a.** My being late to work means that I am going to get into trouble.

The standard form is:

$$\boxed{\text{I was late to work}} \quad \rightarrow \quad \boxed{\text{I am going to get into trouble}}$$

b. Whenever the switch is turned, the light comes on.

The standard form is:

$$\boxed{\text{The switch is turned}} \quad \rightarrow \quad \boxed{\text{The light comes on}}$$

c. A sufficient condition for Smith to have scurvy is that he have a deficiency of vitamin C.

The standard form is obtained by placing the sufficient condition on the left. The sentence also requires some grammatical changes. The standard form is:

$$\boxed{\text{Smith has a deficiency of vitamin C}} \quad \rightarrow \quad \boxed{\text{Smith has scurvy}}$$

d. Having some gas in the tank is a necessary condition for my car to start.

A necessary condition goes on the right, and the sentence requires some grammatical changes in order to make the clauses into complete sentences. The standard form is:

$$\boxed{\text{My car starts}} \quad \rightarrow \quad \boxed{\text{It has some gas in the tank}}$$

e. The match will ignite only if it is dry.

The expression 'only if' conveys that the statement 'It is dry' is a *necessary* condition, which therefore goes on the right. Hence the standard form is:

$$\boxed{\text{The match ignites}} \quad \rightarrow \quad \boxed{\text{The match is dry}}$$

(Note that we have eliminated the future tense in the antecedent, because it is logically irrelevant.)

f. He will pass the course if he passes the final.

It is clear that 'if' introduces a sufficient condition, which therefore goes on the left. Thus the standard form is:

$$\boxed{\text{He passes the final}} \quad \rightarrow \quad \boxed{\text{He passes the course}}$$

To summarize: The aim of changing an implication to the standard form is to show its logical pattern. The standard form must have a proposition or a property on each side. All the expressions used to convey the *relation* of implication (i.e., 'if,' 'then,' 'is a necessary condition for,' 'must,' etc.) should be dropped, since they are replaced by symbols such as '→' or '∴.' Pronouns should be replaced by the nouns they refer to, in order to make the statement as clear as possible. All verb tenses should be changed to the present tense.

The following table summarizes some typical ways of expressing implication.

If . . .	always introduces a sufficient condition.
Only if . . .	always introduces a necessary condition.
Provided that . . .	means the same as 'if'; introduces a sufficient condition.
Whenever . . .	usually introduces a sufficient condition.

7.   Analysis of Arguments

We can now consider some arguments whose implications are not in standard form.

> (8)   **a.**   Taking a taxi is a sufficient condition for Smith to arrive at the meeting on time.
>
> Smith arrived at the meeting on time.
>
> Therefore, he took a taxi.

The first thing we have to do is to change the implication to the standard form. The sufficient condition (taking a taxi) goes on the left, and some grammatical changes are necessary in order to make the clauses into complete sentences. We obtain

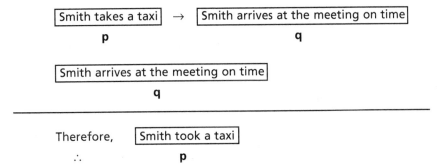

With the implication in the standard form, the rest of the procedure is purely mechanical. We name the antecedent **p** and the consequent **q**, and use the same letters throughout the argument. The result is:

Now we have the form of the argument, a case of the *fallacy of asserting the consequent,* and hence it is invalid.

(8)   **b.** If this is a bird, then it has to be a vertebrate.
This is not a bird.
Hence, this is not a vertebrate.

First we change the implication to the standard form. The expression 'has to' conveys that what follows is a necessary condition. Putting the necessary condition on the right and making the necessary changes, we get the following:

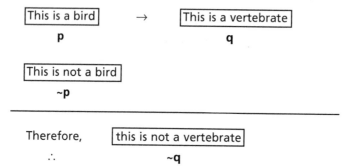

This argument is a case of the *fallacy of denying the antecedent;* it is therefore invalid.

8. Definitions and Biconditionals

Sometimes a sentence is expressed in such a way that it contains two important assertions *in one statement.* For example, suppose someone says 'I will take the job *if and only if* it involves a pay raise.' The statement asserts not only that a pay raise is a *necessary* condition for taking the job, but also that the pay raise is a *sufficient* condition for taking the job. Thus, if **p** stands for 'I will take the job' and **q** stands for 'the job involves a pay raise,' then this person is stating both '**p** → **q**' *and* '**q** → **p**.' Such statements are called '*biconditionals,*' because they express these two conditionals at the same time. Sometimes the expression

$$p \equiv q$$

is used as a shorthand notation for '**p** → **q** *and* **q** → **p**.'

The *definition of a word* normally takes the form of a biconditional. For example, suppose someone says, "A communist is someone who believes in government ownership of the means of production." According to this definition of 'communist,' *if* a person believes in government ownership of the means of production, *then* that person is a communist; *and also,* according to the definition being stated, *if* a person is a communist, *then* that person believes in government ownership of the means of production. Thus, if **p** stands for 'communist' and **q** stands for 'believes in government ownership of the means of production,' then **p** → **q** *and* **q** → **p** or, using the shorthand notation just mentioned, **p** ≡ **q**. In definitions, the conditional implication moves in *both* directions. The word implies its definition and vice versa. In analyzing arguments, we should realize that a biconditional includes two different assertions, and we shall see further examples of this type of argument in a later context.

9.   A Convenient Way to Save Time and Avoid Confusion

Although we have consistently used the letters **p**, **q**, and **r** so far, their use is not required when diagramming the form of an argument. Other letters may be used to stand for the propositions or terms in an argument. In fact, it may often be more convenient *not* to use **p** and **q**. In some cases, their use may cause confusion in analyzing an argument (especially a complex or wordy argument) because we tend to forget which propositions the letters **p** and **q**, etc., stand for in the diagram. This problem can be avoided if we use letters that are the *initial letters in key words of the argument.* For example, consider argument (8)b above. Instead of letting **p** stand for 'This is a bird' and **q** stand for 'This is a vertebrate,' we could have used **B** for 'This is a bird' and **V** for 'This is a vertebrate.'[1] We then would have obtained the form:

$$B \rightarrow V$$
$$\frac{\sim B}{\therefore \quad \sim V}$$

Remembering that **B** stands for 'bird' and **V** stands for 'vertebrate,' we can easily read the argument by looking at the diagram. By inspecting the diagram we notice that it follows the pattern of the *fallacy of denying the antecedent,* even though the letters used are not **p** and **q**. Observe that both of the key concepts change from positive to negative during the course of the argument. The first concept, **B**, becomes negative in the second premise, and the second concept, **V**, becomes negative in the conclusion. We have seen that any argument which follows this pattern is an instance of the fallacy of denying the antecedent, and therefore is invalid. There is no need to rely on the standard formula for the fallacy of denying the antecedent,

$$p \rightarrow q$$
$$\frac{\sim p}{\therefore \quad \sim q}$$

The formula is simply a way of showing that merely to change both terms of an initial premise from positive to negative (without also reversing the *order* of the initial terms) is logically invalid. We can then apply the principle that such a pattern is invalid without having to stop and recite the formula to ourselves.

---

[1]We adopt the convention of using uppercase letters when the letters stand for key words, as a further reminder of this fact. This convention, however, makes no difference to the way we analyze arguments.

In diagramming the form of arguments, there are two advantages in using letters to stand for key words in the argument. The first is that it enables us to skip the step in which we draw boxes around the propositions in the argument; thus there is no need to laboriously rewrite every argument before analyzing it. Instead, we simply write down the letters that stand for the propositions in the order in which they occur.

The second advantage of this method is that it enables us to check more quickly for careless errors in our diagram. We simply read our diagram as a shorthand version of the argument itself, making sure that the concepts occur in the same order as in the argument itself, and with the negatives in all the same places. With the simple arguments we have been considering, this may seem unnecessary, but when we begin analyzing more complex arguments, especially those expressed in long, complex phrases, it will become crucial to be able to check our work for careless errors. Such errors are easier to avoid by using letters that actually stand for key words in the argument. This procedure also allows us to connect the formal techniques of logical analysis more readily to the commonsense kinds of thinking in which we engage every day.

It is also helpful to think of the basic principles of logic, such as *modus ponens* and *modus tollens,* in behavioral terms rather than as memorized formulas. We should remember them in terms of what they tell us we can legitimately do when making logical inferences. For example, *modus tollens* tells us that it is logically legitimate to *negate both terms while reversing their order.*[2] In the argument

$$p \rightarrow q$$
$$\sim q$$
$$\therefore \quad \sim p$$

notice that the **p** becomes **~p**, the **q** becomes **~q**, and the order of the two terms is reversed. Consequently the **~q** on the second line is followed by the **~p** in the conclusion, whereas in the first premise the **p** was followed by the **q**. After the initial premise has been stated, the argument simply negates both of the terms of this initial premise, while reversing their order. If we remember that *modus tollens* always enables us to negate both terms while reversing their order in this sense, then we can apply the principle in any context whatever, regardless of what letters are involved.

We can also apply *modus tollens* in instances where one or both of the terms in the initial premise are *negative.* For example, consider the argument:

(9)   If something is not a vertebrate, then it is not a bird.
This a bird.
Therefore, this is a vertebrate.

---

[2]By 'negating' terms in this context, we simply mean that if the term is positive the first time it occurs, it has become negative the second time it occurs, or if it is negative the first time it occurs, it has become positive the second time. Note that, in both *transposition* and *modus tollens,* the terms are both reversed and negated in this sense.

We can use *modus tollens* to reach this conclusion from these premises, as follows:

$$\sim V \rightarrow \sim B$$
$$B$$
$$\therefore \quad V$$

The conclusion states that 'This is a vertebrate.' We know that this is a valid conclusion, because *modus tollens* tells us that it is logically valid to negate both terms while reversing their order, and this is what the argument does. It negates the ~V by making it V, and it negates the ~B by making it B, while reversing the order of the two terms. We therefore know that the argument is valid. Thus, by thinking of the principle *modus tollens* in behavioral terms rather than as a memorized formula, we can apply it more easily and quickly to a wide diversity of situations.

The same point can be made about all other basic principles of logic. These principles should not be thought of as artificial devices, but as a more precise way to approach the normal process of commonsense thinking that we use every day. The principles tell us what we can legitimately do in certain reasoning contexts, and the fallacies tell us what we cannot legitimately do.

EXERCISES I

These exercises will enable you to become skillful at schematically diagramming a sentence by identifying the two key concepts of each sentence, using the symbol '→' to indicate the relationship of implication between them. Change each of the following implications to the standard form, using boxes to indicate the antecedent and the consequent.

Example 1: I will finish the book tonight if I read half of it this morning.

Solution: *Begin by remembering that the 'if' part of the sentence should go first in the diagram. Since the last part of the sentence contains the 'if' clause, it must go on the left of the diagram, as follows:*

Example 2: We will win the game if and only if we complete this next pass.

Solution: *Remember that 'if and only if' indicates a biconditional. That is, (1) we will win if we complete the pass, and (2) if we are to win, we* must *complete the pass. This relation is indicated by the symbol '/.' The diagram will appear this way:*

Now diagram the following sentences as demonstrated above, showing the relationships of implication that they communicate.

1. They will arrive on time if and only if they leave before noon.

2. Whenever a stranger approaches the dog, it barks.

3. A necessary condition for the motor to function properly is that the brushes be clean.

4. A sufficient condition for Jones to be released from the hospital tomorrow is that his blood pressure be within the normal range.

5. If this animal has eight legs, it must be an arachnid.

6. If Tom goes to the concert tonight, he will have to work two extra hours tomorrow.

7. The banquet will be well attended, provided the weather is good.

8. In order to pass the course, you must pass four of the six exams.

9. A necessary condition for Smith to avoid contracting typhoid fever during his trip is that he be vaccinated.

10. If there is smoke, there must be fire.

11. A necessary condition for Mary to receive a driver's license is that she be at least sixteen years old.

12. All people invited to the party must be members of the fraternity.

13. The fire was caused by a short-circuit if the electricity was left on.

14. We will break even only if we sell at least 100 cars.

15. To Smith, missing work today means losing his job.

16. A necessary condition for John to improve his piano playing is that he practice two hours a day.

17. We will be admitted to the concert only if we arrive before eight o'clock.

18. The economy will improve, provided that inflation is brought under control.

19. If it rains at least ten inches this summer, the crops will be good.

20. All mammals are animals.

EXERCISES II

This set of exercises will develop your skill at schematically diagramming an entire argument by using symbols. To save time, instead of writing out the phrases, use letters to stand for the key concepts in the statements, and in the case of implications, connect the letters with the '→' symbol. Then, by examining the form of the argument, you can tell whether it is valid or invalid.

Example: A necessary condition for John to win the game is that his curve ball must be working. John's curve ball was working today. Therefore, he must have won the game.

Solution: *We begin by choosing letters to stand for the key concepts. Let 'W' stand for John's winning the game, and let 'C' stand for his curve ball's working. We then diagram the entire argument, using the symbol '→' to indicate the relationship of implication between these key concepts. Note that the necessary condition is that John's curve ball must be working, and this necessary condition goes on the right, since if he is to win, then this condition must be met. The entire argument will look this way:*

$$W \rightarrow C$$
$$\underline{ C }$$
$$\therefore \quad W$$

Examining this diagram, we can see that the order of the two key concepts is merely reversed. Therefore, it commits the fallacy of the consequent, and is thus invalid.

Now determine whether the arguments in 1–20 are valid or invalid by diagramming their form. Then answer 21 and 22 as directed.

1. A necessary condition for this match to ignite is that it be dry. The match ignited. Therefore, it was dry.

2. If sulfuric acid is added to the solution, a precipitate will form. A precipitate formed. So, sulfuric acid was added to the solution.

3. The murderer could not have come in through the door if it was not open. The murderer did not come in through the door. Hence, the door was not open.

4. All members of the club are rich. He is rich. So, he is a member of the club.

5. For Jones, losing today's game means losing the series. Jones lost today's game. So, Jones will lose the series.

6. If Smith's knowledge of the situation is accurate, the price of coffee will go down. The price of coffee will go down. Therefore, Smith's knowledge of the situation is accurate.

7. Every time blue and yellow pigments are mixed, green is the result. Green was the result. Hence, blue and yellow pigments were mixed.

8. Mary will not get a raise if she is not successful in her latest assignment. Mary will be successful in her latest assignment. Hence, she will get a raise.

9. This argument cannot be sound if it is not valid. It is valid. Therefore, it is sound.

10. If the murderer was a relative, then the motive was personal hate. The murderer was not a relative. So, the motive could not have been personal hate.

11. If the switch is turned, then the light will come on. The light did not come on. So, the switch was not turned.

12. A necessary condition for Jones to receive his insurance benefits is that he pay his premium. Jones did not receive his benefits. Hence, he did not pay his premium.

13. Being sick is a necessary condition for Al to be late to the meeting. Al was sick. Hence, he was late to the meeting.

14. If **X** is divisible by 28, then it must be divisible by 7. **X** is not divisible by 7. Therefore, it is not divisible by 28.

15. If it rains more than ten inches, the dam will burst. It did not rain more than ten inches. Hence, the dam will not burst.

16. Had the victim seen the assailant, he would have pulled out his gun. The victim did not pull out his gun. Hence, he did not see the assailant.

17. Having an insufficient intake of iodine is a sufficient condition for Jones to have goiter. Jones does not have goiter. Therefore, Jones does not have an insufficient intake of iodine.

18. If penicillin cures all streptococcus infections, it will cure this case. Penicillin did not cure this case. Hence, it does not cure all streptococcus infections.

19. The swift destruction of the enemy's air force was a necessary condition for the attack to succeed. We know that the enemy's air force was destroyed. Therefore, we can be sure that the attack succeeded.

20. If the message is not prepaid, it will not be delivered. The message has been prepaid. Therefore, it will be delivered.

21. Given the following premise, 'If the engineer sees a danger signal, he will stop the train,' what can be inferred from the addition of each of the premises below? (If nothing can be inferred from the two premises together, put that as your answer.)

   (a) 'He saw a danger signal.'
   (b) 'He did not see a danger signal.'
   (c) 'He stopped the train.'
   (d) 'He did not stop the train.'

22. Given the premise, 'If the game is lost, we lose the championship,' what conclusion follows from each of the additional premises below? (If nothing can be inferred, put that as your answer.)

   (a) 'The game is lost.'
   (b) 'The game is won.'
   (c) 'The championship is lost.'
   (d) 'The championship is won.'

CHAPTER 3

Other Fundamental Forms of Argument

1. The Chain Argument

Consider the following argument:

> If our profits continue to increase, we will issue a thousand shares.
> If we issue a thousand shares, we will be able to invest in an extra plant.
> Therefore, if our profits continue to increase, we will be able to invest in an extra plant.

It is fairly obvious that this argument is valid. The first premise asserts that the proposition 'Our profits continue to increase' is a sufficient condition for the proposition 'We will issue a thousand shares' to be true. And the second premise states that the latter proposition is a sufficient condition for the truth of 'We will be able to invest in an extra plant.' Since the first proposition is also a sufficient condition for the third, the conclusion follows. The schema of this argument form is:

$$1. \ p \rightarrow q$$
$$2. \ q \rightarrow r$$
$$\therefore \ p \rightarrow r$$

This form is called *chain argument*. It exemplifies the property that in logic is called *transitivity*. Saying that the hypothetical syllogism is valid is equivalent to saying that implication is a *transitive* relation. In other words, if a first term implies a second, and if *that* term in turn implies a *third*, then the first term implies the third.

Chain arguments are easy to analyze. The implications are reduced to the standard form, then the form is identified by using appropriate letters.

It is important to notice that an argument does not follow the form of *chain arguments* unless its premises are asserted as being true *always* or in *all* cases, rather than merely *sometimes* or in *some* cases. For example, consider the following argument:

> Smith attended the march.
> Some people who attended the march are communists.
> Therefore, Smith is a communist.

We see that the only way the argument *could* be valid would be if the second premise stated that *all* of the people in the march were communists. Then it would be asserting that, if someone was in the march, then that person is a communist. In that case, we could let **p** stand for 'people who participated in the march' and **q** for 'communists,' diagramming the entire sentence as '**p → q**.' But in fact this is *not* what the premise states. Instead, it only states that *some* of the people in the march were communists. Thus it cannot be interpreted as stating that '**p → q**,' and therefore we do not have a valid argument.

Arguments that infer from the premise that *some* **p**'s are **q**'s, to a conclusion which would require that *all* **p**'s would have to be **q**'s, are often called '*faulty generalizations*,' and that is what we shall call them here. Faulty generalization is the fallacy of treating a premise that is asserted as being true *sometimes* or *in some cases* as if it were true for *all* cases.

Logicians call statements that are asserted to be true *sometimes* or in *some* cases '*nonuniversal*' statements. *The principles we have studied so far in this book are not equipped to deal with nonuniversal statements.* Nonuniversal statements require different principles that will be covered in Chapter 5, which discusses '*the logic of syllogisms*.' For now, the important point is that an argument is a *faulty generalization* when it tries to use a nonuniversal premise where a universal one would be required. People are often tricked into accepting such arguments as valid, because they *seem* so similar in form to the *chain argument*. It is therefore important to recognize this type of logical fallacy.

2.   The Disjunctive Syllogism and Implicational Equivalence

A proposition that has the form 'Either **p** or **q**,' or simply '**p** or **q**,' is called in logic an *alternation*, and the two possibilities involved (**p** and **q**) are termed the *alternatives*. Some logicians call alternations *disjunctions*, and the alternatives *disjuncts*. Both terminologies will be utilized in our discussion here.

In English, the expression 'or' and 'either . . . or' are ambiguous. Let's look at some examples. 'John is in New York or in Washington' means that John is in one of the two cities, since he cannot be in both at the same time. However, in the sentence, 'You can buy soap at either a grocery or a drugstore,' the meaning is different. It is obvious that if one can buy soap at a grocery and at a drugstore, one can buy it at both. This latter possibility is not excluded. Thus, an alternation can have two different meanings. In the first example, the meaning is '**p** or **q**, but not both.' In the second, it is '**p** or **q**, or both.' In ordinary speech, no grammatical distinction is made between the two kinds of alternation; the *context* is usually sufficient to determine which of the meanings is intended. In business correspondence the expression 'and/or' is sometimes used when it is essential to specify that '**p** or **q**, or both' is the meaning intended.

In logic, the first meaning, '**p** or **q**, but not both,' is called an *exclusive alternation*. The second, '**p** or **q**, or both,' is termed an *inclusive alternation*. The exclusive alternation is stronger, since it excludes a possibility that is allowed by the inclusive alternation. That is, the exclusive alternation *excludes* the possibility of having both **p** and **q**, whereas the inclusive alternation does not exclude this possibility.

An *exclusive alternation* is really a combination of two statements. It asserts that

(1)   either **p** or **q** must occur;

and it asserts that

(2)   **p** and **q** are *mutually exclusive;* i.e., not both **p** and **q** can occur in the same situation.

The *inclusive alternation* is simpler. It asserts *only the first* of these two statements. For instance, in the example 'John is in New York or in Washington,' both (1) and (2) are meant to be asserted. But in the example 'You can buy soap either at a grocery or at a drugstore,' only (1) is meant to be asserted. Obviously, one could buy some soap at a drugstore *and* buy some soap at a grocery, so (2) is not being asserted in this case.

We shall now consider a fundamental argument form that is based on an alternation. Consider the following argument:

1.   This is an insect or a spider.
2.   This is not an insect.
Therefore, this is a spider.

It is easy to verify that this argument is valid. The first premise asserts that there are only two alternatives, and the second alternative is eliminated by the second premise. Thus only the other alternative is left. Hence, the conclusion follows. Notice that the argument would be valid whether the alternation is meant as an *inclusive* or an *exclusive* one, because the only information that is needed from the first premise is 'either **p** or **q**.' The idea that something cannot be both a **p** *and* a **q** (i.e., both an insect and a spider) is irrelevant to the logic of the argument.

Suppose, however, that we have the following argument with the first premise meant as an *inclusive* alternation:

1.   I will study sociology or physics tonight (or perhaps both).
2.   I will not study sociology tonight.
Therefore, I will study physics tonight.

This argument is valid also. The first premise admits not only the two alternatives (studying sociology or studying physics), but also that I could study both. And the second premise eliminates the alternative of studying sociology; thus only the alternative of studying physics is left, and this is the conclusion. So this argument is valid for the same reason as the previous one, even though the first premise in that argument was an *exclusive* alternation, whereas the first premise of this argument is an *inclusive* alternation. The principle of logic used here applies equally well for an inclusive or an exclusive alternation.

This valid form is called *disjunctive syllogism* and is valid for the two types of alternation. The schema of this form is:

1. **p** or **q**
2.   ~**p**
∴   **q**

It is important to notice that *the order of p and q in the first premise is irrelevant*—'**p** or **q**' means the same as '**q** or **p**.' (In an implication, by contrast, we saw in the last chapter that the order is *not* irrelevant; '**p → q**' is a very different statement from '**q → p**.')

Since the English language is often ambiguous as to whether an alternation is meant to be inclusive or exclusive, and since the disjunctive syllogism is valid for *both* kinds of alternation, *we shall henceforth assume all alternations to be inclusive unless clearly stated otherwise.* That way, we can apply the principle of disjunctive syllogism to all alternations without worrying about whether the speaker intended the alternation to be inclusive or exclusive. We can absolutely rely on the fact that inferences of the form *disjunctive syllogism* will yield a valid conclusion from any either-or premise, whether the either-or is meant inclusively or exclusively.

We shall use the symbol '**V**' (called the wedge) to symbolize the inclusive alternation. It is derived from the initial letter of the Latin word *vel,* which denotes this relation. Thus, the disjunctive syllogism can be rewritten as follows:

1. **p V q**
2.   **~p**
   ───────
∴   **q**

For example, 'Either I must take philosophy or I must take religion. I am not going to take philosophy. Therefore, I will take religion.' Note that the order of the two options is irrelevant. We could also say 'Either I must take philosophy or I must take religion. I am not going to take religion. Therefore, I will take philosophy.'

A slight variation on this form is the following:

   p V q
   ───────
∴   **~p → q**

'Either I must take philosophy or I must take religion. Therefore, if I do not take philosophy, then I will take religion.' Similarly, 'Either I must take philosophy or I must take religion. Therefore, if I do not take religion, then I will take philosophy.' In behavioral terms, an either-or statement always tells us that we can infer that if one of the two options is not the case, then the other must be. We shall call this rule *implicational equivalence* because it allows us to convert a disjunction into an implication or *vice versa.* As a result, we can restate an implication '**p → q**' as the disjunctive statement '**~p V q**.' *Implicational equivalence* can thus be stated as follows:

$$(p \text{ V } q) \equiv (\sim p \to q)$$
$$(p \to q) \equiv (\sim p \text{ V } q)$$

In behavioral terms, both *disjunctive syllogism* and *implicational equivalence* can be seen as reflecting a simple common-sense idea: "Either-or" simply *means* "If not one alternative, then the other."

3. The Principle of Mutual Exclusivity

On those relatively rare occasions when we do need to deal with the assertion that **p** and **q** are mutually exclusive (as asserted by an exclusive alternation), we should notice that the *disjunctive syllogism* is not the appropriate principle to use. When someone asserts that **p** and **q** are mutually exclusive (i.e., that not both **p** and **q** can be true), the statement can be written in the form,

$$\sim (p \ \& \ q)$$

literally, 'Not both **p** and **q**.' For example, someone might state that 'Segregation and true democracy are incompatible. Southern Mississippi is segregated. Therefore, Southern Mississippi is not a true democracy.' Letting **p** stand for 'segregation' and **q** for 'true democracy,' this argument could be diagrammed as follows:

1. ~ (p & q)
2. p
    ∴ ~q

The first premise asserts that not both the alternatives can be true, and the second premise asserts that one of them is true; hence the other cannot be true, which is the conclusion. The argument is valid. We shall call this valid argument form the *principle of mutual exclusivity*. Notice that we could also have let **S** stand for 'segregation' and **D** for 'true democracy,' and then the diagram would have appeared as follows:

1. ~ (S & D)
2. S
    ∴ ~D

It is easy to see that this diagram also follows the pattern of the principle of mutual exclusivity, since it asserts one alternative in the second premise, and then negates the other one in the conclusion. As indicated earlier, since the choice of letters in a diagram is arbitrary, the letters used here stand for the key words in the premises for ease and convenience in evaluating the argument.

Another equally workable way to diagram a statement of mutual exclusivity is to write '~p V ~q.' For example, we could have diagrammed the statement 'democracy and segregation are mutually exclusive' in this way:

$$\sim S \ \ V \ \ \sim D$$

We could read this formulation as 'either we do not have segregation, or we do not have democracy'—which would be equivalent to saying 'we cannot have both segregation and democracy.' However, in order to make inferences from statements diagrammed with these negative terms in an either-or format, we would first have to develop facility with the principle of *double negation,* discussed next. It is often necessary in reasoning to negate a negative. However, since negating a negative can often be confusing, we recommend avoiding it whenever possible. Using the ~(p & q) notation usually avoids this extra complication.

4.   The Principle of Double Negation

We have seen that a negative sentence can be analyzed into two components: an affirmative sentence, and the assertion that this sentence is false. For example, 'John is not a senator' means 'The statement "John is a senator" is false.' Thus, if **p** stands for 'John is a senator,' then the statement 'John is not a senator' is written as **~p**. As another example, if someone says 'I don't have no money,' what this statement *literally* means, at least in standard English, is 'It is not true that I have no money'; and this is equivalent with saying 'I *do* have *some* money.' To negate a negative is to affirm a positive.

Double negation is an important concept because it often happens that we wish to assert that a certain *negative* sentence is *false*. Consider, for example, the following conversation: Mr. **A** says to Mr. **B**, "You did not go to work yesterday," and Mr. **B**, who in fact *did* go to work yesterday, answers, "It is not true that I did not go to work yesterday." This last sentence is another way of saying "I did go to work yesterday." That is, Mr. **A** has asserted that it is not the case that Mr. **B** went to work, and Mr. **B** has asserted that *what Mr. B has asserted* is not the case. In other words, it *is* the case that he went to work. A double negation is equivalent to an affirmation, because if it is not true that **p** is false, then **p** must be true. There is no other possibility; **p** must be either true or false. The form of a double negation is as follows:

'The statement that **p** is not true is not true'—or, simply,

> **Not-not-p**   *or*   **~~p.**

The proposition **Not-not-p** ('the statement that **p** is not true is not true') means the same as **p**; hence we can infer either of these propositions from the other. Thus, we have two valid argument forms:

$$\begin{array}{ccc} 1. \ \textbf{p} & \quad\text{and}\quad & 1. \ \textbf{~~p} \\ \hline \therefore \ \textbf{~~p} & & \therefore \ \textbf{p} \end{array}$$

These two forms constitute the principle of double negation. Any time we have **~~p** as a premise, we can infer **p** as a conclusion, and *vice versa;* **p** and **~~p** are equivalent.

The fact that **p** and **~~p** are equivalent is a very useful point in the context of solving certain problems in logic. For example, suppose we want to deduce a valid inference by applying the principle of *disjunctive syllogism* to the either-or statement

> **~p V ~q**

Using *disjunctive syllogism,* we know that if one of the two alternatives is not true, then the other one must be. That means that if **~p** is not true, then **~q** must be true. This could be written as

> **~~p → ~q**

Using the principle of *double negation* enables us to realize that the '**~p**' in this last statement is equivalent to '**p**,' we can simplify the statement by writing

> **p → ~q**

Thus the principle of *double negation* is an extremely handy one to remember in many contexts when applying logical reasoning.

5. Dilemmas

Consider the following argument:

1. If I stay home tomorrow, I will do some work.
2. If I go out tomorrow, I will waste my time.
3. I will stay home or go out tomorrow.
Therefore, I will do some work or I will waste my time tomorrow.

It is intuitively evident that the reasoning in this argument is valid. The reason is that if we assume an either-or statement is true (for example, 'I will stay home or go out tomorrow'), and we know that each of the two either-or options has certain *consequences* (for example, the consequences mentioned in premises 1 and 2 above), then we can infer that one or the other of these consequences is going to occur.

Arguments of this form are called *constructive dilemmas*. Let's determine the schema by substituting the letters **p**, **q**, **r**, and **s** for the propositions involved. (We need four letters because the premises and the conclusion contain four different propositions.) We obtain the following:

$$
\begin{aligned}
&1. \quad p \to q \\
&2. \quad r \to s \\
&3. \quad p \lor r \\
\hline
&\therefore \quad q \lor s
\end{aligned}
$$

This form is valid. According to the third premise, either **p** is true, or **q** is true, or both are true (since we consider the alternation inclusive). But if **p** is true, then so is **q**, because of the first premise **p** $\to$ **q**. And furthermore, if **r** is true, then so is **s**, because of the second premise (**r** $\to$ **s**). If both **p** and **r** are true, then both **q** and **s** are also true. Thus we have three cases: either **q**, or **s**, or both. And these three cases constitute the meaning of the proposition **q** $\lor$ **s**, which is the conclusion of the argument. Thus, the argument is valid.

Let us now examine another form of dilemma. Consider the following argument:

1. If I work overtime today, I will finish the assignment.
2. If I go home early today, I will get a good night's sleep.
3. Either I will not finish the assignment, or I will not get a good night's sleep.
Therefore, either I will not work overtime today, or I will not go home early.

The form of the argument is:

$$
\begin{aligned}
&1. \quad p \to q \\
&2. \quad r \to s \\
&3. \quad {\sim}q \lor {\sim}s \\
\hline
&\therefore \quad {\sim}p \lor {\sim}r
\end{aligned}
$$

This form is also valid. Premise 3 involves three possibilities: either **q** is false, or **s** is false, or both are false. If **q** is false, so is **p**, because of the first premise. The proposition ~**p** and the first premise together constitute a case of *modus tollens*:

$$p \rightarrow q$$
$$\underline{\hspace{1em} \sim q \hspace{1em}}$$
$$\therefore \quad \sim p$$

Furthermore, if **s** is false, then **r** must be false also, because of the second premise. And if both **q** and **s** are false, then obviously both **p** and **r** will be false too. These three possibilities constitute the meaning of the proposition '~**p** V ~**r**.' Thus the argument is valid. This form is called *destructive dilemma*.

Here is another concrete example of destructive dilemma:

1. If the company performs well, its stock prices will increase.
2. If the company downsizes, it will become more efficient.
3. Either the company's stock prices did not increase, or it became less efficient.
Therefore, either the company did not perform well, or it did not downsize.

6.   Special Cases of the Constructive Dilemma

The constructive dilemma has several special cases that are fairly common. One occurs when the two alternatives in the third premise are a proposition and its denial.

1. If I go to the movie, I will amuse myself.
2. If I do not go to the movie, I will study.
3. Either I go to the movie, or I do not.
Therefore, either I will amuse myself, or I will study.

The schema is

$$\text{(a)} \quad 1.\ p \rightarrow q$$
$$2.\ \sim p \rightarrow r$$
$$\underline{3.\ p \ V \ \sim p}$$
$$\therefore \quad q \ V \ r$$

This form is valid, because it is a particular case of the constructive dilemma.

Another variant of the constructive dilemma in which the consequents of the two implications are one and the same proposition is shown in the following:

1. If I watch television, I will be bored.
2. If I visit Mary, I will be bored.
3. I will either watch television, or visit Mary.
Hence, I will be bored.

If we take the schema of the constructive dilemma and replace the **s**'s in the second premise and in the conclusion with **q**'s, we obtain the following pattern:

1. **p → q**
2. **r → q**
3. **p V r**
∴ **q V q**

But '**q V q**' is the same as '**q**.' Thus, the argument we are considering is a particular case of the constructive dilemma. The schema is:

(b) 1. **p → q**
2. **r → q**
3. **p V r**
∴ **q**

By combining cases (a) and (b), we obtain still another form of the constructive dilemma. Here is an example.

1. If I take the final exam, I will flunk the course.
2. If I do not take the final exam, I will flunk the course.
3. Either I will or will not take the final exam.
Therefore, I will flunk the course.

The form is:

(c) 1. **p → q**
2. **~p → q**
3. **p V ~p**
∴ **q**

This form is obtained by making the appropriate substitutions in the schema of the constructive dilemma. The student should verify this as an exercise. The form is of course valid.

The dilemma forms (a) and (c) both contain a premise of the form '**p V ~p**.' This premise cannot possibly be false, because any proposition must be either true or false. For this reason, a premise of this form is often omitted. It is often regarded as an obvious truth that does not need to be stated. Thus, in our example of type (a) above, we could have omitted the premise 'Either I go to the movie, or I do not,' since its truth is obvious. Similarly, in the above example of type (c), we could have omitted the premise 'Either I will or will not take the final exam.' Thus, the forms (a) and (c) are often reduced to:

1. **p → q**　　　　1. **p → q**
2. **~p → r**　*and*　2. **~p → q**
∴ **q V r**　　　　∴ **q**

However, the premise '**p V ~p**' is implied. The arguments would not be valid unless this premise could be implicitly assumed.

7.   Summary of Argument Forms

1. **p → q**   *Chain Argument*
2. **q → r**
    _____
∴   **p → r**

1. **p V q** *(or vice versa)*   *Disjunctive Syllogism*
2. **~p**
    _____
∴   **q**

1. **~(p & q)**   *Principle of Mutual*
2. **p**   *Exclusivity*
    _____
∴   **~q**

1. **p**   *and*   1. **~~p**   *Principle of*
    _____   _____   *Double Negation*
∴   **~~p**   ∴ **p**

1. **p → q**   *Constructive Dilemma*
2. **r → s**
3. **p V r**
    _____
∴   **q V s**

1. **p → q**   *Destructive Dilemma*
2. **r → s**
3. **~q V ~s**
    _____
∴   **~p V ~r**

EXERCISES I

The arguments in these exercises are either valid instances of **chain argument** *or they are invalid. Determine which ones are valid and which are invalid. The procedure is simply to reduce all implications to the standard form, using letters to stand for the key terms of each sentence, and then identify the form.*

Example: Passing today's test is a sufficient condition to guarantee that I will pass this course. If I pass this course, I will graduate. Therefore, if I pass today's test, I will graduate.

Solution: Using 'PT' for 'passing today's test,' 'PC' for 'passing this course,' and 'G' for 'graduate,' we can diagram the argument as follows:

$$
\begin{array}{r}
PT \rightarrow PC \\
PC \rightarrow G \\
\hline
\therefore\ PT \rightarrow G
\end{array}
$$

The diagram shows that the argument follows the form of **chain argument** *and therefore is valid.*

Now determine whether the following examples are valid instances of **chain argument**, *or whether they are invalid.*

1. If Argentina votes for the resolution, Brazil will vote for it, too. If Brazil votes for the resolution, it will get a majority. Hence, if Argentina votes for the resolution, it will get a majority.

2. Smith will sell his shares only if profits are below 3 percent. If profits are below 3 percent, it will be profitable for us to buy Smith's shares. Therefore, if Smith sells his shares, it will be profitable for us to buy them.

3. Being able to borrow money at 8 percent interest is a necessary condition for our building a new plant. If we are able to borrow money at 8 percent interest, we will have to pay smaller dividends for five years. Hence, if we build a new plant, we will have to pay smaller dividends for five years.

4. If the murderer came through the door, then he had a key. If the murderer was a relative of the victim, he had a key. Hence, if the murderer came through the door, then he was a relative of the victim.

5. If it rains heavily, the roads will get wet. If the roads are wet, traffic conditions will be hazardous. Therefore, heavy rain will cause hazardous traffic conditions.

6. A sufficient condition for the resolution to be killed is that the Russians vote against it. If the resolution is killed, the United States will propose a new one. Thus, if the Russians vote against the resolution, the United States will propose a new one.

7. A necessary condition for John to get his degree in three years is that he finish all general requirements in two. Getting a degree in three years will allow him to spend a year in Europe before going to graduate school. Hence, if John finishes his general requirements in two years, he will be able to spend a year in Europe before going to graduate school.

8. A sufficient condition for the clock to be fast is that the period of oscillation of the pendulum be less than 0.5 seconds. The clock being fast would be a sufficient condition for our time measurements to be wrong. Thus, if the period of oscillation of the pendulum is less than 0.5 seconds, then our time measurements are wrong.

9. If there was a fire in the building, then there was a short circuit. If there was a short circuit, the power lines were overloaded. Hence, if there was a fire in the building, we can be sure that the power lines were overloaded.

10. Our profits will go up, provided that the price of raw materials goes down. We will expand our investments, provided that our profits go up. Thus, if the price of raw materials goes down, we will expand our investments.

EXERCISES II

A. *Rephrase each of the following **either-or** statements into an **if-then** statement with an equivalent meaning.*

Example: Either the economy will remain strong, or we must consider reinvesting our funds.

Solution: *The principle of **disjunctive syllogism,** in behavioral terms, tells us that, given any either-or statement as a premise, we can infer that if one of the two options is not the case, then the other must be. This gives us a way to reformat the either-or as an if-then statement. In this example, we can rephrase the either-or statement as the following implication:*

If the economy does not remain strong, then we must consider reinvesting our funds.

Now rephrase each of the following either-or statements in the form of an implication with equivalent meaning:

1. The nuclear missile defense program will either be too expensive to be practical, or it will be easy for the enemy to counter with new offensive weapons.

2. We must either seek a negotiated settlement with the Palestinians or think of a more effective way to protect ourselves against terrorist attacks.

3. We must either trade Sokolov to the Russians in exchange for Danilov, or give up hope of any summit meeting this year.

4. The President is either joking about his proposed nuclear missile defense program, or he is completely insane.

5. The thief either had a key to the apartment, or was at least six feet tall.

6. It is obvious that John either has run track, or he has played football.

B. *In this part of the exercise, we use the above technique to evaluate arguments containing either-or statements. Determine whether the following arguments are valid.*

Example: Either the economy will remain strong, or we must consider reinvesting our funds. The economy is going to remain strong. Therefore, we need not consider reinvesting our funds.

Solution: *Using 'ES' for 'the economy will remain strong,' and 'CR' for 'we must consider reinvesting our funds,' we obtain the following form:*

$$ES \lor CR$$
$$ES$$
$$\therefore \quad \sim CR$$

*This argument has attempted to use **disjunctive syllogism,** but has done so incorrectly. The 'ES' in the diagram should be negative, and the 'CR' should be positive. The argument is therefore invalid.*

Another way to see this is to rephrase the either-or as an equivalent if-then statement, yielding the following diagram:

$$\sim ES \rightarrow CR$$
$$ES$$
$$\therefore \quad \sim CR$$

We know this reasoning is invalid because it is always invalid to merely negate the terms of an argument without also reversing their order. Using either method of analysis, then, the argument is invalid.

Now determine whether the following are valid or invalid:

1. We must either seek a negotiated settlement with the Palestinians or think of a more effective way to protect ourselves against terrorist attacks. We are seeking a negotiated settlement with the Palestinians. Therefore, we need not protect ourselves against terrorist attacks.

2. We must either trade Sokolov to the Russians in exchange for Danilov, or give up hope of any summit meeting this year. We have already given up hope of any summit meeting this year. Therefore, we should not trade Sokolov to the Russians in exchange for Danilov.

3. It is obvious that John either has run track, or he has played football. I know from talking to his roommate that he ran track in high school. Therefore, we can conclude that he did not play football.

EXERCISES III

*The following exercises cover examples of both **chain argument** and the **dilemmas**. Determine whether each one is valid or invalid by determining their form. If an argument contains an implicit premise, state it.*

Example: If I show up, I will lose the match. If I do not show up, I will lose the match. Therefore, I will lose the match.

Solution: *This argument contains an unstated premise, namely 'Either I will show up, or I will not show up.' Using '**p**' for 'I will show up,' and '**q**' for 'I will lose the match,' we can diagram the argument as follows:*

$$p \to q$$
$$\sim p \to q$$
$$\therefore \quad q$$

*Alternatively, we could use '**SU**' for 'I will show up,' and '**LM**' for 'I will lose the match,' in which case the diagram would look this way:*

$$SU \to LM$$
$$\sim SU \to LM$$
$$\therefore \quad LM$$

*Either way, we can recognize the pattern as a special case of **constructive dilemma**, and can see that it is valid.*

Now diagram each of the following arguments, and determine in each case whether the reasoning is valid or invalid.

1. If the building that burned down had insurance, then National Paper Company will not go bankrupt. If someone at National Paper did not forget to pay the premium, then the building that burned down did have insurance. Therefore, a sufficient condition for National Paper Company to go bankrupt is that someone there forgot to pay the insurance premium.

2. If I go to work in my car, I will save time. If I go to work on the bus, I will save money. I will either go to work in my car or on the bus. Therefore, either I will save time or I will save money.

3. If the result of the test is positive, the patient will be transferred to a hospital. If the result of the test is not positive, the patient will be released. The result of the test is either positive or it is not. Thus, the patient will be transferred to a hospital or released.

4. If the rate of inflation in the next two years is less than 5 percent, our profits will remain about the same in real terms. If the rate of inflation in the next two years is more than 5 percent, we will lose a lot of money. The rate of inflation in the next two years

will be less than 5 percent or it will be more. Therefore, either our profits will remain the same in real terms, or we will lose a lot of money.

5. If I take two courses this semester, I will have to pay full tuition. If I take four courses this semester, I will have to pay full tuition. I will take two or four courses this semester. Hence, I will have to pay full tuition.

6. If I work on the report tonight, it will be mailed tomorrow. If I do not work on the report tonight, it will be mailed out tomorrow. Therefore, the report will be mailed out tomorrow.

7. If I reinvest my share profits, I will be richer in the long run. If I spend my profits now, I will be able to get some things I need. Either I will reinvest my share profits or spend them now. Hence, either I will be richer in the long run, or I will be able to get some things I need.

8. If Smith accuses the opposing candidate of being immoral, he will be getting into risky personal matters. If Smith does not accuse the opposing candidate of being immoral, many will say that he is avoiding important issues. Therefore, Smith will be getting into risky personal matters or many will say that he is avoiding important issues.

9. This bottle contains either ethyl or methyl alcohol. It does not contain ethyl alcohol. Hence, this bottle contains methyl alcohol.

10. If I apologize to Smith, I will suffer a great embarrassment. If I do not apologize, he will never talk to me again. Hence, either I will suffer a great embarrassment or Smith will never talk to me again.

EXERCISES IV

Convert each of the following into a schematic diagram and then state whether valid or invalid.

Example: A necessary condition for the Packers to win is that Brett Favre must have a big game. The wide receivers will have a good game only if Brett Favre has a big game. Hence, if the Packers are to win, the wide receivers must have a good game.

Solution: *Let's use* **'PW'** *for 'Packers win,'* **'FBG'** *for 'Favre has big game,' and* **'WRG'** *for 'Wide receivers have good game.' Since a necessary condition does not guarantee the outcome, it goes on the right. Thus our schematic diagram looks this way:*

$$PW \rightarrow FBG$$
$$\sim FBG \rightarrow \sim WRG$$
$$\therefore PW \rightarrow WRG$$

Since there is no way to reformat the argument to make it follow the form of a valid 3-term chain argument, the argument is invalid.

Now evaluate the following arguments using the same method.

1. I cannot both work hard and fail the course. I am working hard, so I won't fail the course.

2. Since minimum wages are price controls, and price controls have always been disastrous, minimum wages must be disastrous.

3. If one is a self-lover, then one takes the greatest good for oneself. One takes the greatest good for oneself if one chooses to live life in accordance with reason. Hence the self-lover is the one who chooses the life according to reason.

4. Either Duke will win the NCAA championship, or we will have to see Shane Battier cry. Shane Battier is crying, so Duke did not win the NCAA championship.

5. I will go to the party only if you go, and you will go only if Chivon goes. Therefore, if I go, then Chivon will go.

6. You will not be able to master logic if you are not serious about it. But if you were not serious, you would not have read this far. So, if you have not read this far, you will not be able to master logic.

7. The stranger cannot be both a knave and a fool. The stranger is no fool, so he must be a knave.

8. That man is either drunk or he is stoned. He is stoned, so he cannot be drunk.

CHAPTER 4

Troubleshooting Techniques:
Seeing the Logical Structure in Language

Applying the principles we have discussed to determine the deductive validity of arguments would be an easy matter except for one unfortunate complication. Human languages, unlike computer languages, do not express themselves with mathlike precision. Instead, there is an almost infinite variety of ways to express a given meaning in words, some more clear than others. Life would no doubt be less interesting if people did talk in the way that computers do. Jesus' statement that "A little child shall lead them" would hardly have been as inspiring if he had expressed himself with a more precise sentence, such as "On the whole, it is frequently desirable to cultivate a childlike quality of innocence." Nonetheless, the variety of linguistic expressions poses problems if we want to interpret the meaning of statements precisely, so that we can clearly see the logical structure of arguments, and decide whether their reasoning is valid.

The purpose of logic is to determine the *validity* of arguments, aside from their emotional or artistic merits, and without being distracted by intuitive insights that may be obliquely suggested but not *logically demonstrated* on the basis of the evidence given. But before we can determine whether the logical structure of an argument is valid or not, we must first see what that structure *is*.

Suppose someone expresses the following argument:

(1) We will play ball today unless it rains.
It is not going to rain.
Therefore, we will play ball today.

It is easy to see that this argument is valid by the principle of *modus ponens*. The reason is that 'We will play ball today unless it rains' obviously *means* the same thing as 'If it does *not* rain, then we will play ball today.' So the whole argument can be taken to mean the same thing as:

(2) If it does not rain, then we will play ball today.
It is not going to rain.
Therefore, we will play ball today.

Letting **p** stand for 'it does not rain,' and **q** for 'we will play ball today,' the logical structure of the argument should be familiar by now:

$$p \rightarrow q$$
$$p$$
$$\overline{}$$
$$\therefore \quad q$$

The argument is clearly valid according to *modus ponens*.

But now notice that the same reasoning *could* have been stated in different words, somewhat less straightforward in their logical meaning:

(3)   Barring rain, we'll knock around the old rawhide today. And the forecast is sunny, so the bats will be cracking.

Notice what goes on in your mind as you interpret this argument. Before we can grasp the meaning of the argument and determine whether it is valid, we must first see that 'The bats will be cracking' means the same thing as 'We'll knock around the old rawhide,' both of which mean 'We will play ball.' We must also see that 'barring rain' means 'if it does not rain,' and 'the forecast is sunny' means 'it is not going to rain.' We then see that the meaning of argument (3) is *exactly the same* as (1) and (2). Just as above, a diagram of the form of the logic in the argument would look like this:

$$p \rightarrow q$$
$$p$$
$$\overline{}$$
$$\therefore \quad q$$

Once we are able to see the form of an argument, deciding whether it is valid or not is easy. But seeing the form of an argument is not always so easy. Consider now this argument:

(4)   All taxpayers who claim business expenses, including depreciation or lease payment deductions for any listed property, must complete Part III of Form 4562, unless the taxpayer in question operated a business as a sole proprietorship. John Smith did not operate a business as a sole proprietorship, and he did claim a lease payment deduction for a listed property. Certainly, he must complete Part III of Form 4562.

At first glance, a person not trained in real estate law might give up on deciding whether the logic in this argument is valid or not. Actually, one need not know anything about the *content* being discussed to analyze its logic. It is the *form*, or *structure*, of the argument that we are interested in. Before analyzing such a cumbersome expression, however, it will be helpful to discuss several techniques for handling problems that such expressions pose. The main problems are:

1.   Premises and conclusions may not be easily identifiable as such.

2.   Phrases may be so long and cumbersome that we lose track of their structural relationship to the overall argument.

3. Synonyms may be used, as well as unclear terms and phrases.

4. Some premises may require reformatting.

5. Some premises may be unstated.

6. The statements in the argument may not seem to be expressed in terms of the *if-then* or *either-or* relationships with which logical principles are typically expressed.

The first three of these problems can be resolved without much difficulty. The fourth, fifth, and sixth require the development of certain specific skills. After discussing all six of these potential pitfalls, we will then be equipped to handle tricky arguments like the one in example 4 above.

1.   Identification of Premises and Conclusions

The first thing we must do to make logical sense of a complex verbal expression is to understand what the speaker is trying to prove, demonstrate, or convince us of. No mechanical formula can be applied here. This is one of the main reasons that using logic is as much an art as it is a science. Nonetheless, whatever the speaker is trying to convince us of by means of the argument must be taken as the *conclusion* of the argument. Everything else in the argument that appears to support or prove the conclusion comprises the *premises* of the argument. Everything that is *irrelevant* to supporting or proving the conclusion should be ignored.

For example, consider this argument:

(5)   It is well known that communists participated in the march against aid to the Chinese dissidents. Obviously, John Smith is as red as hell, because he was in the march, right in the front row!

If we attend to the meaning of what is being said, rather than just mechanically focusing on the words, it becomes clear that what the speaker is trying to convince us of is that Smith is a communist. This is what is meant by 'as red as hell.' We should not expect that the conclusion will necessarily be the last statement in the argument, or the first statement, or that it will be clearly identified with such words as 'therefore' and 'thus.'

Notice also that the fact that Smith was 'right in the front row' of the march is irrelevant to the logic of the argument. The logic is that there were communists in the march, and Smith was in the march, therefore Smith must be a communist. Which row he marched in is thus irrelevant and should be completely ignored in analyzing the logic of the argument. Accordingly, a correct symbolic diagram of the structure of the argument will make no mention of this irrelevant fact.

As soon as we are able to interpret the meanings of the statements in a clear way, it is easy to see that the argument cannot be valid unless its first premise asserts that *all* people who attended the march were communists. But all it really asserts is that *some* people who attended the march were communists. It is therefore an example of a *faulty generalization*. Letting **p** stand for 'Smith,' **q** for 'person(s) who attended the march,' and **r** for 'communist(s),' we see that the argument exhibits the following form:

$$p \rightarrow q$$
$$\textit{Some } \textbf{q}\text{'s are } \textbf{r}\text{'s.}$$
$$\therefore \quad p \rightarrow r$$

Such an argument cannot be interpreted as following any of the *valid* forms we have considered. Instead, it is clearly an example of a faulty generalization. But to make such an assessment, we must often *interpret* the language in an argument to see what its structure really is. Close reading and thoughtful assessment of statements is necessary; much the same point applies to the cases below.

2.　Dealing with Long, Cumbersome Phrases

As a general rule, nothing tends to discourage us from the task of analyzing the logic in arguments more than long or overly complex phrases. Devious or manipulative speakers will often use this technique as a rhetorical device to disguise an argument that is not valid. However, the truth is that long or complicated phrases are easy to deal with, given some practice. You can use a simple device to help avoid being confused by the length of phrases. Consider this example:

(6)　If there were a tendency for the presence of multinational corporations in Third World countries to stimulate economic growth in those countries, then there should be a significant and positive statistical correlation between growth in average real income in Third World countries (defined as countries with an annual average income under $400) and the presence of multinational corporations, measured in terms of the percentage of the gross national product of the countryin question that is accounted for by multinational corporations, over an extended period of time such as, say, twenty years. But studies by Bornschier and others show that the correlation between growth in average real income and the presence of multinational corporations, as measured in these terms over a twenty-year period from 1950 to 1970, is negative. Therefore, the evidence would indicate that the presence of multinational corporations in these countries does not, on the whole, stimulate economic growth as defined by growth in average real income.

The key to analyzing such a wordy argument is to notice that the first sentence, which is quite long, asserts a logical connection between two complex ideas. The connection asserted is an *'if-then'* relationship. Let's call the two items that are connected by this relationship **p** and **q**. We then notice that idea **p** is repeated in the conclusion of the argument, although what is asserted in the conclusion is that **p** is *not* the case. Finally, we see that idea **q** is repeated in the second sentence, although here again what is asserted is that **q** is *not* the case. Thus the whole argument follows the following schematic form:

If	There were a tendency for the presence of multinational corporations in Third World countries to stimulate economic growth in those countries	*then*	there should be a significant and positive statistical correlation between growth in average real income in Third World countries (defined as countries with an average income under $400) and the presence of multinational corporations, measured in terms of percentage of gross national product of the country in question that is accounted for by multinational corporations, over an extended period of time such as, say, twenty years

It is not true that | there is a significant and positive statistical correlation between growth in average real income in Third World countries and the presence of multinational corporations, as measured in the way described above, over a twenty-year period

Therefore, it is not true that | There is a tendency for the presence of multinational corporations in Third World countries to stimulate economic growth in those countries (as defined in the way described above)

A simpler diagram of the argument is as follows:

$$p \rightarrow q$$
$$\frac{\sim q}{\therefore \quad \sim p}$$

When looked at in this way, it can be seen that the argument is valid by the principle of *modus tollens*. The *logic* in the argument is not complicated. Nor do we need to know anything about economics, statistics, or international relations to analyze this logic. It is exactly the same structure of reasoning found in the following simple argument:

If the car were out of gas, it would stop running.
The car has not stopped running.
Therefore, the car is not out of gas.

Or, diagrammed, it reduces to the following:

$$p \rightarrow q$$
$$\sim q$$
$$\therefore \quad \sim p$$

The key to handling arguments with long, complex phrases is to focus on the *overall* relationships between large chunks of information. First we look for important *connective* words, such as 'if,' 'then,' 'either,' 'or,' etc. Then we look for repetitions of the same concept in different sentences. This too helps establish the logical connections between one thought and the next, so that we can achieve a useful focus on the overall structure of the argument, without getting lost in the details.

3.   Synonyms and Fuzzy Terms and Phrases

Sometimes a writer or speaker will phrase the same idea with several different forms of expression, either to achieve variety of style, to conform with the practices of specialized "professional" writing, or perhaps out of a malicious intent to mislead. Whichever is the case, it is important that we recognize an idea as the *same* idea each time it occurs, and that we treat it as such in analyzing the logic of the argument. We saw a simple example of the use of synonyms and of terms and phrases somewhat fuzzy in meaning when we analyzed argument (3). We saw that 'We'll knock around the old rawhide today' and 'The bats will be cracking,' in the context of the argument, were meant to denote the same meaning. 'Barring rain' was the same as 'If it does not rain,' and 'The forecast is sunny' was the same as 'It will not rain.' If we had not seen the equivalence of the synonymous words and phrases, we would not have been able to analyze the logic in the argument.

Now consider a more complicated example of an argument that uses synonymous and less-than-clear words and phrases:

(7)   The delusions that mislead men arise from their tendency to believe that to be true which corresponds to their wishes. One of the strong desires that affects human belief is the hope that man will escape extinction at death and live eternally in some ideal haven of bliss. No one who has any understanding of the origin of delusional systems in human wishes can fail to conclude that this belief in immortality is a delusion.

The main obstacle to understanding the logical structure of this argument is that the phrasings are wordy and imprecise. Nonetheless, these phrasings are no more wordy or imprecise than many arguments one hears or reads almost every day in the statements of politicians, businessmen, schoolteachers, or sports commentators. If we want logic to be relevant to the real world, we must realize that people do not communicate like computers (or logic textbooks).

We note first that the last sentence of the argument is its conclusion, and that the meaning of this statement is to assert a connection between two ideas—immortality and delusions. The connection asserted is that immortality is a delusion. Remembering the definition of implication in Chapter 1, we see that the speaker is asserting that the relationship between 'immortality' and 'delusion' is a type of implication. If we let **I** stand for 'belief in immortality' and **D** for 'delusion,' the speaker is asserting that '**I** → **D**.' As we attempt to understand the rest of the argument, then, the question we must continually ask ourselves is: How are these other statements *relevant* to immortality and to delusions, and how do they attempt to establish a connection between them? We should also remember that most logical arguments that attempt to establish connections between two ideas do so by linking them both in some way to some third idea; logicians call this linking idea the '*middle term*' of the argument because in a valid argument it must connect the first term with the last term of the argument.

So the main thing we need to find out is: What is the third idea (or *middle term)* that connects the two ideas of '*immortality*' and '*delusions*,' and how does it attempt to establish this connection? As soon as we pose the question in this way, it becomes apparent that the first sentence of the argument asserts a connection between delusions and something else—people's wishes. What it is saying is that people tend to believe that whatever they wish to be true *is* true. Thus all delusions are beliefs that something we wish were true is true. So we now know that '*wishes*' is going to be the *connecting link* between 'immortality' and 'delusions.' We then see that in the second sentence there is a *synonym* for '*wishes*'—namely, '*desires*.' What is it saying about *desires* that would be relevant to proving the conclusion that immortality is a delusion? It is saying that immortality is one of the desires (or wishes) that we human beings have. It says this in a complicated way, of course, but the complications are irrelevant to the logic of the argument. Consequently, the logic of the whole argument can be reduced to:

(8)   All *delusions* are beliefs that we *wish* to be true.
       Immortality is a belief that we *wish* to be true.
       Therefore, *immortality* is a *delusion*.

The argument can be simplified still further by using letters to stand for the concepts being connected. We shall use **D**, **W**, and **I** to stand for the three key concepts in the argument.

(9)   All **D**'s are **W**'s   **D** → **W**

                  I is a **W**   *or*   **I** → **W**
          ─────────────   ─────────────
          ∴   **I** is a **D**   ∴   **I** → **D**

By now, the perceptive reader will have noticed that this reasoning is invalid, since it is the same as the reasoning we would be using to advance such an absurd argument as:

(10) All Frenchmen are Europeans.
       Fritz is a European.
       Therefore, Fritz is a Frenchman.

Compare the reasoning in arguments (7), (8), (9), and (10) and notice that their structure is exactly the same. Their form is:

$$p \rightarrow q$$
$$r \rightarrow q$$
$$\therefore \quad r \rightarrow p$$

All arguments of this form are invalid because, *even if the premises were true, it would still be possible for the conclusion to be false.*

Notice that a *valid* argument using a middle term to establish a connection between two other terms would have to follow the form of *chain argument,* as we saw earlier. That is, it would have to follow the form:

$$p \rightarrow q$$
$$q \rightarrow r$$
$$\therefore \quad p \rightarrow r$$

In this form, notice that **q** functions as a *middle term,* establishing a relationship of implication between **p** and **r**. Note the difference between this valid form and the invalid form of the previous argument. In the previous argument, the **q** of the second premise is in the wrong place, and thus does not function as a middle term. Some logicians therefore call this invalid form the *'fallacy of the misplaced middle term.'* In effect, this is also essentially the same mistake made in the *fallacy of the consequent,* since in effect it tries to infer '**q** → **r**' from '**r** → **q**,' thus confusing this statement with its own converse (i.e., it turns the statement around backwards from the way it would need to be in a valid argument).

Remember that the key to analyzing arguments that contain synonymous or imprecise terms and expressions is to see that the key concept expressed by two different phrases is really *the same* concept. The speaker or writer has probably chosen to express the same idea in different ways to add variety to the writing or speaking style, to appear learned, or to evade the need for clarity and coherence.

4.   Premises that Require Reformatting

We saw in Chapter 2 that, according to *transposition,* the statement '**p** → **q**' is equivalent in meaning to the statement '**~q** → **~p**.' The reason is that '**p** → **q**' entails '**~q** → **~p**,' while at the same time, '**~q** → **~p**' entails '**p** → **q**.' For example, the statement 'All Spelman students are women' is equivalent with the statement 'If someone is not a woman, then that person is not a Spelman student.'

In the same way, we saw in Chapter 3 that, according to *disjunctive syllogism,* the statement '**p V q**' is equivalent with the statement '**~p** → **q**,' and also with the statement '**~q** → **p**,' since '**p V q**' entails both these statements, and they both entail it. We noted at that point that in some contexts it is useful to be able to 'reformat' an *either-or* statement into the form of an equivalent *if-then* statement. In many real life instances, a premise will occur in a form that is not convenient to work with, and in order to make sense of the argument in which it occurs, we need to reformat the premise into an equivalent form that is convenient to work with.

For example, consider this argument:

$$\sim a \rightarrow \sim x$$
$$a \rightarrow q$$
$$\therefore \quad x \rightarrow q$$

To see whether the argument is valid, we need to 'reformat' the first premise, so that it becomes more convenient to work with. We know that, according to *transposition,* '$\sim a \rightarrow \sim x$' is equivalent with '$x \rightarrow a$.' We can therefore substitute '$x \rightarrow a$' in place of '$\sim a \rightarrow \sim x$' in the argument, and the result is a much simpler formulation:

$$x \rightarrow a$$
$$a \rightarrow q$$
$$\therefore \quad x \rightarrow q$$

This formulation expresses the same information as the above, but is easier to analyze. It follows the form of *chain argument,* and is therefore valid.

Here is a verbal example of an argument requiring the same kind of reformatting:

> If I don't study, I won't pass the test. But if I do study, I'll have to skip the fraternity party. So if I want to pass the test, I'll have to skip the party.

Using '**S**' for 'study,' '**PT**' for 'pass the test,' and '**SFP**' for 'skip the fraternity party,' we obtain:

$$\sim S \rightarrow \sim PT$$
$$S \rightarrow SFP$$
$$\therefore \quad PT \rightarrow SFP$$

To see that the argument is valid, we must reformat the first premise, so that the argument appears this way:

$$PT \rightarrow S$$
$$S \rightarrow SFP$$
$$\therefore \quad PT \rightarrow SFP$$

The same problem often occurs with *either-or* statements. For example, consider the following:

> I must either study, or fail the test. If I study, I'll have to skip the fraternity party. So, if I want to pass the test, I'll have to skip the fraternity party.

A diagram of this argument, using the same symbols as before, would look this way:

$$S \quad V \quad \sim PT$$
$$S \rightarrow SFP$$
$$\therefore \quad PT \rightarrow SFP$$

To see whether this reasoning is valid, we need to reformat the *either-or* statement. *Disjunctive syllogism* tells us that, given an either-or statement, we can infer that if one option is not the case, the other must be. We can then write the first premise as follows:

$$\sim\sim PT \rightarrow S$$

Since the order of the two options is irrelevant in an either-or statement, we have chosen to begin with the right-hand term because we can see that the first term in the conclusion, 'PT' needs to be matched by the upper-left term, if the argument has any hope of being valid. Simplifying the resulting if-then statement still further, by cancelling the double negative, we obtain:

$$PT \rightarrow S$$

We can then substitute this statement in place of 'S V ~PT' in the original argument, so that it now appears in a much simpler form:

$$PT \rightarrow S$$
$$S \rightarrow SFP$$
$$\therefore \quad PT \rightarrow SFP$$

By reformatting statements, we can convert arguments that appear to be confusing into ones that are simple to evaluate.

5.   Arguments with Unstated Assumptions

Often in everyday language, people do not explicitly state all of their assumptions, because they assume that the context of their language makes them obvious. For example, someone might argue as follows:

> If we cut the state's education budget, we will have to spend more money on prisons.

The speaker means for us to assume the missing premises, so that the overall reasoning would go like this:

> If we cut the state's education budget, fewer students will become qualified for good jobs. People who are not qualified for good jobs tend to have trouble making a living. Statistically, people who have trouble making a living are more likely to commit crimes. If people are more likely to commit crimes, then we'll have to spend more money on prisons. Therefore, if we cut the state's education budget, we'll have to spend more money on prisons.

When there are missing assumptions in an argument, we can determine what they are by thinking of additional concepts that could logically connect the stated assumptions and the conclusion of the argument. It also helps to remember that, when all the assumptions are explicitly spelled out, each key concept will occur twice in the overall argument. The above argument, for example, uses all the key concepts twice, as the following schematic diagram shows:

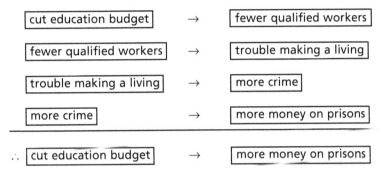

With several assumptions needed to prove the conclusion, this argument follows the form of a *chain argument* with several intermediate middle terms, a type of argument discussed in Chapter 3. Since we have an unbroken chain of key concepts that imply each subsequent key concept in turn, leading from 'cut education budget' in the upper left to 'more money on prisons' in the lower right, this argument obviously is valid.

6.   Statements Not Expressed in 'If-Then' or 'Either-Or' Terms

By far the most substantial problem to be overcome in understanding the logical form of an argument and determining whether it is valid is that the logical relationships involved may not be expressed straightforwardly as *if-then* or as *either-or* relationships. Such expressions as 'unless,' 'with the exception of,' 'Every **A** exhibits the qualities of a **B**,' and '**A** and **B** cannot both be true' do not initially *appear* to express relationships of implication. We must examine these kinds of statements to discover the relationships of implication that they express.

Almost any statement can be regarded as an implication. For instance, if we reflect for a moment on the principle of *disjunctive syllogism,* explained in Chapter 3, we see that the real reason this principle enables us to deal effectively with *either-or* statements is that an *either-or* expression is really just *another way of expressing implication.* For example, consider the statement,

Either you stop insulting my wife, or I will hit you.

This statement is expressed in *either-or* terms, but it really means the same thing as:

If you do not stop insulting my wife, *then* I will hit you.

Carrying this reasoning a step further, we realize that the meaning of *any* either-or statement can just as well be expressed as an appropriately chosen *if-then* statement.

The same is true for 'unless' statements, as we saw at the beginning of this chapter. The statement 'We will play ball today unless it rains' means the same thing as '*If* it does *not* rain, *then* we will play ball today.'

Think what a wonderfully simple thing logic would become if it were to turn out that virtually all logical relationships could be expressed as *if-then* statements! Then all we would need to know to determine the validity of *all deductive arguments whatever* would be the principles that we have already examined in this book. Surprisingly, it really is almost that simple. There is virtually no form of expression that, if we think about it, cannot be expressed as an *if-then* statement. Consider the statement just made, for example.

There is no form of expression that cannot be expressed as an *if-then* statement.

Although it might sound a little odd, we could express the same logical relationship by saying,

If something is a form of expression, *then* it can be expressed as an *if-then* statement.

Or take the statement,

All Spelman students are women.

We could just as well say,

If a person is a Spelman student, then that person is a woman.

Even the following type of statement can be expressed as an *if-then:*

Mary is a Spelman student.

Although it would sound a little odd, we could express this meaning by saying,

If something is Mary, then it is a Spelman student.

Why would we want to say something that sounds so odd? Because things become much simpler if we can convert every statement into the format of an implication. Then all arguments, if they are valid, could be expressible as a simple chain of implications:

$$p \rightarrow q$$
$$p$$
$$\therefore \quad q$$

OR

$$p \rightarrow q$$
$$q \rightarrow r$$
$$\therefore \quad p \rightarrow r$$

OR

$$p \rightarrow q$$
$$q \rightarrow r$$
$$r \rightarrow s$$
$$\therefore \quad p \rightarrow s$$

Some arguments might be expressed in the form of even longer chains of such implications, with each term serving as a middle term for the ones before and after it, until the last term is reached.

As soon as we realize that things are this simple, then we can approach the task of doing logic with an unprecedented self-confidence. For now we realize that there is virtually nothing that we can't determine about the deductive validity or invalidity of any deductive argument whatever—as long as we can clearly understand what it is that the speaker or writer is trying to communicate.

With this kind of confidence, let's return to that argument that seemed so hopelessly cumbersome at the beginning of the chapter—argument (4).

(4)　All taxpayers who claim business expenses, including depreciation or lease payment deductions for any listed property, must complete Part III of Form 4562, unless the taxpayer in question operated a business as a sole proprietorship. John Smith did not operate a business as a sole proprietorship, and he did claim a lease payment deduction for a listed property. Certainly, he must complete Part III of Form 4562.

We can begin to simplify the argument by replacing the cumbersome legal phrases with symbols that stand for them. As mentioned earlier, it is often helpful to use letters or symbols that suggest the actual words in the relevant phrase, so that we do not forget what the letters and symbols stand for later on in the analysis. In this argument we use the following symbols in place of the phrases.

T　=　'taxpayer'
C　=　'claim business expenses, including depreciation or lease payment deductions for any listed property'
P　=　'must complete Part III of Form 4562'
O　=　'operate a business as a sole proprietorship'
J　=　'John Smith'

Then the first statement of the argument can be written much more simply:

If　　$\boxed{\text{T \& C}}$　　*then*　　$\boxed{\text{P}}$　　*unless*　　$\boxed{\text{O}}$

Here we have used the technique of converting statements into 'if-then' form whenever possible. The meaning of the statement remains the same if we state it in the form, '*If* someone is a taxpayer and claims business expenses, *then* that person must complete Part III,' etc.

We can simplify the statement still further by converting the *unless* clause into an *if-then* relationship. We saw earlier that

| We will play ball | ***unless*** | it rains |

means the same thing as

If | it does ***not*** rain | ***then*** | we will play ball |

Applying the same principle to the example we are now analyzing, we can say that the statement

| If **T & C** then **P** | ***unless*** | **O** |

means the same thing as

If not | **O** | ***then*** | If **T & C** then **P** |

Or, equivalently,

If | **~O** | ***then*** | If **T & C** then **P** |

And we can simplify this still further to mean

If | **~O & T & C** | ***then*** | **P** |

Or, equivalently,

If | **T & C & ~O** | ***then*** | **P** |

And it becomes even more simple if we use the symbolic notation for implications:

$$(T \text{ \& } C \text{ \& } {\sim}O) \rightarrow P$$

Now if we can similarly simplify the second and third statements in the argument, it will be easy to decide whether the argument is valid. Using the same symbols we just chose, the second statement in the argument becomes:

$$J \rightarrow (T \text{ \& } C \text{ \& } {\sim}O)$$

That is, John Smith is a taxpayer and claims a business expense (i.e., a lease payment deduction for a listed property) and did not operate a business as a sole proprietorship. The third statement, which is the conclusion, can be written:

$$J \rightarrow P$$

That is, John Smith must complete Part III of Form 4562.

Notice that it is easier to see the logical relations if we reverse the order of the two premises, so that the statement beginning with '**J**' is the first statement in our diagram. (It is usually easier if the first term in the first premise is the same as the first term in the conclusion.) We can then write the entire argument in the form:

$$J \rightarrow (T \,\&\, C \,\&\, \sim O)$$
$$\underline{(T \,\&\, C \,\&\, \sim O) \rightarrow P}$$
$$\therefore \quad J \rightarrow P$$

When we simplify the argument to this extent, it becomes evident that it is valid, because it says that **J** implies **(T & C & ~O)**, which in turn implies **P**. Therefore, **J** implies **P**.

Using the techniques we have discussed so far should enable us to determine whether any argument whatever is deductively valid, provided that the statements in the argument are in universal form. (To analyze arguments involving nonuniversal statements requires one additional technique, which will be discussed in Chapter 5 on 'syllogistic logic.') Given a reasonable amount of practice, this entire analytical process can become virtually second nature.

EXERCISES I

A. *Remembering that it is often useful to transform various kinds of statements into the form of an implication, rephrase each of the following **unless** statements as an **if-then** statement with equivalent meaning.*

Example: I will fail the course unless I pass this test.

Solution: *The statement initially connects two key concepts in this way:*

| I fail the course | **unless** | I pass this test |

The unless clause becomes simply a condition whose negative is sufficient to ensure failing the course. So the statement can be written in the form of an implication as follows:

~| I pass this test | → | I fail the course |

The implication can be read as: 'If I don't pass this test, then I will fail the course.'

*Now rephrase each of the following into the form of an **if-then** statement:*

1. Persons not covered under section 6(c) will qualify for this policy unless they have dependents.

2. With the exception of those who have a strong background in both physics and chemistry, prospective physics majors should begin by taking Physics 101 and Chemistry 101.

3. The Republicans will lose unless they can attract the religious fundamentalist vote.

4. If we can complete a twenty-yard pass and get out of bounds before the clock runs out, then we will be in field goal range unless the pass play is called back because of a penalty or the wind shifts away from the direction of the kick.

B. *In this part of the exercise, we use the above technique in the context of an argument to determine its validity. Determine whether each of the following arguments is valid.*

1. Persons not covered under section 6(c) will qualify for this policy unless they have dependents. John Smith is not covered under section 6(c), and he has dependents. Therefore, he qualifies for the policy.

2. If the Republicans can raise enough funds for an effective media campaign and attract the blue-collar vote, they will win the election, unless they alienate the religious fundamentalists and blacks turn out in large numbers. They already have enough money for an effective media campaign, as we have seen in their TV ads, and they do have the blue-collar vote, as evidenced by the AFL endorsement. Although blacks are expected to turn out in large numbers, the Republicans have not alienated the religious fundamentalists. Therefore, they will win the election.

EXERCISES II

In each of the following arguments, notice that the first premise asserts one simple logical relationship between two lengthy concepts. Bearing this in mind, diagram the structure of each argument and deduce your own valid conclusion from the premises given. State your conclusion in words.

1. A significant decrease in the flow of cocaine shipments into any large American city has been proven sufficient to cause a substantial increase in the average price of cocaine on the streets of that city, adjusted for inflation. But police statistics show that there has been no substantial increase in the average price of cocaine on the streets of large American cities after adjusting for inflation, since the Drug Czar initiated his "war on drugs." We may therefore conclude that . . .

2. If being victimized by serious child abuse were not one of the factors that cause people to become criminals later in life, then there would be no statistical correlation, in a randomly selected group of criminals and noncriminals, between the incidence of child abuse victimization and later criminal activity on the part of the abused child. But statistics have consistently shown that there is a highly significant correlation between child abuse victimization and later criminal activity in studies focusing on randomly selected groups of criminals and noncriminals. From these assumptions, it follows logically that . . .

3. We must either begin now to restructure the entire sociopolitical system so that large segments of the next generation are not robbed of the opportunity to compete economically because of such social problems as poverty, poor schools, malnutrition, hopelessness of being able to attend college, and the domination of neighborhoods by street gangs, or else face the bleak prospect of an ever-increasing number of disenfranchised, hopeless, and angry people who will eventually turn to rioting and violence which, coupled with the increasing social expense of dealing with more crime, unemployment, drug use, and the increased health problems of the poor, will result in political destruction of society as we know it. The conservative philosophy which now dominates American thought will prevent the restructuring of the sociopolitical system so as to solve these problems of the poor and unemployed. Therefore . . .

4. If the method used by salmon to find their way upstream to hatch their young were dependent on the sense of smell, then salmon with their olfactory glands severed would not be able to find their way upstream to their original spawning areas. Evidence shows that salmon with severed olfactory glands find their way easily to their original spawning areas. This shows that . . .

EXERCISES III

Determine whether each of the following is valid or invalid, reformatting whenever necessary.

Example:
$$X \rightarrow \sim Q$$
$$\sim Z \rightarrow Q$$
$$\therefore \quad X \rightarrow Z$$

Solution: *We notice that the 'X' in the conclusion already matches the first term in the first premise, so there it no need to reformat the first premise. The second premise, on the other hand, can be reformatted to read '~Q → Z.' We then see that the total argument can be written as follows:*

$$X \rightarrow \sim Q$$
$$\sim Q \rightarrow Z$$
$$\therefore \quad X \rightarrow Z$$

It is now obvious that the argument is valid, since it follows the familiar form of a three-term chain argument. Now evaluate the following arguments in the same way:

1. $\sim Z \rightarrow F$
   $Z \rightarrow \sim S$
   ─────────
   $\therefore \quad S \rightarrow F$

2. $B \lor F$
   $\sim Z \rightarrow \sim F$
   ─────────
   $\therefore \sim Z \rightarrow B$

3. $M \rightarrow H$
   $\sim H \rightarrow Q$
   ─────────
   $\therefore \sim M \rightarrow Q$

4. $R \lor Z$
   $Z \lor B$
   ─────────
   $\therefore \sim B \rightarrow \sim R$

5. $\sim t \rightarrow \sim g$
   $g \rightarrow v$
   ─────────
   $\therefore \quad t \rightarrow v$

6. $y \rightarrow b$
   $\sim y \rightarrow c$
   ─────────
   $\therefore \quad b \rightarrow \sim c$

7. No non-Scythians are Ethiopians, and all Ethiopians are vegetarians, so all non-vegetarians are Scythians.

8. If I do not return the book, I will get a fine, and I will return the book only if it is overdue; hence, if the book is not overdue, I will not get a fine.

9. The people of the United States are gullible, since if a group of people is not gullible, they would not be taken in by such pathetic tactics, and the people of the United States were taken in by those tactics last night.

10. No apple pies are good when served cold, since all fruit dishes are best served warm, and apple pies are fruit dishes.

EXERCISES IV

For the following arguments, make a symbolic diagram and fill in the missing premise.

Example: If the war succeeds, the president will be a hero. Therefore, if the war succeeds, the -president will be re-elected.

Solution: *The stated premise and the conclusion can be diagramed as follows:*

$$WS \rightarrow PH$$
─────────
$$\therefore \quad WS \rightarrow PR$$

To make a valid argument, we need the terms **'PH'** *and* **'PR'** *to repeat themselves in the second premise, as follows:*

$$WS \rightarrow PH$$
$$PH \rightarrow PR$$
─────────
$$\therefore \quad WS \rightarrow PR$$

Now follow a similar procedure with each of the following:

1. Since that which is ever in motion is immortal, the soul is immortal.

2. A nation without a conscience is a nation without a soul. A nation without a soul is a nation which cannot live. Therefore. . . .

3. Since history turns out badly for them, small countries tend to remember history especially well.

4. No enthymemes are complete, so this argument is incomplete.

5. All arguments for distributive justice are flawed, since all arguments for distributive justice make an illicit assumption.

CHAPTER 5

The Logic of Syllogisms

So far, we have not discussed any rules of logic that would enable us to make inferences from nonuniversal premises—premises that are presented as being true sometimes (but not always) or in some cases (but not all cases). For example, consider the statement 'Some Democrats are liberals.' If we take as a second premise that John Smith is a Democrat, we cannot deduce the conclusion that Smith is therefore a liberal. Even if the first premise were 'Most Democrats are liberals,' we still could not make this inference.

To cover situations in which premises are not universal (and this includes many situations in real life), we need to learn a few additional techniques for making deductive inferences. These additional techniques often go under the name *'syllogistic logic'* because they deal with 'syllogisms.' Such arguments can involve either *universal* generalizations ('All dogs are animals') or *nonuniversal* generalizations ('Some Democrats are liberals').

Many logic textbooks require students to learn two completely different systems of logic—*'sentential'* logic, which deals with logical relations between whole sentences ('If Tom invites Mary to the party, she will go'), and *'syllogistic'* logic, which deals with logical relations between *concepts* ('All Harvard students are men'). Traditionally, the two main systems for handling syllogistic logic are those devised by Aristotle in ancient Greece ('traditional syllogistic theory') and more recently by Gottlob Frege ('modern predicate logic')—and both systems are very complex.[1]

Our definitions avoid this extra complexity. Remember that we defined the relation of 'implication' to refer to both relations between sentences ('If Tom invites Mary, then she will go') *and* relationships between concepts ('All Democrats are liberals'). Consequently, we can still use all the rules we have learned about arguments involving generalizations and concepts by adding a few new rules to cover nonuniversal statements.

The rules we have covered so far allow inferences from premises that are universally true, ('All Harvard students are men, therefore anyone who is not a man is not a Harvard student'). These rules also allow inferences from premises about particular individuals ('My dog is a collie, therefore any dog that is not a collie is not my dog'). But they do *not* cover inferences from nonuniversal premises: '*Some* Democrats are liberals, therefore anyone who is not liberal is not a Democrat,' for example, would be an invalid inference. To cover nonuniversal situations, we need to introduce a new logical symbol and two new rules.

---

[1]For an interesting and readable comparison of these two systems, see Jacques Maritain, *An Introduction to Logic* (New York: Sheed and Ward, 1937); or Kenton Machena, *Basic Applied Logic* (Glenview, IL: Scott, Foresman, 1982).

We shall use the notation

$$\text{Some } p \rightarrow q$$

to mean 'Some **p**'s are **q**'s,' or '**p**'s are sometimes **q**'s.' This notation can also be used to symbolize nonuniversal relations between *statements*: 'In some cases, if a person stops breathing, the person is dead.' But this last type of situation is rare. Usually, a nonuniversal statement asserts a relation between concepts rather than between statements.

A typical example of negative concepts used in this context, 'Some Harvard students are not women' can be written

$$\text{Some } H \rightarrow \sim W$$

Notice that a statement of the form '*No* Harvard students are women' is written

$$H \rightarrow \sim W$$

and is handled just as any other universal statement would be handled, according to the rules already learned.

1.   The Four Types of Propositions

Propositions in which a predicate is asserted of a subject can have four patterns. Using the letters **p** and **q**, we can write them as follows:

1.	**All ps are qs.**	or	$p \rightarrow q$
2.	**No ps are qs**	or	$p \rightarrow \sim q$
3.	**Some ps are qs**	or	Some $p \rightarrow q$
4.	**Some ps are not qs**	or	Some $p \rightarrow \sim q$

The relation between the subject and the predicate in each of these sentence patterns can be regarded as a relation between two concepts or between two classes or kinds of things.

We already know that a proposition of the form '$p \rightarrow q$' can be reformatted by transposition as '$\sim q \rightarrow \sim p$.' Now, with the nonuniversal statements we have a different situation. Consider the sentence "**Some cats are black**." It is easy to see that the relationship stated can also be expressed by saying that "**Some black things are cats**." The two statements assert that the class of cats and the class of black things have at least one member in common. Hence we can state the following equivalence:

$$(\text{Some } p \rightarrow q) \ \equiv \ (\text{Some } q \rightarrow p).$$

And by the same reasoning we can assert that

$$(\text{Some } p \rightarrow \sim q) \ \equiv \ (\text{Some } \sim q \rightarrow p).$$

This new equivalence we shall call ***Nonuniversal Transposition.***

The recognition that each of the four types of subject-predicate propositions has two equivalent forms will be important for the process of determining validity and invalidity in syllogisms.

2.   Syllogisms

The argument type called syllogism consists of two premisses, each of which can be a universal or a nonuniversal proposition. The conclusion is also a sentence of one of the two types. Further, a syllogism contains a total of three concepts or terms, each being used in two propositions. The term that is present in both premisses is called *the middle term*. This term shows the connection between the two premisses.

We shall now discuss the patterns of syllogism that are valid. First, let us consider a syllogism that consists of universal premisses with a universal conclusion, like the following:

All moths are insects.
All insects are invertebrates.
Therefore, all moths are invertebrates.

Using the letters **M** for 'moths,' **I** for 'insects' and **N** for 'invertebrates,' we can symbolize the argument as follows:

$$M \rightarrow I$$
$$I \rightarrow N$$
$$\therefore \quad M \rightarrow N$$

We know that this pattern is valid; it is a chain argument This pattern is a case of transitivity, which means that a predicate of a given subject can be transferred to another subject. A syllogism is valid if transitivity can be established for it. It is not difficult to examine the different patterns of syllogisms to determine in which cases transitivity occurs. Let us begin with the pattern

$$\text{Some } p \rightarrow q$$
$$q \rightarrow r$$
$$\therefore \quad \text{Some } p \rightarrow r$$

There are a number of ways to show the validity or invalidity of syllogisms. We shall use simple diagrams in which circles represent the different classes represented by the terms. Since all **q**'s are **r**'s, we draw the circle of the **q**'s inside that of the **r**'s. And since there is at least one **p** hat is **q**, we represent it by a cross. Now, we can see that that **p** *is* inside the circle of the **r**'s. Hence it follows that "**Some p is r**." Thus, the argument pattern is valid. We shall call this valid form *Chain Argument II*.

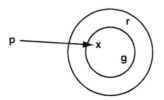

Now let us take up the pattern

$$p \rightarrow q$$
$$\text{Some } q \rightarrow r$$

$$\therefore \quad \text{Some } p \rightarrow r$$

Let us diagram it. The circle of **p**s lies inside the circle of **q**s. Now, the **q** that is r may lie inside of the **p** circle, but it may also lie outside of it, as we have shown in the diagram. This possible situation shows that the argument pattern is invalid. It is possible for the premises to be true and conclusion false. I should be noticed that if the conclusion were universal, the pattern would also be invalid.

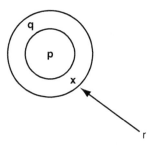

Another possible pattern is

$$\text{Some } p \rightarrow q$$
$$\text{Some } q \rightarrow r$$

$$\therefore \quad \text{Some } p \rightarrow r$$

As we diagram the relationships involved, we see that the **p** that is **q** may not coincide with the **q** that is **r**. Thus, the pattern is invalid. Of course, if the conclusion were universal, the resulting pattern would be with a stronger reason invalid.

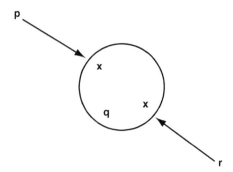

Hence we can conclude that there are only two cases of transitivity and thus only two valid patterns of syllogism, which we have called **Chain Argument I** *and* **Chain Argument II:**

Chain Argument I	Chain Argument II
$p \rightarrow q$	Some $p \rightarrow q$
$q \rightarrow r$	$q \rightarrow r$
$\therefore\ p \rightarrow r$	$\therefore$ Some $p \rightarrow r$

3. Determining Validity and Invalidity in Syllogisms

We have seen that there are only two valid patterns of syllogism. However, since each of the four types of propositions has two equivalent forms, the validity or invalidity of a syllogism often not apparent upon inspection. It is often necessary to use transpositions in order to state the argument in a way that shows whether it has a valid form or not.

Given a syllogism, the first thing we must look at is the nature of the premises. If the syllogism has two universal premises and a universal conclusion, then to be valid it must conform to *Chain Argument I*. If it has one universal and one nonuniversal premise, and a nonuniversal conclusion, then it must conform to *Chain Argument II*. Any other arrangement of premises immediately shows that the syllogism is invalid. Thus, we have only two situations in which validity is possible. Let us now see how to work out the comparison of specific arguments with the valid forms.

Consider the argument

Some flying creatures are mammals.
No snakes are flying creatures.
Therefore, some mammals are not snakes.

Let us symbolize the argument, using **F** for 'flying creatures,' **S** for 'snakes,' and **M** for 'mammals.' We get:

$$\text{Some } F \rightarrow M$$
$$S \rightarrow \sim F$$
$$\therefore\quad \text{Some } M \rightarrow \sim S$$

First we notice that there is one universal and one particular premise, and the conclusion is particular. This argument *could* be a case of *Chain Argument I*, but we don't know yet.

Now we seek to put the terms in the same order as they are in the *Chain Argument I* form. We use one or two transpositions to do this. The middle term **F** should be on the right in the first premise and on the left in the second. Now *we write just the premises*, and transpose both premises to obtain

Some $M \rightarrow F$	*Nonuniversal Transposition*
$F \rightarrow \sim S$	*Transposition*

Then we find out if something follows from these premises. We can see that the conclusion

$$\text{Some } M \to \sim S$$

follows from the premises. The argument is valid.

Let us consider another argument:

Lizards are not snakes.
Copperheads are snakes.
Therefore, lizards are not copperheads.

Since the two premises and the conclusion are universal propositions, we know that the argument must conform to the form of *Chain Argument I* if it is valid. Let us name the terms in the argument as follows:

lizards—L
snakes—S
copperheads—C

The argument can then be symbolized:

$$L \to \sim S$$
$$\underline{C \to S}$$
$$\therefore \quad L \to \sim C$$

Now we make whatever changes we need to follow the pattern of *Chain Argument I* in the premises. We must place the middle term once on the right and once on the left. If we transpose the second premise we obtain

$$L \to \sim S$$
$$\sim S \to \sim C$$

The middle term is $\sim S$ and we can see that the conclusion $L \to \sim C$, which is the conclusion given. Thus, the argument is valid.

4.   Two Important Cases of Invalid Syllogisms

Consider the following syllogism.

All doctors administer first aid.
Some nurses administer first aid.
Therefore some nurses are doctors.

Let us name the terms as follows:

Doctors—D
Nurses—N
Administers first aid—A

The argument can now be stated as:

$$D \rightarrow A$$
$$\text{Some } N \rightarrow A$$
$$\therefore \quad \text{Some } N \rightarrow D$$

We can now rewrite the argument, placing the nonuniversal premise on top, and transposing the universal premise to place the middle term in the correct position. Thus we get

$$\text{Some } N \rightarrow A$$
$$\sim A \rightarrow \sim N$$

Now we notice that the middle term in the first premise is **A**, but in the second it is negative, **~A**. Hence, *the two premises do not really have a term in common, and nothing follows from them.* This is a common cause of invalidity. We shall call it ***middle term affirmative and negative.***

Another common form of invalid argument that is often persuasive is found in the following example: "Some Americans are Democrats. Some Democrats favor nationalized health care. Thus some Americans favor nationalized health care." The reason this argument sounds intuitively appealing, even though it is not valid, is that we are tempted to assume additional information that is not stated. Since we naturally assume that all Democrats in the example are Americans, we intuitively are inclined to treat this assumption as part of the argument even though it is not stated.

If we do assume explicitly that all Democrats are Americans, and that some Democrats favor national health care, it *is* a valid inference that some Americans favor national health care. The argument would look this way:

$$\text{Some } D \rightarrow FNHC$$
$$D \rightarrow A$$
$$\therefore \quad \text{Some } A \rightarrow FNHC$$

It is necessary to reformat this argument to see that it is valid. The principle of *nonuniversal transposition* tells us that '**Some D → FNHC**' is equivalent with '**Some FNHC → D**,' and that the conclusion, '**Some A → FNHC**,' is equivalent with 'Some **FNHC → A**.' So the argument can be re-written this way:

$$\text{Some } FNHC \rightarrow D$$
$$D \rightarrow A$$
$$\therefore \quad \text{Some } FNHC \rightarrow A$$

This is the familiar form of *Chain Argument II*, in which the three terms form a chain, and the second premise is a universal statement. Notice that if this were not a universal premise, the conclusion that some Americans favor national health care would *not* be a valid conclusion.

5.   The Question of Existence

As we have seen, a categorical proposition can be interpreted as a relation between two *classes* or as a relation between two *concepts*. A universal proposition can be understood in two ways. The proposition "All cats are mammals" asserts that there are cats and that they are mammals. The existence of cats is implicitly asserted. But there is another possibility. The statement can be meant in a *hypothetical* sense. Suppose I don't know whether there are snakes in Ireland, but I know that snakes are cold-blooded. Hence, I can say "All snakes in Ireland are cold-blooded," although I don't intend to assert that there are snakes in Ireland. Other examples are "All unicorns have tails," "All animals on Jupiter are made of cells."

The first interpretation (that asserts the existence of a class of things) we shall call the *existential*, while the second we will term the *hypothetical* interpretation.

Particular propositions can also be interpreted in the same two ways. Thus, "Some cats are black," means that there are cats and some are black (the existential interpretation). Now suppose that I don't know whether there are cats in Madagascar, but I know that if there were any cats there, some would have to be female. I can express this by saying, "Some Madagascar cats are female," thus intending the statement in a hypothetical sense. In general, the statement "Some **p**'s are **q**'s may mean that there are **p**'s and some of them are **q**'s (existential meaning), or it may mean 'If there are any **p**'s, then some of them must be **q**'s' or 'being **p** and being **q** are compatible concepts.'

What is the importance of all this for reasoning? If we have a syllogism in which the premises make *hypothetical assertions*, it would be incorrect to interpret the conclusion as existential, and vice versa.

Consider the argument "All dragons are fire-breathing creatures. All fire-breathing creatures are dangerous to humans. Hence, all dragons are dangerous to humans." Since the premises are true hypothetically, the conclusion is true, but only hypothetically. Dragons, if they existed, would be dangerous to human beings.

In the following argument the premises are intended hypothetically. Suppose I don't know that in fact there are people with perfect pitch at Clark High School. But I can make an argument hypothetically, as follows. Let us put an **E** or an **H** preceding each proposition to indicate whether it is meant existentially or hypothetically.

(H)	1. Some people at Clark High School have perfect pitch.
(H)	2. All people who have perfect pitch are good musicians.
(H)	Therefore, some people at Clark High School are good musicians.

It should be clear now that the conclusion must also be hypothetical. From the hypothetical premises we cannot conclude that *in fact* there are people at Clark High School who are good musicians.

The essential point of the preceding discussion is that sometimes we construct arguments on the basis of hypothetical statements, and sometimes from existential ones. And we need to know what our premises mean in order to interpret the conclusion correctly. The rule that follows from our discussion is very simple. First, we have to have a syllogism in the form of

Chain argument I or II. If the first premise is hypothetical the conclusion must be hypothetical. If the first premise is existential the conclusion is existential.

The second premise is irrelevant. Let us see why. Consider the form *Chain Argument I*:

$$p \rightarrow q$$
$$q \rightarrow r$$
$$\therefore \quad p \rightarrow r$$

If the premise is intended existentially, then there are **p**s. Thus, since all of them are **q**s, there are **q**s also. And since there are **q**s, and all **q**s are **r**s, there are also **r**s. Hence, the conclusion refers to really existing things. If the first premise is hypothetical, then we are not asserting the actual existence of any **p**. Hence, the conclusion that all **p**s are **r**s must be hypothetical. The reasoning is analogous for the *Chain Argument II*.

There is an important inference that can be made from a universal proposition. Let us first consider an existential one. It is clear that if all horses are mammals, then it is true that some horses are mammals—although this is an obvious and rather trivial inference.

If a universal proposition is stated hypothetically the inference is also valid, but the conclusion must be interpreted hypothetically. So if all dragons are fire-breathing creatures (hypothetically) then some dragons are fire-breathing creatures (also hypothetically). Hence we have the inference form

$$p \rightarrow q,$$
$$\therefore \quad \text{some } p \rightarrow q$$

with the proviso that a hypothetical premise leads to a hypothetical conclusion, and an existential premise to an existential conclusion.

6. Using Counter-Examples to Prove Invalidity

A useful way to prove an argument invalid is to construct an argument with the same form as the given one, and with true premises and a false conclusion. For example we can show that the syllogistic form

$$\text{Some } p \rightarrow q$$
$$\text{Some } q \rightarrow r$$
$$\therefore \quad \text{Some } p \rightarrow r$$

is invalid by the following argument.

Some men are professors.
Some professors are women.

Some men are women.

The fact that we can reach a false conclusion from true premises proves that this argument pattern is invalid. Such an argument is called a counter-example to the given pattern.

Let us take another example. The following argument:

All cats are mammals.

Some mammals are dogs.

Therefore, some cats are dogs.

shows that the syllogistic form is

$$p \rightarrow q$$
$$\text{Some } q \rightarrow r$$
$$\therefore \quad \text{Some } p \rightarrow r$$

is invalid, since the argument has true premises and a false conclusion.

EXERCISES I

Determine whether each of the following arguments is valid or invalid.

Example: No quarks have negative spin. Some particles composed of superstring constituents have negative spin. Therefore, some particles composed of superstring constituents are not quarks.

Solution: *We begin by assigning the letter '**Q**' to stand for 'quarks,' '**NS**' for 'negative spin,' and '**CSC**' for 'composed of superstring constituents.' It is important to remember that a statement beginning with the word 'no' is a universal negative statement; that is, 'no quarks have negative spin' means that if something is a quark, then it does not have negative spin, written as follows:*

$$Q \quad \rightarrow \quad \sim NS$$

We can then write the entire argument this way:

$$Q \quad \rightarrow \quad \sim NS$$
$$\text{Some } CSC \quad \rightarrow \quad NS$$
$$\text{Some } CSC \quad \rightarrow \quad \sim Q$$

Next, we change the order of the two premises, writing the bottom one on top, since the order of premises is arbitrary, and we know that the only way the argument can be valid by Rule 2 is to have the 'some' statement stated first:

$$\text{Some } CSC \quad \rightarrow \quad NS$$
$$Q \quad \rightarrow \quad \sim NS$$
$$\text{Some } CSC \quad \rightarrow \quad \sim Q$$

Notice that 'Q → ~NS' is equivalent to 'NS → ~Q' according to **transposition***; we can see that rewriting this premise in this equivalent way would be helpful, since it would move the 'NS' term to the left, where it could be diagonal to the 'NS' in the upper right, which would allow it to serve as a middle term. So the argument can be reformatted to look this way:*

$$\begin{array}{rcl} \text{Some} \quad \text{CSC} & \to & \text{NS} \\ \text{NS} & \to & \text{~Q} \\ \hline \therefore \quad \text{Some} \quad \text{CSC} & \to & \text{~Q} \end{array}$$

Since this pattern matches the pattern of **Chain Argument II***, we know that it is valid.*

Now diagram and reformat the following examples to determine whether they are valid or invalid.

1. Some modern art is abstract. No abstract art is easy to grasp. Hence, some modern art is not easy to grasp.

2. Some lawyers are not good speakers. All good speakers are entertaining. Hence, some lawyers are not entertaining.

3. No politician is shy. All shy people are introverted. Hence, no introverted person is a politician.

4. Some senators are not intelligent. Intelligent people solve problems. Some people who solve problems are not senators.

5. Some actors are vain. Anyone who is an actor is self-centered. (1) Hence, some vain people are self-centered. (2) Some self-centered people are not vain.

6. All mathematicians are good reasoners. All astronomers are mathematicians. Hence, all astronomers are good reasoners.

7. No crows are white. Some white things are winged. Hence, some winged things are not crows.

8. All lawyers know the law. Some court clerks know the law. Hence, some court clerks are lawyers.

9. Some people are liars. No liars are to be trusted. Therefore, some people are not to be trusted.

10. Some insects are not moths. All insects are invertebrates Therefore, no invertebrates are moths.

11. Some good teachers are not good athletes. All professional tennis players are good athletes. Therefore, no professional tennis players are good teachers.

12. All textbooks are books that are hard to read. Some novels are books that are hard to read. Hence, some novels are textbooks.

13. Some insane people are not criminals. All thieves are criminals. Therefore, some insane people are not thieves.

14. No actors are boxers. All actors are egomaniacs. Hence, no boxers are egomaniacs.

15. No people whose first concern is to win elections are good statesmen. All politicians running for office this year are people whose first concern is to win elections. Hence, no good statesmen are politicians running for office this year.

EXERCISES II

Determine whether the following syllogisms are valid. They are not given in the standard logical order, with the conclusions at the end. You must first determine which of the propositions is the conclusion and then rearrange the argument.

1. All creative people are people who come up with original ideas, so all creative people are intelligent, since all intelligent people are people who come up with original ideas.

2. No writers of cheap sentimental novels are honest artists, but some novelists are not writers of cheap sentimental novels; consequently, some novelists are honest artists.

3. All men are entitled to due process because all men are citizens and all citizens are entitled to due process.

4. Some animals are not animals that should be protected because although all endangered species are animals that should be protected, some animals are not endangered species.

5. All teachers are good lecturers. Hence, some good administrators are not good lecturers, since some teachers are not good administrators.

6. Some cars are expensive to maintain for all cars are complicated machines and some complicated machines are expensive to maintain.

7. No gentlemen are liars. Therefore, no dishonest men are gentlemen because all liars are dishonest men.

8. Since some books are boring things and all boring things are a waste of time, it follows that some books are a waste of time.

9. Since all conservatives are against budget deficits, and all right-wing fanatics are against budget deficits, it is clear that all conservatives are right-wing fanatics.

10. Since all good astronomers are competent scientists, and some astrophysicists are competent scientists, some astrophysicists are good astronomers.

CHAPTER **6**

Solving Complex Problems

1. Determining Validity in Extended Arguments

Once we know the basic rules of logic, it becomes possible to solve problems of any degree of complexity. The key to success is to transform each premise into the form of an implication so that, quite literally, we can see what its implications are. If given a premise of the form '**A V B**,' it is crucial to see that an equivalent way to state the same information would be '**~A → B**.' Another equivalent way would be '**~B → A**.' In solving problems, the important thing is to choose the equivalent form most useful to us in the context of solving that particular problem.

The second thing to remember in solving complex problems is that the human brain is constituted so as to yield the answer to any deductive question, *provided that we formulate the right question to begin with.* If we know what the conclusion is that we are trying to prove, we should then ask ourselves, "Of all the information contained in this set of premises, which one tells me what would imply that particular conclusion?"

This process is easiest to see in a specific example. Suppose we want to know whether the following argument is valid or invalid:

1. **A**	→	**~X**
2. **~A**	→	**~Q**
3. **X**	**V**	**~P**
4.	**Q**	

∴   **~P**

We begin by asking, "Which premise tells me what would imply ~**P**?" We know it has to be premise 3, because it is the one that talks about the concept '**P**.' How could we transform premise 3 into an equivalent form in which something would imply ~**P**? We know that '**X V ~P**' is equivalent to '**~X → ~P**.' On scratch paper, begin writing the equivalent forms of each premise as they become useful in the process of trying to prove **~P**. It is helpful to begin with the conclusion and work backward until we have constructed an obvious proof from the information given in the premises. In this case, we write

$$
\begin{array}{ll}
\text{~X} \;\rightarrow\; \text{~P} & \text{(premise 3)} \\
\hline
\therefore \qquad \text{~P} &
\end{array}
$$

We now see that if only we could prove **~X**, then we could prove **~P**, since **~X** implies **~P**. How could we prove **~X**? We have another premise that talks about the concept **X**. It says '**A → ~X**.' This means that if we could prove **A**, then we could prove **~X**, which in turn would prove **~P**. Add this to the notation on the scratch paper, so that we don't forget it, remembering to continue working *backward* from the conclusion:

$$
\begin{array}{ll}
\text{A} \;\rightarrow\; \text{~X} & \text{(premise 1)} \\
\text{~X} \;\rightarrow\; \text{~P} & \text{(premise 3)} \\
\hline
\therefore \qquad \text{~P} &
\end{array}
$$

Then ask, 'What implies **A**, according to these premises?' The answer, of course, is to be found in premise 2 (since it is the one that talks about **A**), but only after we transform it into an equivalent form. We know that '**~A → ~Q**' is equivalent with '**Q → A**.' Now we see that, if only we could prove **Q**, we could prove **A**, and thus **~X**, and thus **~P**. Add this information to the diagram on the scratch paper:

$$
\begin{array}{ll}
\text{Q} \;\rightarrow\; \text{A} & \text{(premise 2)} \\
\text{A} \;\rightarrow\; \text{~X} & \text{(premise 1)} \\
\text{~X} \;\rightarrow\; \text{~P} & \text{(premise 3)} \\
\hline
\therefore \qquad \text{~P} &
\end{array}
$$

Now if only we could prove **Q**, then we could prove **A**, and thus **~X**, and thus **~P**. But wait! **Q** is given unconditionally as a premise. So the entire set of premises we were originally given has now been rewritten in an equivalent form that is more useful:

$$
\begin{array}{ll}
\text{Q} & \text{(premise 4)} \\
\text{Q} \;\rightarrow\; \text{A} & \text{(premise 2)} \\
\text{A} \;\rightarrow\; \text{~X} & \text{(premise 1)} \\
\text{~X} \;\rightarrow\; \text{~P} & \text{(premise 3)} \\
\hline
\therefore \qquad \text{~P} &
\end{array}
$$

Writing the problem in this equivalent form is more useful to us because it enables us to see clearly, and with no hesitation, that the argument is valid. Using the same procedure, we can determine the validity or invalidity of any complex problem.

2.   Showing Invalidity

We can also prove the invalidity of arguments using the same method just described. Suppose, in working backwards from the conclusion in the way just indicated, we reach the point where no information provided in the premises, even when reformatted, yields a statement with the consequent we are trying to prove at that point. We then know definitively that the argument is invalid.

For example, consider the following argument:

1. **A   V   Q**
2. **X   →   ~Q**
3. **A**
4. **~X   →   R**
5. **R   →   Z**

∴   **Z**

We begin by working backwards from the conclusion we are trying to prove, and ask ourselves what implies **Z**. The answer, of course, is that **R → Z**, according to premise 5. So we can write thus much of our proof:

R → Z   (from premise 5)

∴   **Z**

Now we must ask ourselves: What implies **R**? The answer here is equally obvious: premise 4 tells us that **~X → R**. So we can add this information to our proof, as follows:

~X → R   (from premise 4)
R → Z   (from premise 5)

∴   **Z**

Our next question is: What implies **~X**? Obviously, the answer comes from premise 2. We must reformat the premise using the principle of *transposition* (i.e., by negating and reversing the terms). This yields '**Q → ~X**' so we can add this piece of information to our chain of inferences:

Q → ~X   (from premise 2, **transposition**)
~X → R   (from premise 4)
R → Z   (from premise 5)

∴   **Z**

Then we ask ourselves: What implies **Q**? Premise 1 provides the answer when we reformat the premise by using the reformatting rule *implicational equivalence*, which we noted in Chapter 3 enables us to reformat an either-or statement. In this case, we convert the premise 'A V Q' to its equivalent implicational form, ~A → Q. We can now write:

$$
\begin{array}{ll}
\text{~A} \rightarrow \text{Q} & \text{(from premise 1, \textbf{implicational equivalence})} \\
\text{Q} \rightarrow \text{~X} & \text{(from premise 2, \textbf{transposition})} \\
\text{~X} \rightarrow \text{R} & \text{(from premise 4)} \\
\text{R} \rightarrow \text{Z} & \text{(from premise 5)} \\
\hline
\therefore \quad \text{Z} &
\end{array}
$$

Finally, we ask ourselves: What implies ~A? The answer is: None of the information given tells us that anything implies ~A. A is stated as an assumption (premise 3), but we have no way to prove that ~A is true. Thus we are at the end of our rope. There is no way to prove ~A, thus there is no way to prove any of the subsequent terms that follow from ~A—i.e., Q, ~X, ~R, and so on. If we cannot prove ~A, then we cannot prove any of the subsequent terms, and thus in the final analysis cannot prove Z. Thus the argument is invalid.

Strictly speaking, we have not provided formal rules to cover all of the most complex situations. However, the needed rules can be derived from the rules we have already stated in this book. For example, while attempting to prove Q, we may be given the premise

P & (P → Q)

Common sense tells us that 'P' and 'P → Q' can be treated as two separate premises, yielding

P

and

P → Q

Obviously, we can now use *modus ponens* to deduce Q.

So, while we have not elaborated in this book all of the inference rules that logicians have identified, we have covered enough of them to allow the student to infer the needed rules whenever necessary. And this is the main goal of the book: to provide enough commonsense principles to guide in evaluating any pattern of reasoning that may be encountered in everyday situations.

The next section will explain how to construct a formal proof of a conclusion based on a set of premises.

3.   Formal Proofs of Extended Arguments

There is a procedure that facilitates the process of formally proving an extended argument of the type we have been considering. Let us begin with an example:

Either the computer arrived defective or it broke down in the warehouse.
The computer did not break down in the warehouse.
If the postal service treated the package properly, the computer did not arrive defective.
Therefore, the postal service did not treat the package properly.

In order to symbolize the argument, we must pull out the simplest propositions present in the premises and conclusion. These are the statements that contain none of the logical connectives "not," "or," "if . . . then," etc. Then we give them names.

The computer arrived defective—CAD
The computer broke down in the warehouse—BDW
The postal service treated the package properly—TPP

It should be noticed that the negative statements are *not* simple propositions. Now we can symbolize the argument with the letters we have chosen. After the last premise, we write "*//*," followed by the conclusion we wish to reach.

1. **CAD V BDW**
2. **~BDW**
3. **TPP → ~ CAD // ∴ ~TPP**

Now we examine the premiese and seek to derive new statements by means of the valid rules of inference we know. Any validily drawn statement is acceptable. Thus, we notice that premises 1 and 2 make up a case of *Disjunctive Syllogism* so we can write

4. **CAD**   **from 1,2 Disjunctive Syllogism**

We now notice that if we use double negation on 3, changing it to

5. **~~CAD**

then this statement (5) together with premise 3 makes up a case of *Modus Tollens*. The result is

6. **~TTP**   **from 3,5 Modus Tollens**

And this is the conclusion we wanted. We have proved that it follows from the premises.
Let us prove another example, this time it is given already symbolized.

1. **~T V S**
2. **~S**
3. **~T → ~W**
4. **D → W // ~D**
5. **~T**   **from 1,2 Disjunctive Syllogism**
6. **~W**   **from 3,5 Modus Ponens**
7. **~D**   **from 4,6 Modus Tollens**

It is important to notice that there are usually many different paths to make a proof.

4.   Proving Inconsistency

In Chapter 1, Section 7, we learned that a proposition that has the form '**p & ~p**' is an *explicit contradiction*. Also, a set of propositions is said to be *inconsistent* if and only if an explicit contradiction can be deduced from them.

Thus, given a set of statements, we can prove that it is inconsistent if we can build a proof (as in an extended argument) that leads to a conclusion that has the form 'p & ~p.'

In order to prove inconsistency we use, as a final step an inference that is very obvious. If we have two separate statements we can state them together as one by means of the &. Formally stated:

1. p
2. q
_____
∴   p & q

This rule is called **conjunction.** It allows us to dramatize the fact that a contradiction has been found. Now let us consider an example. We proceed as in an extended argument, except that our aim is to reach *any contradiction we can.* Usually several are possible. Let us show that the following set of five propositions is inconsistent.

1. A V T
2. S → ~N
3. ~T
4. A → N
5. S
_____
6. A   from 1,3 Disjunctive Syllogism
7. N   from 4,6 Modus Ponens
8. ~~N   from 7 Double Negation
9. ~A   from 4,8 Modus Tollens
10. A & ~A   from 6,9 Conjunction

We have found a contradiction. Others could be found as well.

The importance of inconsistency lies in the fact that if a set of statements are inconsistent, they cannot all be true.

EXERCISES I

Determine whether each of the following arguments is valid or invalid by using the method of analysis discussed in this chapter.

Example:

1. p V ~p
2. ~q → ~p
3. ~q → p
4. ~r → ~q
_____
∴   r

Solution: *Working backward from 'r,' we see that applying* **modus tollens** *to premise 4 would show that* **q → r**. *So we know that* **if** *we could prove* **q**, *then we could prove* **r**. *We then see that applying* **modus tollens** *to both premises 2 and 3 would convert them, respectively, to '***p → q***' and '***~p → q***.' Since premise 1 tells us that either* **p** *or* **~p** *must be true, we know by* **constructive dilemma** *that* **q** *is true. We can reformat the entire argument to look this way:*

step 1	p	V	~p	
step 2	p	→	q	(from premise 2, **modus tollens**)
step 3	~p	→	q	(from premise 3, **modus tollens**)
step 4		q		(from 1, 2, and 3, **constructive dilemma**)
step 5	q	→	r	(from premise 4, **modus tollens**)
∴		r		(from 4 and 5, **modus ponens**)

Thus we have shown that the argument is valid.

Now determine the validity of the following arguments on your own. (Arguments continue on next page.)

(1)
1. (p & q) → r
2. ~p → ~s
3. s
4. ~t V q
5. t

∴ r

(2)
1. p → q
2. ~r V p
3. s → r
4. s

∴ q

(3)
1. (A & B) → C
2. D → A
3. ~D → A
4. D V ~D
5. E → B
6. A → E

∴ C

(4)
1. p V ~q
2. r → s
3. t → u
4. ~s & ~u
5. (~r & ~t) → w
6. ~q → ~w

∴ p

EXERCISES II

From the premise given in each of the following exercises, deduce a valid conclusion.

Example 1:   ~x V y

Solution: *Disjunctive syllogism tells us that we can reformat the statement to say that if one of the two options in the alternation is* not *the case, then the other* must *be. From the premise given, we can deduce the conclusion '~~x → y.' Simplifying this expression yields 'x → y.' Thus we can make the following inference:*

$$\frac{\text{~x V y}}{\therefore \quad \text{x} \rightarrow \text{y}}$$

Example 2:   x → (y & z)

Solution: *The terms within parentheses can be treated as one unit. Applying* **transposition** *to this statement yields the following:*

$$\frac{\text{x} \quad \rightarrow \quad \text{(y \& z)}}{\therefore \text{ ~(y \& z)} \quad \rightarrow \quad \text{~x}}$$

In common sense terms, the premise of this argument states that if **x** *is true, then both* **y** *and* **z** *will be true. This entails the conclusion that if it is* not *the case that* both **y** *and* **z** *are true, then* **x** *cannot be true.*

Now deduce your own valid conclusion from each of the following premises:

(1)   ~P   V   ~Q

(2)   ~(~A & ~B)

(3)   (X & Y)   →   ~A

EXERCISES III

Directions: Evaluate for validity, showing your work.

1.   q V ~z
        s → ~r
        s V z
        f → ~q
    ∴ r → ~f

2. $\sim$w   V   p
      m $\rightarrow$ $\sim$g
    $\sim$w $\rightarrow$ $\sim$r
      g   V $\sim$p
    _____
    $\therefore \sim$r   V $\sim$m

3. 1. p $\rightarrow$ m
    2. r V $\sim$t
    3. $\sim$s V a
    4. $\sim$s $\rightarrow$ $\sim$r
    5. $\sim$t $\rightarrow$ $\sim$m
    _____
    $\therefore$ p $\rightarrow$ a

4. 1. r $\rightarrow$ z
    2. $\sim$t V q
    3. m
    4. $\sim$t $\rightarrow$ $\sim$z
    5. $\sim$m V r
    _____
    $\therefore$ q

5. No interesting poems are unpopular among people of real taste, no affected poetry is popular among people of real taste, and no modern poetry is free from affectation. Now, all your poems are on the subject of soap bubbles, and only a modern poem would be on the subject of soap bubbles; hence, all your poems are uninteresting.

EXERCISES IV

Construct a proof for the following extended arguments.

1. If the victim was shot from above, then he did not commit suicide. If the victim did not commit suicide, he was murdered. If the victim was murdered, then his wife murdered him. His wife did not murder him. Hence, the victim was not shot from above.

2. Either the alarm was turned off or it was not in good working order. The alarm was in good working order. If the night watchman was not careless, the alarm was not turned off. Therefore, the night watchman was careless.

3. Either China votes for the resolution, or Russia will note vote for it. If Russia does not vote for the resolution, its Eastern European allies will not vote for it. China will not vote for the resolution. The sufficient condition for the Eastern European allies of Russia to vote for the resolution is that they become alienated from Russia. Hence, the Eastern European allies of Russia have become alienated from it.

4. If Russia does not support the resolution, then Japan will. If Japan supports the resolution, then the U.S. doesn't need to seek more votes to win. The U.S. needs to seek more votes to win. Hence, Russia supported the resolution.

5. Jones will not get a raise. If Jones is successful in his current assignment, he will get a recommendation from his department head. If Jones gets a recommendation from his department head, he will get a raise. Hence, Jones will not be successful in his current work assignment.

6. I will make the sale, if I am persuasive. Either I act incompetently, or I am persuasive. My making the sale will allow me to buy a new car. I will not buy a new car. If I act incompetently, then I run the risk of being fired. Therefore, I run the risk of being fired.

7. If we don't take a vacation this year, we will pay for our car within a year. If we pay for our car within a year, we will save $450 on interest. If we save $450 on interest we will not need to borrow money for our vacation next year. We won't take a vacation this year if my wife agrees. If my wife is fairly happy with things as they are, she will agree. Either my wife is fairly happy with things as they are, or I am not a good husband. I am a good husband. Therefore, we won't need to borrow money for our vacation next year.

8. Either the driver was not watching the road when the accident happened or he did not see the man cross the road. If the driver was paying attention, he was watching the road when the accident happened. If visibility in the area was adequate at the time of the accident, the driver saw the man cross the road. If the driver was not watching the road when the accident happened, he would be tried for manslaughter. The driver was not tried for manslaughter. Hence, visibility in the area was not adequate at the time of the accident.

9. If the litmus paper turns pink, the solution is acidic. The solution being acidic is sufficient condition for our experiment not to be successful. The litmus paper turned pink. Our experiment will be unsuccessful only if we do not follow the instructions correctly. Hence, we did not follow the instructions correctly.

10. If the gardener did not leave the bar before 12:30 on the night of the murder, he was not in the victim's house at 11 o'clock. If the gardener was not in the victim's house at 11 o'clock, he did not murder him. Either the gardener murdered the victim, or else the secretary murdered him. If the secretary murdered the victim, then her alibi is false. If the secretary's alibi is false, we will have to prove it. The gardener did not leave the bar before 12:30 on the night of the murder. Hence, we have to prove the secretary's alibi is false.

EXERCISES V

Prove that these sets of statements are inconsistent.

1. If Mary accepts Tom's invitation to the prom, she has a romantic interest in him. If Mary is romantically interested in Tom, Dick will be jealous of Tom. If Mary does not accept Tom's invitation to the prom, Tom will not go to the prom. Dick is not jealous of Tom. Tom will go to the prom.

2. Thomas will take biology or an elective course this semester. If Thomas takes an elective course this semester, he will make a bad grade in it. Thomas will not take biology this semester. Either Thomas doesn't get a bad grade in the elective course or he will not get a car from his father. Thomas will get a car from his father.

3. Either the solution we obtained was not acidic or the litmus paper we used to test it does not work. If the solution was not acidic, then our experiment to obtain hydrochloric acid was not correctly performed. The experiment was correctly performed. The litmus paper we used works.

4. 1. ~B → N
   2. ~N
   3. ~B

5. 1. ~S V ~N
   2. P → N
   3. S
   4. ~P → ~T
   5. T

6. 1. ~S → ~B
   2. ~N → ~T
   3. ~B → ~N
   4. T
   5. S → ~G
   6. G

7. 1. B → S
   2. F → D
   3. B V F
   4. ~S
   5. ~D

8. **1.** ~A V ~C
    2. D →   C
    3. A
    4. ~D → ~W
    5. W

9. **1.** S
    2. D → ~T
    3. ~T →   A
    4. ~F → ~A
    5. D
    6. ~F V ~S

10. **1.** K
    2. ~G V ~X
    3. X   V ~D
    4. D   V ~W
    5. G
    6. ~W→ ~F
    7. K   →   F

CHAPTER 7

Thinking Logically about Value Issues

1.   The Importance of Logic in Value Discussions

It has become increasingly fashionable in recent years to think of ethical and value beliefs as issues that do not lend themselves to reasoned argument and logical analysis. Even early twentieth century philosophers began to despair of their attempts to "prove" the truth of their basic value assumptions. More recently, social scientists have demonstrated the diversity of different value systems among various cultures, subcultures, and individuals. And media exposure of the frequent moral hypocrisy and self-absorption of public figures, coupled with control of public institutions by power politics and economic interests, has led to a general cynicism about the rationality of value beliefs.

It still seems true, however, that value beliefs are not merely arbitrary whims on the part of those who believe in them. Most people, after momentary reflection, can think of reasons for their beliefs. Most of us do not mindlessly adopt the value assumptions of our general culture, or even of our parents and teachers. Most people can think of at least a few important ethical questions on which they disagree with the beliefs of their parents' generation, and with the majority of people in their contemporary culture.

This continual rethinking of assumptions is why ethical thinking continues to evolve. Ethical thinking has changed considerably since Old Testament times, when virtually all cultures considered it morally acceptable to slaughter all the members of a foreign city to resolve a military conflict, or to take their land. Just a few hundred years ago in Europe, one of the most immoral acts was considered to be usury—the charging of interest for loans. This belief changed, not for purely arbitrary, emotional, or religious reasons, but because people decided that it no longer made *sense*, in a rapidly industrializing economy that could promise greater prosperity for everyone, to impede economic progress by discouraging usury.

Today, similar rethinking is proceeding, often on rational grounds, of controversial issues such as birth control, regulation of environmental pollution, racial and gender conflicts in both economic and political contexts, the distribution of educational resources, and methods of reducing criminal behavior. And much of this rethinking involves purely *logical* analysis of whether a given viewpoint makes sense.

Even when people cite religious beliefs as justification for their moral assumptions, it is clear that practitioners of the same religion often have diametrically opposed beliefs on their most basic value assumptions; they *interpret* their religious texts to support their preferred ethical beliefs. Very often people choose how they interpret their religious beliefs based on ethical beliefs that seem to make sense for independent reasons. Otherwise, members of the same religion would not so frequently interpret the ethical implications of their religion so differently. If God is all-knowing, it would be safe to assume that, whatever God's ethical beliefs are, they can be supported with good logical reasoning. The idea that ethical reasoning can be based on logic in no way conflicts with the role that religion seems to play in thinking about moral issues. The important point for our purposes is that people usually have reasons for their beliefs, and those reasons can be submitted to logical analysis.

Rational inquiry into the nature and justification of ethical beliefs often begins when those beliefs are challenged. We may find our fundamental beliefs about good and bad, right and wrong, challenged for several reasons. First, we may be confronted with a situation that brings two or more of our fundamental beliefs into conflict with each other. Confronted with the decision whether to engage in illegal activities to protect Jews from the Gestapo during World War II in Germany, many conscientious Germans became persuaded that one should choose the action that produces the most desirable consequences measured by human well-being (in this case, saving the lives of the Jews), even when doing so involved extensive illegal activities, sometimes including murder of Nazi informants. They adopted an essentially utilitarian position; that is, they believed that one should do whatever produces the greatest human well-being in the given circumstances, rather than obeying preconceived rules of conduct presumed to be valid regardless of the consequences.

This utilitarian principle of judging actions by their tendency to maximize human well-being also led to assassination attempts against Hitler and to dropping the atomic bomb. President Truman believed that using the atomic bomb, even though it would kill many thousands of innocent civilians, would also save more lives in the long run than it would destroy, by forcing the Japanese government to admit defeat and end the war.

Despite the commonsense appeal of the utilitarian principle, its problems become more apparent when we realize that essentially the same reasoning can be used to support the terroristic activities of the Islamic Jihad and other extremist groups that, like Truman, also think that the bombings and killings in which they engage will ultimately produce good consequences that will outweigh the undesirability of the deaths of a small number of innocent people—consequences expected to relieve thousands from starvation, misery, and political tyranny. The terrorist groups challenge us to consider, for example, the number of deaths that occur each year among Palestinian refugees from inadequate medical facilities, poor nutrition, and generally impoverished conditions. If this large number of lives can be saved by means of a few well-chosen terrorist killings, they ask, then how can anyone disapprove of the killings? But for many people, the outcome of this discussion is just the opposite of what the terrorist thinks: Rather than accept terrorism because it can be justified on utilitarian grounds, many reject the utilitarian value assumption because it appears to lead to the justification of terrorism.

Juxtaposing such life experiences as the German situation during World War II and the contemporary situation involving the Islamic Jihad reveals an ethical dilemma of the most fundamental kind: Should we decide what to do in a given situation on the basis of action expected to produce the most desirable consequences in the long run, or are there certain rules of conduct that no one has the right to disobey, regardless of the consequences? Does a political tyrant have a moral right not to be murdered, even if his murder would probably produce beneficial consequences so far-reaching as to outweigh the life or death of one individual? Both alternatives seem to have their problems, since if we choose utilitarianism, terrorism seems defensible, at least in principle; on the other hand, if we choose against utilitarianism, we seem committed to the strange position that it is sometimes all right to act according to the rules even if we know that it will produce disastrous consequences—for example, telling the truth even when doing so causes Jews to fall into the hands of the Gestapo. Part of the challenge of ethical thinking is to realize that, in many situations, conflicting values are at stake, and to develop defensible principles to choose the best balance between the conflicting values. We shall examine strategies used in this kind of thinking later in this chapter.

Another way in which people sometimes find themselves having to justify or defend their ethical beliefs occurs when the members of one culture develop a sophisticated knowledge of the variety of attitudes and lifestyles cherished by various other cultures and subcultures. An obvious example of the influence of this kind of cross-cultural knowledge was ancient Greece. One can make a good case that the cosmopolitan and pluralistic nature of the Greek society, together with its somewhat democratic political institutions that popularized the public debate of crucial issues, was one of the chief factors promoting the open-mindedness and radical reexamination of attitudes and beliefs for which the most famous of the Greek philosophers are noted.

For many ancient Greek philosophers, the discovery that different cultures had different ethical norms was so great as to lead them to regard all ethical norms as based on mere social conventions or customs rather than on any objective validity. This view was especially popular among the Greek Sophists, such as Lycophron and Protagoras, and has been championed more recently by some (but by no means all) analytic philosophers and empirical social scientists, notably the cultural anthropologist Edward Westermarck.[1] It is generally called *ethical relativism*. A popular argument for this type of basic assumption about value issues will be discussed and analyzed later in this chapter.

While simple solutions such as ethical relativism may result from the shock of encountering societies with ethical norms vastly different from our own, another consequence is more careful and sophisticated philosophical thinking. Such philosophical thinking further clarifies the rational basis of ethical beliefs. In ancient Greece, Socrates, Plato, and Aristotle exemplified this response to the challenge of culture shock. Rather than throwing up their arms and saying "It's all arbitrary!" or "One person's opinion is as good as another's!", these thinkers met the challenge by settling down to the hard work of weighing different arguments against each other in terms of their logical validity and soundness. Before rejecting the possibility of discussing value issues

---

[1]Edward Westermarck, *Ethical Relativity* (New York: Harcourt Brace, 1932).

reasonably, we should remember that it is impossible to honestly hold any political policy belief without basing it on at least one value belief. A political policy, is, among other things, a decision to act in certain ways. As such, the validity of the policy can be defended only to the extent that either the results of the action, or the action itself, are believed preferable to a different action or its results. Thus ethical assumptions—that is, assumptions about what kinds of things are more worthwhile than others—are needed to support the policy position. The more democratic a society becomes, the more important it is that citizens critically evaluate the rational justification of value assumptions that support conflicting political policies.

One further factor that often forces us to reexamine our ethical thinking is the realization that many people seem to be dishonest in their ethical views, believing in just those moral principles that either allow them to enjoy moral complacency while condemning others, or to pursue crassly their own personal gain. In fact, examples of the coincidence between moral beliefs and self-interest or self-adulation suggest themselves so obviously that it is only natural to ask ourselves whether our own value structures are completely free of these kinds of intellectual dishonesty. To answer this question, we must inquire into the rational justification for the beliefs in question.

In sum, rational and critical examination of ethical beliefs becomes imperative whenever the beliefs of one individual or culture seem to conflict with those of others, and whenever they seem to harmonize too well with the self-interest and/or the self-promotion of the person who expounds them.

The remainder of this chapter will apply the analytic techniques we have learned to arguments involving value issues. This will require determining the validity of arguments, the same as in any other context. But it also will involve many instances in which the assumptions of an argument are missing or unclear. The next section examines ways of identifying these missing assumptions and clarifying the meaning of what is being said.

2.   Spotting and Clarifying Missing Assumptions

Missing (or covert) assumptions occur as frequently in ethical arguments as in any other. In many cases, a speaker will state one premise and a conclusion, and assume that the unstated premise is understood. Often the first step toward establishing fruitful communication in such instances is to identify and clarify just what is the missing premise of the argument.

Consider this example:

(1)   The law against homosexuality is a law supported by the majority of people.
Therefore, the law against homosexuality is morally justifiable.

In this case, identifying the missing assumption is easy. Remembering that each key concept in an argument must occur at least twice, we see that 'the law against homosexuality' is a key

majority of people' and 'morally justifiable' occur only once, and need to occur twice. Therefore, the missing premise must contain them both. The stated premise and conclusion can be diagrammed in this way:

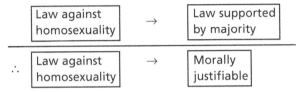

Using 'LAH' for 'the law against homosexuality,' 'LSM' for 'law supported by the majority of people,' and 'MJ' for 'morally justifiable,' this diagram can be simplified still further.

$$\text{LAH} \rightarrow \text{LSM}$$
$$\therefore \quad \text{LAH} \rightarrow \text{MJ}$$

We can see that the missing assumption needs to fill in the connection between 'LSM' and 'MJ,' so it must assert that 'LSM' implies 'MJ.' The argument would then read as follows:

$$\text{LAH} \rightarrow \text{LSM}$$
$$\text{LSM} \rightarrow \text{MJ}$$
$$\therefore \quad \text{LAH} \rightarrow \text{MJ}$$

This argument is unsound, because the missing assumption is completely implausible. It would be virtually impossible for anyone to agree with the premise that *all* laws supported by the majority are morally justifiable, because that would mean that mutually contradictory laws have been morally justifiable. Once slavery was supported by the majority of people, but now the majority do not support it. That would suggest that slavery was morally justifiable when the majority supported it, but not when they did not. While it is logically possible to hold such a position, obviously most people would not, and the burden of proof is on the person asserting the premise to convince people that it is so. As it is, no reason has been offered as to why we should believe that all laws supported by the majority of people are morally justifiable, so the speaker in example (1) has not adequately proved that the law against homosexuality is morally justifiable.

And yet, by filling in the missing assumption, we have facilitated a more fruitful dialogue, because it is now clear that the real basis for the controversy hinges on whether this premise is true. Are *all* laws supported by the majority of people morally justifiable? That is the real question. By shifting the discussion to focus on that missing assumption, we can facilitate a more constructive dialogue on the real reason for disagreement between the opposing parties.

In some instances, the crucial question about a moral argument is whether its assumptions are true in all instances or only in some instances. In syllogistic logic, the crucial question is whether the assumptions of the argument are meant as 'some' statements, or as 'all' statements. We saw in Chapter 5 that whether an argument is valid often depends on the pattern in which 'some' and 'all' statements occur in the argument.

Here is an example of an ethical argument containing a missing assumption, in which 'some' *versus* 'all' becomes the crucial issue:

(2)   Adopting Senator Smith's amendment would balance the budget.
       Therefore, adopting Senator Smith's amendment would be beneficial.

At first glance, it may seem as if the missing assumption is that "Balancing the budget would be beneficial"—which sounds plausible enough. We might then be tempted to diagram the argument as follows, using 'ASA' to stand for 'adopting Smith's amendment,' 'BB' for 'balancing the budget,' and 'B' for 'beneficial':

$$
\begin{array}{rcl}
\text{ASA} & \rightarrow & \text{BB} \\
\text{BB} & \rightarrow & \text{B} \\
\hline
\therefore \quad \text{ASA} & \rightarrow & \text{B}
\end{array}
$$

However, this would be an incorrect way of diagramming the argument! The reason is that 'adopting Senator Smith's amendment' is only a *method* of balancing the budget. To clearly show what the statement implies, we must be careful in the use of the concept of 'implication,' bearing in mind the discussion of the meaning of implication in Chapter 2. Recall the three types of implications. Any of the following types of statements could be written in the form of an implication.

(1)   ____ is a ____.
(2)   All ____s are ____s.
(3)   If ____, then ____.

A statement beginning with an individual thing or event, such as 'adopting Senator Smith's amendment' can be an implication if it follows the form '____ is a ___.' To put this statement into that type of form, it must read 'Adopting Senator Smith's amendment is a ___.' The implication, then, can be captured with the statement 'Adopting Senator Smith's amendment is a method of balancing the budget.'

Bearing this in mind, we then see that, for the two middle terms to match each other, the first term in the *second* premise must also deal with '*methods* of balancing the budget.' To reflect this fact, we must recognize that both premises, the stated one and the missing one, are about *methods* of balancing the budget. The diagram would then follow this form:

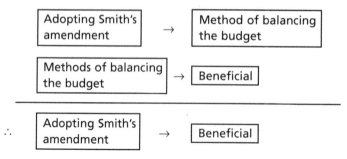

To simplify still further, we can let '**MBB**' stand for '*methods* of balancing the budget,' combined with the same abbreviations used above, and the argument becomes:

$$\begin{array}{rcl} \text{ASA} & \to & \text{MBB} \\ \text{MBB} & \to & \text{B} \\ \hline \therefore \quad \text{ASA} & \to & \text{B} \end{array}$$

Notice that the second premise, '**MBB** → **B**,' as we have diagrammed it here, asserts that *all* methods of balancing the budget are beneficial. It seems to be unclear in the mind of the speaker, however, whether this assumption is meant to be true in all cases, or only in *some* cases. To validly entail the stated conclusion, it must be assumed to be true in *all* instances. But to assume that *all* methods of balancing the budget are beneficial is obviously implausible. We can easily imagine many ways of balancing the budget that would *not* be beneficial. If the speaker means to assume that this premise is true in *all* instances, then the argument is clearly unsound. It does not prove what it is trying to prove.

On the other hand, if the assumption is only that *some* methods of balancing the budget are beneficial, then the argument would be diagrammed this way:

$$\begin{array}{rcl} \text{ASA} & \to & \text{MBB} \\ \text{Some MBB} & \to & \text{B} \\ \hline \therefore \quad \text{ASA} & \to & \text{B} \end{array}$$

If this is what the speaker means, then the argument is clearly *invalid*. In syllogistic logic, we learned that when there are any 'some' statements in an argument, the *second* premise must be an 'all' statement. The fact that *some* methods of balancing the budget would be beneficial is not enough to prove that Senator Smith's method would be beneficial.

On either interpretation of the second premise, then—whether it is meant as an 'all' statement or only as a 'some' statement—the argument is unsound. If we interpret the second premise as asserting that *all* methods of balancing the budget are beneficial, it is clearly an *implausible* assumption. But if we interpret it as asserting that *some* methods of balancing the budget are beneficial, then the premise itself may be plausible, but it is too weak to support the conclusion of a syllogistic argument. The argument could be valid only if we were to assume that *all* methods of balancing the budget are beneficial. As it is, the argument has not provided us with any reason to believe that Senator Smith's method is beneficial. For all we know, it may just as well be harmful.

Another example illustrates the same kind of missing assumption, except that in this case the first assumption is the one that is missing.

(3) The prevention of rape is an important goal that ought to be achieved.
     Therefore, the castration of all rapists is a practice that is morally justifiable.

We can see a missing premise in this argument because each key concept must occur at least twice in the course of an argument. In this argument two of the important concepts, 'the prevention of rape,' and 'castration of all rapists,' occur only once. The missing sentence, then, is the one that would contain both these concepts, and would establish some sort of connection between them. What would this additional assumption have to be to make the argument work?

Following the usual analytical method, we can begin by noticing that one of the key concepts contained in this argument already *does* occur twice, although it is worded a little differently each time. The idea of 'ought to be done' is contained in both sentences. The stated premise asserts that the prevention of rape ought to be done (or "is an important goal that ought to be achieved"), and the conclusion asserts that the castration of rapists ought to be done ("is a practice that is morally justifiable").

To identify the missing assumption, it is evident that the speaker needs to assume some sort of connection between 'castration of all rapists' and 'prevention of rape.' And, as in the above examples, we need to write the missing statement in the form of an implication, and the relevant type of implication must take the form '_____ is a _____.' The plausible relationship between 'castration of rapists' and 'prevention of rape' is that castration is one method of preventing rape (not, of course, the only possible method). Just as in the form of example (2), here 'methods of preventing rape' is a common term shared by both premises.

Bearing this in mind, we are now prepared to diagram the entire argument, including the missing premise. We could diagram the entire argument in two possible ways, depending on whether the second premise is meant as a 'some' statement or as an 'all' statement. If the second premise is meant to assert that *'some methods of preventing rape ought to be used,'* then the appropriate diagram would take the form:

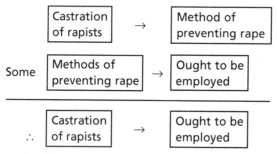

We can simplify still further by using 'CR' for 'castration of all rapists,' '**PR**' for 'prevention of rape,' and 'O' for 'ought to be done,' showing that the form of the argument is:

$$CR \rightarrow MPR$$
$$\text{Some } MPR \rightarrow O$$
$$\therefore \qquad CR \rightarrow O$$

Since this is a syllogistic argument containing a 'some' statement, it can be valid only if its second premise is an 'all' statement. In this case, the second premise is a 'some' statement, so the argument is invalid. The assumption that castrating rapists is a method of preventing rape does not entail that castrating rapists is a method that ought to be used.

On the other hand, if the speaker means for the second premise to be taken as an 'all' statement, then the diagram would look this way:

$$CR \rightarrow MPR$$
$$MPR \rightarrow O$$
$$\therefore \quad CR \rightarrow O$$

In this case, the argument follows a valid form, but it is unsound, because its second premise is extremely implausible. No one would accept the assumption that *all* methods of preventing rape ought to be used regardless of how extreme, and no matter what other negative consequences they might cause.

Completing this analysis is useful not only because it shows that the argument is invalid, but also because it helps clarify the logical reasoning behind this belief, to establish better communication. We can clearly explain why we disagree: The argument would be valid only if we were to assume that *all* methods of preventing rape are morally justifiable. If we assume that only *some* methods are justifiable, and that there are others besides castrating rapists, then the argument is invalid.

3.   The Concept of *Prima Facie* Value

One of the most difficult aspects of discussing value issues from a logical standpoint is that few value statements are absolutely true in all instances. For example, people generally agree that telling lies is morally wrong in most cases, but not when telling the truth would cause the death of an innocent person. Similarly, killing is commonly regarded as wrong, but not when it is the only way to defend oneself against being killed. If such statements are technically mere 'some' statements rather than 'all' statements, it is difficult to see how any specific conclusions can be validly deduced from them. As in example 2, if *some* methods of balancing the budget are beneficial, we still cannot infer that the specific method advocated by Senator Smith is beneficial.

In general, we cannot deduce a conclusion about an individual case from a 'some' statement. Yet most value statements cannot plausibly be asserted as 'all' statements.

To avoid this difficulty, we need a way to attach qualifications to a statement without making it into a mere 'some' statement. The concept of *'prima facie* value' is useful for this purpose. In the context of value theory, *'prima facie'* simply means 'unless some more important value takes priority.' For example, someone might say that "Freedom of speech has *prima*

facie value." This would mean that "Freedom of speech has value, unless some more important value takes priority over it in the given situation." In this speaker's view, the importance of
protecting small children from extreme forms of pornography, or preventing a demagogue
from stirring up a lynch mob, might in some cases take priority over the value of the freedom
of speech. The speaker leaves open the possibility that other values might, in certain instances,
take priority over the value of the freedom of speech. He or she does not specify which types
of instances these might be, but simply leaves open the possibility that there might be some
such instances. Thus to say that "Freedom of speech has *prima facie* value" is to make a more
moderate statement than "Freedom of speech is the most important value in every possible situation, no matter what, and nothing can ever take priority over freedom of speech." Similarly,
someone might say "Telling the truth is something that you ought to do, at least *prima facie*." By
adding the phrase "at least *prima facie*," the speaker leaves open the possibility that there might
be other values that, in certain situations, could take priority over telling the truth—for example,
if telling the truth were to help a group of criminals find a man they are intent on murdering.

Most disagreements about value issues—and therefore also about social and political
policy—have nothing to do with what kinds of things have value. The disagreements usually
deal with the comparative *importance* of these agreed-upon values in those situations when
the values conflict with each other. And that is when the concept of '*prima facie* value'
becomes very useful. By modifying their value assumptions in this way, the opponents in a
dispute can recognize that the other party's goals are worthwhile *prima facie*. Time then is not
wasted arguing about whether those goals have value or not, but can be spent focusing on the
real source of the disagreement—the disagreement as to which one of the conflicting values
is more important in the given situation.

For example, someone might attempt to justify the statement 'Murderers ought to be exe-
cuted' by means of this argument:

(4)   Executing murderers deters crime.
      Therefore, executing murderers is a method that ought to be used.

If '**EM**' stands for 'executing murderers,' '**MDC**' stands for 'method of deterring crime,' and
'**O**' stands for 'ought to be done,' then this person's argument can be diagrammed as follows:

$$\frac{EM \rightarrow MDC}{\therefore \quad EM \rightarrow O}$$

Clearly, this is not a valid argument until we add the missing assumption, which the speaker
obviously has tacitly assumed without explicitly stating it. The tacit assumption is that '**MDC**
implies **O**'—that 'Any method that deters crime ought to be used.' The argument then reads:
'Executing murderers is a method of deterring crime. Any method that deters crime ought to
be used. Therefore, executing murderers ought to be done.' Or, schematically,

$$\frac{\begin{array}{c} EM \rightarrow MDC \\ MDC \rightarrow O \end{array}}{\therefore \quad EM \rightarrow O}$$

Now it is easy to see that this argument is logically *valid,* in the sense that the assumptions do indeed imply the conclusion; but the problem remains that the argument is *unsound,* because its second assumption is extremely questionable, and in fact is almost certainly false. It would imply, for example, that executing petty thieves or marijuana users, or depriving defendants of the right to a fair trial, among other things, ought to be done, to help deter crime. The problem, obviously, is that not everything that would deter crime ought to be done. Thus the assumption that 'Any method that deters crime ought to be used' ('**MDC** implies **O**') *is not true.* And there certainly is no reason why anyone should accept the conclusion of an argument that has obviously untrue assumptions, and is therefore unsound. (Because this chapter concerns value assumptions, we are ignoring for the moment the *empirical* question as to whether the death penalty does in fact deter crime. This type of assumption will be discussed in Chapter 9, which deals with scientific reasoning.)

The qualification that must be added to these statements, to make the argument both valid and sound, involves the use of the term '*prima facie.*' As stated above, in the context of value theory, '*prima facie*' means 'unless some more important value takes priority.' The addition of this qualification to the argument about the death penalty changes it as follows:

> Executing murderers deters crime.
> Any method that deters crime ought *prima facie* to be used.
> Therefore, executing murderers is something that ought *prima facie* to be done.

Bearing in mind the definition just stated for the term '*prima facie,*' this argument can be paraphrased as follows:

> Executing murderers deters crime.
> Anything that deters crime ought to be done *unless some more important value takes priority.*
> Therefore, executing murderers ought to be done *unless some more important value takes priority.*

We now have a more moderate argument that is not only valid; it is also very likely that its value assumption is *true,* provided that the qualification '*prima facie*' is added. We can therefore use value assumptions to logically justify political policy beliefs, provided the value assumptions are true. The conclusion, however, is now much more qualified. Instead of arguing that the death penalty ought to be used as a method to deter crime, no matter what other bad consequences it might involve, the argument asserts more modestly that the death penalty ought to be used unless there are reasons important enough to outweigh the reasons for using it.

But this solution immediately raises another problem. Someone could equally well argue the following:

> (5) Abolishing the death penalty would prevent the execution of innocent men.
> Preventing the execution of innocent men ought *prima facie* to be done.
> Therefore, abolishing the death penalty ought *prima facie* to be done.

This also appears to be a sound argument, but its conclusion conflicts with the other one. We now have two conflicting *prima facie* policy opinions, both of which have been demonstrated to be true. The question that remains to be resolved, concerning the value component of the arguments, is which should take priority over the other: Which is more important—deterring crime, or preventing the execution of innocent men?

To resolve this deeper level value dispute, we must penetrate the overall value *systems* of the two opponents. We must ask what their criteria are for believing that deterring crime is more important than preventing the execution of innocent men, or *vice versa*. When we pose this question, we have entered into a meaningful discussion of the real basis for the disagreement. To do so, we need methods to clarify what the basic value systems are that could lead to the opposing opinions on the specific issue of the death penalty. The next section will discuss these methods.

4.   Intrinsic *versus* Extrinsic Value

We have seen that most value disputes hinge on the real disagreement about the comparative importance of conflicting *prima facie* values. To understand the disagreement, then, we must examine the differing basic value systems that engender differing criteria for the comparative importance of conflicting values. To do that, we need to be able to know enough about a given value system to infer its essential criteria.

A useful tool for this purpose is the distinction philosophers make between intrinsic and extrinsic values. An *extrinsic* value (also called an 'instrumental' value) is something valued because it will help us to realize something beyond itself, rather than for its own sake. We value money not really for its own sake, but because we can *use* it, for example, to buy a car. The car itself has only extrinsic value; we value it not simply for its own sake, but to accomplish other purposes, such as getting to work, impressing our friends, or simply experiencing the pleasure of driving it.

By contrast, an *intrinsic* value is something valued simply for its own sake, not because we can use it to accomplish some further purpose. For example, consider the pleasure that we get out of driving a new car. Do we value this because the pleasure helps us to achieve something beyond itself, or simply for its own sake? Generally, people value pleasure for its own sake, not to achieve something else. Exceptions to this rule can occur, as perhaps when an over-worked businessman takes a pleasure trip so that he can work more efficiently after the vacation is over. In this case, the pleasure of the trip functions both as an intrinsic value (because the pleasure is not completely dependent on an ulterior purpose) *and* as an extrinsic value (because it does help accomplish an ulterior purpose, namely, working more efficiently).

The distinction between intrinsic and extrinsic values is useful because it enables us to understand *why* people value the outcomes that they value. When we understand this, we can then identify the components of basic value systems. And when we have done that, then we know the criteria people use to decide about the comparative importance of conflicting *prima facie* values. It is not that people fail to recognize the issue of competing values, but rather that the person's criteria for weighing the comparative importance of those conflicting values differs from the criteria asserted by opponents.

Many value conflicts are automatically resolved when this distinction is made. If the only purpose of two extrinsic values is to promote the same intrinsic value, yet they conflict with each other, then the conflict can be resolved by determining which will *most effectively* promote the intrinsic value at stake. For example, I might extrinsically value an ice cream cone because eating it would make me happy; and I might extrinsically value losing weight because that too would make me happy. The conflict (I cannot both eat the ice cream and lose weight) can be resolved by determining which alternative will make me happier. The reasoning here is that happiness is the intrinsic value both of these extrinsic values are meant to promote. (This does not imply, necessarily, that happiness is the *only* intrinsic value, as we shall soon see.) As another example, a government might have to choose between the extrinsic value of paving roads and the extrinsic value of keeping taxes low—both of which have value because they promote an intrinsic value, the general happiness. If the general happiness is the only intrinsic value at stake, then the conflict can be resolved by deciding which of the two policies will *most effectively* promote the general happiness.

Notice that, if two people disagree about whether the government should pave roads or keep taxes low, each believing that his or her preferred policy will promote the general happiness, then they do not really disagree about *values*, but about *facts*. Each of the opponents believes that his or her proposed policy will promote *the same* value—the general happiness. The disagreement has to do with which method of accomplishing this purpose is likely to be more effective. This is a factual issue that can be resolved, as any other factual issue, by collecting empirical evidence and interpreting it as accurately as possible. The proposed actions in this case are extrinsic values, meant to promote the common intrinsic value of maximizing the general happiness.

Any disagreement that is genuinely a value dispute must be one in which different and conflicting intrinsic values are opposed. One politician may favor eliminating the Legal Services Corporation, which provides free legal services to those who cannot afford to hire lawyers, to save money for the government (so that the general public can pay lower taxes and thus be happier). An opponent, however, could argue that although eliminating the Legal Services Corporation might promote a slight increase in the general happiness, it would not be fair to do so, because the poor would then have no recourse to their basic legal rights. If this second politician believes that the intrinsic value of fairness exceeds the intrinsic value of maximizing the general happiness, he or she may conclude that the Legal Services Corporation ought *not* to be eliminated. In this case, we have a genuine value disagreement, because the two politicians fundamentally disagree about the priority of intrinsic values. In such situations we must resort to a more difficult mode of analysis to clarify and evaluate the reasoning behind opposed values.

5. Evaluating Basic Criteria for Value Decisions

When the basis for a disagreement is that the disputing parties use different criteria for deciding which conflicting value should have priority, we must examine the reasoning behind those criteria (that is, the differing basic value systems). It is convenient to divide different value systems, or criteria for value decisions, into five broad types. Within each of these types, there may be many variations, but they share a certain type of reasoning with which to reach decisions in cases of conflict. For our purposes here, it will be useful to identify these five basic types of value systems.

(a) Egoistic hedonism.   An egoistic hedonist follows a very simple criterion for all value decisions: that there is only *one* intrinsic value; namely, his or her own personal happiness. The egoistic hedonist may, of course, believe that other people's happiness has *extrinsic* value—but only when and if it eventually leads to the egoistic hedonist's *own* happiness. For example, the egoistic hedonist may help other people so that they will help him later; the intrinsic value for the person remains, however, his or her own happiness. Some people would maintain that everyone should act on the principle of their own self interest. This position is sometimes called '*universal* egoistic hedonism'—the belief that *all* individuals should simply do whatever best promotes their own happiness.

Egoistic hedonism as a pragmatic criterion for value decisions seems to have increased in popularity in recent years. Why are so many people, especially those born after 1950 or 1960, egoistic hedonists? From a psychological perspective, it may be that the increasing complexity of contemporary economic and social realities makes people wish for a simple criterion for resolving conflicting priorities. And what could be simpler than a value system that contains only one intrinsic value? But the question that must be addressed from a *logical* point of view is: What rational arguments can be given for accepting egoistic hedonism as a criterion for value decisions?

A typical argument to support such a position is:

(6)   1. Human psychology is such that people *cannot* do anything but seek their own happiness.

    2. If people *cannot* do something, then it makes no sense to claim that they *ought* to do it ('ought implies can').
    Therefore, people *ought* not to do anything other than seek their own happiness.

This argument has a somewhat persuasive effect because it seems to follow a valid form. Schematically, it would look this way:

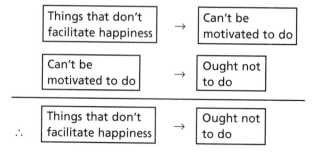

If we use 'C' for 'can,' 'O' for 'ought,' and 'OH' for 'one's own happiness,' the argument sounds as if it would follow this form:

$$\begin{array}{ccc} \sim\!\textbf{OH} & \rightarrow & \sim\!\textbf{C} \\ \sim\!\textbf{C} & \rightarrow & \sim\!\textbf{O} \\ \hline \sim\!\textbf{OH} & \rightarrow & \sim\!\textbf{O} \end{array}$$

The number of negatives in this reasoning make it somewhat confusing, but if we read the diagram in verbal form, it would say "If something does not promote our own happiness, then we cannot do it. If we cannot do something, then it can't be true to say that we ought to do it. Therefore, if something does not promote our own happiness, then it can't be true to say that we ought to do it." This conclusion equals the statement, "We ought not to do anything other than promote our own happiness."

Is this argument valid? We saw in Chapter 4 that, if an argument *appears* to follow a valid form, we must still ask some additional questions about it. For example, does the argument use terms to mean the same thing each time they are used, or are the terms ambiguous? If the terms do not mean the same thing each time they are used, then the concepts communicated by the words are not really the same, and should not be treated as such in the diagram.

Consider the word 'happiness.' It is plausible to believe that everyone always seeks their own happiness *if* what is meant by happiness is 'whatever a person chooses to do whether or not it actually makes them feel good'. We might call this a *weak sense* of the word 'happiness.' In this weak sense, to commit suicide, or to sacrifice self-interest for the sake of a just cause would be to do what makes us happy. It would be doing what we choose to do. But happiness in this weak sense—in the sense of 'whatever we choose to do'—can include things that do not make us happy in the *stronger* sense meant in the egoistic hedonist's conclusion. Egoistic hedonism means that we should seek happiness in the sense that we should do only what makes us actually feel good. If it meant only that we should do 'whatever we choose to do' (the weak sense of the word 'happiness'), it would have no content. Even the most altruistic people do what they choose to do when they sacrifice their own self-interest for the sake of a social cause or a concept of justice, but egoistic hedonism does not suggest that people should act altruistically. Rather, it denies that people should act for altruistic reasons (for the sake of promoting social justice, etc.). Consider the white integrationist ministers in the Southern United States in the 1960s who knowingly sacrificed their careers to work toward desegregation. A pure egoistic hedonism would advise such people *not* to act for the sake of these altruistic social values.

The first premise of the egoistic hedonist's argument is plausible only if 'happiness' is taken in its weaker sense. However, since the conclusion clearly implies 'happiness' in the stronger sense, the argument contains an equivocation. It changes the meaning of a key term in the middle of an argument, making the argument sound as if it proves a conclusion that it really does not prove. Other examples of this fallacy of equivocation will be examined in Chapter 8, which focuses on how to recognize different types of logical fallacies.

(b) Utilitarianism.   Like egoistic hedonists, utilitarians believe that the only true intrinsic value is to maximize human happiness; but, rather than only one's own happiness, they believe that the *general* happiness should be maximized. That is, we should do whatever is most likely to facilitate the greatest possible happiness for the greatest number of people, counting every person's happiness as having the same value. Notice that the value of maximizing the amount of happiness may sometimes conflict with doing what is most fair or just, according to some concepts of justice (see section (c) on page 116).

Here is a typical argument for a utilitarian value system, derived from the argument by John Stuart Mill, one of the most influential advocates of utilitarianism during the nineteenth century.[2] For simplicity, we divide Mill's argument into two parts. The first part is not very controversial and meant only to prove that maximizing the general happiness has *prima facie* intrinsic value.

(7)   1. Maximizing the general happiness is the most effective way to facilitate each person's happiness, insofar as possible.
   2. Each person's happiness is valued by that person.
   3. For something to have *prima facie* intrinsic value requires that someone does value it, could value it, or should value it. This means that if someone values their own happiness, then that happiness does have at least *prima facie* value (unless some more important value takes priority over it). Therefore, maximizing the general happiness has *prima facie* intrinsic value.

There is no need to diagram this much of Mill's argument to see that, granted the premises, the argument is valid. If anything that people value has at least *prima facie* value, and people do value happiness, then maximizing happiness has at least *prima facie* value.

Are these premises plausible? The first asserts that if we maximize the general happiness, we will achieve, insofar as possible, each person's happiness. While maximizing the general happiness may not make everyone happy, it is the closest we can come to that goal. The premise could be questioned, but does not seem very controversial.

The second premise states that each person values his or her own happiness. This premise seems based on observed fact, and is not very controversial. It can be observed in a variety of ways that people do value their own happiness, at least *prima facie.*

The third premise is that "For something to have *prima facie* intrinsic value requires that someone does value it, could value it, or should value it." We should ignore the irrelevant information in this premise, and concentrate on the point that Mill needs for his argument to work: that if something is valued by someone, then it has *prima facie* value (that is, unless some more important value takes priority).

Given Mill's premises, which seem fairly plausible, this part of the argument is valid. But the second part of the argument is more controversial: Here, Mill introduces a fourth assumption to prove that maximizing the general happiness is the *only* intrinsic value.

[2]John Stuart Mill, *Utilitarianism* (New York: Dutton, 1857/1931), esp. 3–4.

4.   No one can demonstrate that we intrinsically ought to do anything other than maximizing the general happiness.
Therefore, maximizing the general happiness is the only thing we intrinsically ought to do.

Schematically, this reasoning would look this way:

4. | Other intrinsic values | → | Can't be demonstrated |

(5. | Can't be demonstrated | → | Have no intrinsic value |) (missing premise)

∴ | Other intrinsic values | → | Have no intrinsic value |

Notice that the verbal argument contains a missing assumption, which we have added as a fifth premise (within parentheses) in the above diagram—the assumption that, if no one can demonstrate that something has *prima facie* value, then it does not have any. Obviously, Mill must assume this to make his conclusion follow—otherwise there would be nothing to connect the "can't be demonstrated" of the fourth premise with the "have no intrinsic value" of the conclusion.

We can schematize this logic still more simply by using 'D' to stand for 'can be demonstrated to have intrinsic value,' 'OIV' for 'other intrinsic values other than maximizing happiness,' and 'IV' for 'intrinsic value,' as follows:

4.   OIV   →   ~D
5.   ~D   →   ~PFV   (missing premise)
∴   OIV   →   ~PFV

Certainly, the conclusion follows logically from the premises. But are the premises true? The fourth premise asserts that no one can demonstrate that anything other than maximizing happiness has value. Mill seems to base this assumption on his study of the history of philosophy. But whether it is really true is questionable. The next section will examine at least one attempt to demonstrate that something other than maximizing happiness has intrinsic *prima facie* value—namely, distributive justice. If that demonstration succeeds, then Mill's fourth premise will have been proven wrong. That remains to be seen.

The fifth premise was not explicitly stated in the original argument, but clearly must be assumed if the argument is to work. Is it true? That is doubtful as well. Many things are true that cannot be demonstrated to be true. However, it might be unwise to act according to an ethical principle that cannot be demonstrated to be true, even with some degree of probability, because we would then be acting according to a principle that is as likely to be false as it is to be true. It might do less harm not to act at all than to act on the basis of a principle that is just as likely to be false as true. Many people might feel prone to give Mill the benefit of the doubt and accept this premise. If so, the crucial question becomes whether the fourth premise is true. Can anyone demonstrate that something other than maximizing the general happiness has *prima facie* intrinsic value? The next section considers this question.

(c) Value systems based on concepts of justice (often called *'deontic' systems*) intrinsically value not only the general happiness (including one's own happiness) but also fairness in the distribution of happiness. They also maintain that, at least in some cases, the value of fairness should take priority over the value of the general happiness. Those who use a justice system as a criterion for value decisions, for example, may believe that it is intrinsically valuable to respect certain basic rights, even if doing so causes a decrease in the general happiness; or they may believe that goods should be distributed in a fair way; or that people should get what they "deserve" in some moral sense; or that certain rules of conduct should be followed regardless of the consequences.

Duties and rights, of course, are correlative: If John has a duty toward Fred, this means that Fred has a right for John to behave in a certain way toward him. Rights can be viewed as the most fair way for people to behave toward each other: Every right is ultimately the right to be treated fairly. There are, of course, many possible interpretations of what is most 'fair.' But fairness is ultimately the intrinsic value that is meant to be promoted by 'rights' and 'duties.'

It is often useful to divide value systems based on concepts of justice into two broad categories, based on two entirely different kinds of 'justice'. In many instances, the same person may believe in both kinds of justice, but it is still important to realize that they are different.

Retributive justice refers to the belief that giving people what they 'morally deserve' has intrinsic (not merely extrinsic) value. That is, there should be a proportion between the rewards and punishments people receive and the moral worth of their actions, intended actions, personality dispositions, etc. A retributive justice thinker would believe that people should be punished in direct proportion to the seriousness of the crime committed, even if rehabilitating them or making a deal with them (in exchange for evidence against some other criminal for example) would contribute more to the well-being of society, or even if doing so requires a painful tax increase to pay for additional prison space. In this case, retributive justice conflicts with the utilitarian value of maximizing the general happiness.

Distributive justice refers to the belief that 'distributing opportunities and/or benefits equitably' (in one sense or another) has intrinsic value, even if doing so conflicts with the value of *maximizing* the amount of such opportunities and benefits. A distributive justice thinker might well be in favor of increasing the minimum wage, even if doing so causes employers to lay off other workers to pay for the increase, thus slowing down production and hurting the economy, which could mean that the minimum wage increase would not be beneficial for the population in general. As another example, a distributive justice thinker would favor government programs to help ensure equitable educational opportunities, even if this required tax increases paid by taxpayers whose children do not benefit from the programs. Some would argue that this is contrary to *retributive* justice, which asserts that people should be allowed to benefit in proportion to how hard they have worked, so that parents who have worked hard to earn money for their children's schooling should not have to pay taxes to send other people's children to school. Of course, this argument would assume that well-to-do parents have worked harder to earn money, which is a questionable assumption.

Whether justice is meant in the retributive or the distributive sense, many different ideas exist about what such justice consists of, and many arguments are given about these ideas. Since this general introduction to logic is not a textbook in ethics, we cannot take the time to survey this interesting field. But one argument for a concept of distributive justice is particularly persuasive. The argument was given by John Rawls,[3] whose thinking has been influential in the American Civil Rights movement, and has laid important groundwork for recent liberal political thinking:

(8)   1.   'Fairness' means the best way to distribute opportunities and benefits (as opposed to the best way to maximize them).

2.   Objectively speaking, the best way to distribute opportunities and benefits can be decided only by a completely unbiased observer whose self-interest is not affected by the decision.

3.   A person in the 'original position' (one who would not know any personal facts that might prejudice his or her judgment) would make an objective decision as to what is fair (how opportunities and benefits should be distributed).

4.   In such a position, this person would realize that a given amount of *very necessary* goods are more valuable than an equal amount of *less necessary* goods (defining the 'degree of necessity' as the extent to which the goods in question affect the person's total sense of well-being). The person judging from this neutral standpoint would not be willing to risk deprivation of very necessary goods for the chance of gaining less necessary goods. If this person were to favor an extremely unequal distribution of goods, in which some must go without very necessary goods so that others may enjoy less necessary (or luxury) goods, this would be taking an illogical risk. The reason is that the person in the original position knows that he or she is going to occupy one of the resulting social positions, but not necessarily which one; thus he or she would not want to risk being in a deprived position. On the other hand, it would be illogical to favor exactly equal distribution because this would lessen the incentive to work hard and would contribute to an unproductive economy. The person in this 'original position' would thus favor a decision principle that would distribute goods with the minimum amount of inequality necessary to give people incentives to work hard, and give priority to extremely necessary benefits and opportunities compared with equal amounts of less necessary benefits and opportunities.

Therefore, the decision principle just described is the one that defines fairness, according to the definitions given in steps 1, 3, and 4, along with the assumption in step 2.[4]

[3]For example, see John Rawls, *A Theory of Justice* (Cambridge, Mass: Harvard University Press, 1971).

[4]This summary of Rawl's argument is paraphrased from Ralph D. Ellis, *Just Results: Ethical Foundations for Policy Analysis* (Washington: Georgetown University Press, 1998).

The argument can be schematized as follows:

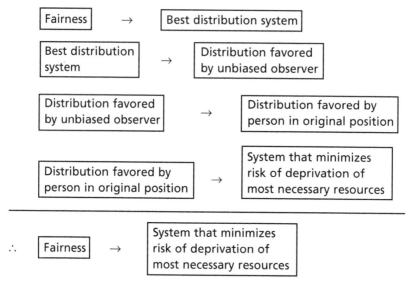

If we use 'F' to stand for 'fairness,' '**BDS**' for 'best possible distribution system,' '**UO**' for 'unbiased observer whose self-interest is not at stake,' '**OP**' for 'person in the original position,' and '**DSMRD**' for 'distribution system that minimizes the risk of deprivation of necessary opportunities and resources while, as a secondary priority, maximizing the chance of gain,' then we can diagram the argument as follows:

$$
\begin{aligned}
F &\rightarrow BDS \\
BDS &\rightarrow UO \\
UO &\rightarrow OP \\
OP &\rightarrow DSMRD \\
\hline
\therefore \quad F &\rightarrow DSMRD
\end{aligned}
$$

Whether the argument is sound depends on whether each premise is plausible. The fourth premise, in particular, is complicated, and to prove it would involve constructing still further arguments. However, it seems initially to be plausible. We shall not pursue this question, but simply note that, if the premises are accepted, the conclusion seems to follow. Rejecting the conclusion requires also rejecting at least one of the premises.

(d) **Personalism** (also called '*self-actualizationism*'). The most complex of all value systems is the one that intrinsically values not only the general happiness, and/or one's own happiness, and/or fairness, but also *self-actualization,* i.e., the opportunity to realize one's full potential as a human being. This does not mean merely that self-actualization is *extrinsically* valuable when doing so promotes the intrinsic value of *happiness*. Personalists *intrinsically* value self-actualization—facilitating opportunities for people to realize their potential as human beings—*even if doing so does not lead to an increase in happiness,* and sometimes even if it *decreases* one's happiness. For example, they believe that we should strive to increase our consciousness by developing our intellects, even if remaining ignorant would keep us happier by protecting us from the pain of acknowledging unpleasant realities.

A simple argument for this position is that, if given the choice to be a very happy dog or a less happy human being, most of us would choose the less happy human being. This implies that the purpose of human life is not merely to be happy, contented, or in an enjoyable frame of mind, but also to exercise certain capacities of the human mind (or 'soul') that cannot be understood in terms of a happiness-maximizing motivational theory. Martin Luther King was a well-known personalist. He believed that creating opportunities for people to realize their potential as conscious beings was more important than the general happiness, although he recognized the importance of the latter. Boston University was a stronghold of personalist philosophy when King did his graduate work there. One of the most important developers of personalism in ethics taught there, Edgar Brightman,[5] who in turn was influenced by B. P. Bowne, the originator of the philosophy of personalism.[6]

(e) Ethical relativism.   Ethical relativists hold that value beliefs are only expressions of emotion or cultural traditions. They therefore perceive no one value system as any more or less correct than another. Hitler's value system was no more or less correct than Martin Luther King's. Things can 'have value,' in the opinion of ethical relativists, only if and because someone values them; the values are only subjective emotions and have no objective validity or invalidity. One person's emotions are no more valid than another's; one culture's customs are no more valid than another's.

In everyday life, one often hears this kind of viewpoint expressed, and it often seems based on the following reasoning:

(9)   1. If rational, well-informed people cannot reach agreement on some given issue, then there can be no objective truth on that particular issue.

       2. But when it comes to value issues, rational and well-informed people can argue indefinitely without reaching agreement.

Therefore, when it comes to value issues, there is no objective truth.

The first question we must ask, to schematize the pattern of this logic, is whether the two premises are meant as 'some' statements or as 'all' statements. Is premise 1 assuming that *all* value issues (even *prima facie* beliefs, such as the belief that human life has *prima facie* intrinsic value) are issues on which rational, well-informed people disagree; or, does it assume only that *some* value issues are lacking in widespread agreement?

An example of evidence for thinking there is no agreement on such issues is that, if we survey different cultures, we find that some (such as the United States) approve taking human lives in certain instances, whereas others (most other industrialized countries) do not. And,

[5]See Edgar Brightman, *Nature and Values* (New York: Holt, 1945).
[6]See B. P. Bowne, *Principles of Ethics* (New York: Harper & Brothers, 1892).

within each culture people disagree on this issue. But does this mean that people do not agree that human life has *prima facie* intrinsic value? Most people who believe in the death penalty do not deny that human life has *prima facie* intrinsic value, but argue that protecting and respecting the lives of the victims of murderers requires the execution of murderers. Even people who advocate killing in certain instances still do not deny that human life in general has *prima facie* intrinsic value. So the second premise seems plausible only if we interpret it as a 'some' statement. *Some* value issues are issues on which there is widespread disagreement.

The same is true for the first premise. People disagree on various issues for many reasons, and not always because of a lack of objective truth. It is sometimes because they lack information that would enable them to make a better assessment of the truth. And in some instances, judgment is unconsciously distorted by self-interest. There was a time of widespread disagreement as to whether the earth went around the sun, but this certainly did not mean there was no objective truth as to whether it did or not. Even while people were arguing about it, the earth was continuing to go around the sun, whatever people's beliefs or feelings about it. So the second premise, that disagreement occurs because of a lack of objective truth on the issue in question, is true in some instances, but not in others. We can accept it as a plausible assumption if meant as a 'some' statement. *Some* disagreements result from a lack of objective truth on the issues.

Since both premises must be interpreted as 'some' statements, the argument takes a syllogistic form.

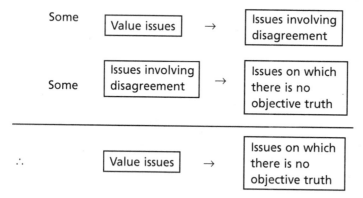

Using '**VI**' to stand for 'value issues,' '**D**' to stand for 'issues on which there is disagreement between rational, well-informed people,' and '**~OT**' to stand for 'issues on which there is no objective truth,' we can further simplify the diagram.

$$
\begin{array}{lccc}
\textbf{Some} & \textbf{VI} & \rightarrow & \textbf{D} \\
\textbf{Some} & \textbf{D} & \rightarrow & \textbf{~OT} \\
\hline
\therefore & \textbf{VI} & \rightarrow & \textbf{~OT}
\end{array}
$$

We know from our study of syllogistic logic that two 'some' premises cannot support an 'all' conclusion. But the argument above seeks to conclude, as a sweeping generalization, that *all* value issues are issues on which there is no objective truth, based on premises that are true only in *some* instances. The argument would be valid only if we were to assume that the premises were true in *all* instances. Since both premises are true only in *some* instances, there is no reason to accept the conclusion of the argument as true. That is, there is no reason, based on this reasoning, why we should believe that all value statements are devoid of objective truth and are only cultural traditions or subjective emotions. Of course, other arguments can be given to support the idea of ethical relativism. We have examined only one popular type of reason for believing in it.

In this chapter we have considered only a few arguments demonstrating some of the prevailing types of value systems. But there are other arguments that people have used to try to establish the truth of each of the value systems we have discussed. If the goal were to discover the complete truth about value theory, we would be only at the very modest beginning of a long road indeed. But at least applying the tools of logical analysis can point us in a useful direction, and can provide us with a road map to help ensure that we can continue to move closer to the goal. It is only necessary to consider more and more arguments in support of more and more value systems, and then logically scrutinize them and compare the results.

EXERCISES I

Diagram the following arguments, which pertain to value issues, to determine whether they are valid or invalid.

Example: If human beings had complete free will, then there would not be systematic correlations, in well-controlled studies, between childhood environmental factors and adult behavior problems. But we do find these systematic correlations in well-controlled studies (e.g., child abuse correlates with subsequent criminal behavior, childhood religious training correlates with subsequent moral beliefs, etc.). Therefore, human beings do not have complete free will.

Solution: *Noticing which concepts occur at least twice in the argument, we see that the key concepts are 'complete free will,' and 'correlation between childhood environmental factors and adult behavior problems.' Using* **'CFW'** *(for 'complete free will') and* **'CEAB'** *(for 'correlation between environment and adult behavior'), we can diagram the argument this way:*

$$\text{CFW} \quad \rightarrow \quad \sim\text{CEAB}$$
$$\underline{\text{CEAB}}$$
$$\therefore \quad \sim\text{CFW}$$

Obviously, this argument is valid according to **modus tollens.**

Now determine the validity of the following arguments:

1. To vote against the new Highway Safety Construction Bill is to vote against spending $10 million per year to save an estimated 20 lives per year, or $1/2 million per life. To vote against spending $1/2 million to save a life is to place a value of less than $1/2 million on a human life. Therefore, anyone who votes against the bill is placing a value of less than $1/2 million on a human life.

2. Killing is *prima facie* wrong, and the death penalty is an instance of killing. So the death penalty is wrong, whether it deters crime or not.

3. In many instances, the right of free speech must be infringed upon to protect more important values—for example, when someone insists on distributing pornography to children or inciting mobs to riot. The value that takes priority over free speech in such instances is the well-being of the people involved. It follows that the well-being of people should always take priority over freedom of speech.

4. In cases where killing is a necessary means of self-defense, killing is morally acceptable. The death penalty is an instance of killing as a necessary means of self-defense. Thus, the death penalty is morally acceptable.

5. Killing is wrong, unless necessary for an individual or group to defend their safety or basic rights when no other means of defense is available. The death penalty is a form of killing, and is not necessary in order for an individual or group to defend their safety or basic rights because another means (life imprisonment of murderers) is available. This shows that the death penalty is wrong.

6. The death penalty would be *prima facie* extrinsically valuable if it prevented even one murder. It is known that John Smith would have killed his victim when he robbed the bank, except that he was afraid of the death penalty. Therefore, in the final analysis, the death penalty ought to be used, regardless of whatever other arguments might be brought against it.

EXERCISES II

In each of the following arguments, fill in the missing assumption needed to support the conclusion of the argument, and state whether that assumption would be plausible or implausible.

Example: Reducing the capital gains tax is a method of stimulating economic growth.
(Missing Assumption)
Therefore, a reduction in the capital gains tax ought to be adopted.

Solution: *Notice that the term that occurs twice in the argument is 'reduction in capital gains tax.' The other two key concepts occur once each, but need to occur twice; they are 'methods of stimulating economic growth' and 'ought to be adopted.' Thus the missing assumption will contain both these concepts. Filling it in where it belongs, the overall argument becomes:*

Reducing the capital gains tax is a method of stimulating economic growth.
All methods of stimulating economic growth ought to be adopted. (Missing assumption)
Therefore, the reduction of the capital gains tax ought to be adopted.

As soon as we state the missing assumption, we realize how implausible it really is.
  Now state the missing assumption in each of the following:

1. Affirmative action is a policy that does not promote the interests of the majority of Americans.
   (Missing Assumption)
   Therefore, affirmative action ought to be abolished.

2. Making deals with criminals who can provide evidence is a means of increasing the deterrent effect of the criminal justice system.
   (Missing Assumption)
   Therefore, making deals with criminals who can provide evidence is a good policy, at least *prima facie.*

3. The food stamp program is a way to help the poor.
   (Missing Assumption)
   Therefore, the food stamp program is a *prima facie* good.

EXERCISES III

*For each of the following value statements, state whether the decision principle being used is a **utilitarian** principle or a **nonutilitarian** principle (e.g., a principle based on a concept of hedonism or one of the forms of justice).*

Example: "A government works project could guarantee that everyone could have a job, but that would reduce the profitability of American industry, which would lead to a less productive economy for everyone. Therefore, I'm against the works project."

Solution: *First ask: What **intrinsic value** is a productive economy "for everyone" meant to promote? The fact that the benefits are measurable by economic prosperity, the purpose of which is **happiness,** combined with the phrase "for everyone" suggests the utilitarian intrinsic value of **maximizing the general happiness.** To achieve this purpose, the speaker is willing to sacrifice a program that would increase the fairness of the **distribution** of benefits (the jobs program). Therefore the speaker is assuming a **utilitarian** criterion for resolving the conflict between these two values. (That is, the speaker considers maximizing the general happiness to be more important than increasing distributive fairness.)*
  Now determine whether each of the following statements indicates a utilitarian or nonutilitarian criterion for decision.

1. I believe that people who receive welfare should have to work for their welfare checks, even if such a policy would cost more than it would save.

2. I don't believe in affirmative action, even if it does increase the overall productivity of the work force, because it gives the minority applicant an automatic advantage over others.

3. I believe that a college education should be considered a privilege, not a right, because our society simply cannot afford to pay for everyone to go to college.

4. Everyone will be better off if we all look out for our own interests. Therefore, free enterprise capitalism is best.

5. I believe in making deals with petty criminals and settling minor criminal cases out of court to save money on court costs—tax money that could be used for other badly needed government programs to benefit everyone.

CHAPTER 8

Informal Fallacies, Ambiguity, and the Art of Definition

A fallacy is traditionally defined as an argument that appears valid, but is not. We have seen many examples in earlier chapters. At this point we need some further exploration and qualification of the definition.

Arguments are mainly used in two kinds of situations: reasoning and debate. In the process of reasoning, a person sets out to find what, if anything, follows from a given set of premises. In a debate, two persons who hold contradictory (or at least contrary) theses about a certain subject, face one another, each trying to persuade the other (and the audience, if there is one), that his or her thesis is the true one.

In reasoning, characteristic mistakes of inference or logical form, which, as we have seen, can often arise, are called fallacies. In debate, logically defective techniques are often used by a contender to compel his or her opponent to accept a thesis. Some of these techniques are actually defective forms of logical argument. Others are not arguments at all, and have nothing to do with reasoning. They are tricks used to influence the opponent and audience to agree with a thesis (even if not persuaded of its truth), or to act in a certain way. These techniques are also called fallacies.

Since mistakes in deductive reasoning and the sometimes intentional errors of logic in debating are different things, it is useful to have different terms to refer to them. We shall call the fallacies that usually occur in reasoning *reasoning mistakes*. Those that arise from an attempt to persuade or otherwise influence an opponent in debate we shall term *debating fallacies*.

The fallacies of *asserting the consequent* and *denying the antecedent,* which we studied in an earlier chapter, are invalid because of their incorrect *form.* These are called *formal fallacies*. The fallacies in this chapter do not depend on the form of the arguments, but on other factors, such as a hidden, erroneous assumption. They are traditionally called *informal fallacies.*

There is no universally accepted classification of fallacies. Since there are many ways in which people can make logical mistakes, it is not really possible to name and analyze all of them. On the other hand, certain kinds of errors occur so often and tend to have such a persuasive effect (even though they do not contain sound reasoning), that it is useful to name and analyze them. Such an analysis helps us avoid these fallacies and recognize them when they occur. We can also gain insight into why these errors continue to be persuasive.

In this chapter, we will examine the most common fallacies analyzed by philosophers and rhetoricians, although the list is not exhaustive. We begin with a group of fallacies characterized by the fact that the premises do not provide sufficient evidence for the conclusion. They are usually called *fallacies of irrelevance*.

1.   Fallacies of Irrelevance

The Ad Hominem Argument. The *ad hominem* argument is a debating fallacy that occurs when a debater attempts to refute an opponent's thesis by making assertions about the opponent's character or situation. The refutation is addressed 'to the man' rather than 'to the thesis.' We shall discuss the two distinct types of this fallacy separately.

When a debater attempts to refute an opponent's thesis by attacking the opponent's character, the argument is called an *abusive ad hominem.* For example:

> Ladies and gentlemen, what Mr. Smith has just told you about the bond issue now being considered by this council is not worth taking seriously, because Mr. Smith is an irresponsible and prejudiced person, and an alcoholic as well.

The irrelevant nature of the statement is clear. Instead of giving reasons why Mr. Smith's statement about the bond issue is incorrect, the speaker attempts to discredit his character. Mr. Smith's character defects (if they are true, which they may not be) are not directly relevant to the truth of what he says. The abusive *ad hominem* argument gives no evidence against the opposing thesis; thus *it is not a valid deductive argument.*

However, although the personal qualities of a speaker cannot constitute a *deductive proof* of the falsity of a statement the person has made, in many situations such qualities have a bearing on the truth of what the person says. For example, if we know that the speaker is a habitual liar, we have good reason to think that the person may be lying in the debate. Or if the person has something to hide, he or she may be lying to avoid revealing something personally unfavorable. Such factors do not prove that the person is lying, although they certainly diminish his or her credibility. Thus, the abusive *ad hominem* argument is invalid if regarded as a deductive argument, but it can be used to present considerations that legitimately diminish the persuasiveness of the statement. If, for example, it can be shown that a person has consistently lied in similar situations in the past, there is a strong probability that he or she is lying now. This differs greatly from arguing that the person has some irrelevant character defect, and therefore his or her position on the specific issue at hand should be rejected. As a rhetorical strategy, this form of the abusive *ad hominem* is often used by a debater to hide the fact that he or she has no real arguments against the opponent.

The second type of *ad hominem* argument is called *circumstantial ad hominem*. It arises when a debater argues that an opponent has to accept or reject a certain proposition because of his or her special circumstances. For example:

> Mr. A's arguments for the increase in machinists' salaries are worthless because he is a machinist himself, and therefore stands to gain by any such increase.

The statement provides no evidence against the thesis that machinists' salaries should be increased and is invalid if regarded as a deductive argument.

However, a person's circumstances may, in some cases, be relevant in evaluating the truth of what the person says. Assume, for example, that a professional soldier, who has remained in the military by choice, argues in favor of pacifism. It would be relevant to point out that a belief in pacifism is inconsistent with the commitments of his profession, and that such a person has not clearly thought out the implications of his own beliefs. This circumstance does not deductively prove that the soldier's statements are false, but it does raise a reasonable doubt about his beliefs and the consistency of his thinking because his actions (as a soldier) would seem to contradict his avowed belief (in pacifism).

To summarize: Both the abusive and the circumstantial *ad hominem* arguments are invalid as deductive arguments. But both types of information can, in certain specific cases, be legitimately used as inductive evidence to weaken the case of an opponent, if the information cited indicates good reasons for doubting a speaker's credibility on an issue. However, in most cases, the character or particular circumstances of a speaker are not relevant to whether the speaker's reasoning is invalid or unsound. The reasoning still must be assessed on its own merits.

The Argument from Ignorance (Argumentum ad Ignorantiam). This fallacy arises when it is argued that the absence of evidence for a particular proposition proves that it is false. It can arise as a reasoning mistake or as a debating trick. The following argument is a typical example:

> There is no evidence whatsoever of the existence of intelligent life on Jupiter; hence, there is no intelligent life on Jupiter.

This type of argument is obviously invalid. The fact that we do not know that a proposition is true does not imply that it must be false. When this fallacy is used in debate, it can be an insidious and very effective tool used by a debater to browbeat an ignorant opponent into accepting his or her position. Suppose, for example, that a person knowledgeable in physics argues with someone who knows very little about the subject. Suppose that the former argues that there is no evidence for Einstein's theory of relativity and it must therefore be considered false. The latter, ignorant of the available evidence, cannot cite it in the debate, and thus he or she and the audience may be persuaded to agree with the opponent, even though the opponent's position is false.

Although the argument from ignorance is not deductively valid, the same type of information may constitute, under certain conditions, important inductive evidence. Suppose that we have known a person for many years, and everything we know about him shows that he is an honest person. The weight of the evidence lends overwhelming probability to the belief that he is honest, although it is not deductive proof that he is. In this situation, as in many others, our knowledge depends on inductive evidence, rather than deductive proof. On the other hand, in many situations, the fact that we have no evidence to prove that someone is dishonest does *not* constitute evidence that the person is honest. The situation must be one in which the person's behavior has been observed over a long period of time, and in a fairly systematic way, with no evidence of dishonesty. This kind of reasoning will be discussed in the next two chapters, which deal with scientific reasoning. For now, we should realize that, when no investigation has been made to discover evidence in support of a thesis, then the lack of evidence either pro or con does not provide any reason to either accept or reject the thesis. Thus, when a person argues that such a lack of evidence *does* constitute a reason to accept or reject the thesis, then this person is using the fallacy of *argument from ignorance,* which should be exposed as the illegitimate trick of reasoning that it is.

Appeal to Authority (Argumentum ad Verecundiam). This fallacy consists of the claim that a proposition is true because a certain authority supports it, as in the following arguments:

> There is no God. Freud, the greatest psychologist of our time, stated that the idea of God is an illusion.

or,

> God exists because many great thinkers have held this belief.

Obviously the fact that someone has a belief is not deductive proof that the belief in question is true. This type of argument appeals to the feeling of reverence toward authorities.

However, we must often deal with situations, or face decisions, in which we have to judge the truth of a statement without the special knowledge required. In such cases, we must depend on the authority of those who have that knowledge. For example, when most of us go to a physician, we accept the diagnosis and prescriptions on the authority of the physician's specialized knowledge. And it is rational for human beings to trust the authority of those with more knowledge than they on a particular subject. Hence, an appeal to authority, although not deductively valid, may in certain instances constitute inductive evidence. Every appeal to authority must be judged on its merits, but the following general considerations are useful in evaluating them:

1. If the authority is appealed to in a subject that lies outside his or her field of competence, then the argument is worthless. An example is the argument that a certain economic theory is true because a famous novelist supports it. This form of the argument may be called the 'appeal to celebrity.'

2. The authority should be identified as clearly as possible. A statement such as "Leading physicians say that X is the most effective remedy against arthritis" is inadequate. It raises questions: Do *all* physicians agree with this statement? Who are these 'leading' physicians? What makes them 'leading'? And what does 'leading' mean? It may be that the 'leading' physicians are simply those who agree with the speaker.

In general, the more precise the identification of the authority, the better the argument. If the authorities are clearly identified, it is easier for us to judge how knowledgeable and representative they are.

3. The authority should be known to be competent in the relevant field at the present time. Suppose someone invoked the opinion of a scientist who was an authority on a certain subject forty years ago. It is possible that this scientist's opinion is not shared by any expert in the field today.

4. It should be stated whether the authority's opinion represents the consensus of the experts in the field, or whether there is disagreement among them. If the opinion is not generally accepted, then this fact should be clearly stated. It is clear that, if all the experts in the field do not agree, then the opinion of a single expert does not carry as much weight as it would if it were universally or generally accepted by the experts. When experts disagree, then we must analyze their reasoning to determine which experts should be believed.

The Fallacy of Ignoring Qualifications (Secundum Quid). It often happens that a statement is made that is true with certain qualifications, but the qualifications are not stated. Under these conditions, it is possible to use the statement as a premise while neglecting the tacit qualifications. The result is a fallacious argument. Consider this example:

> You reap what you sow.
> Therefore, if you sow some peas your father gave you, you will reap some peas your
> father gave you.

The source of the mistaken inference in this argument is that the premise contains a tacit qualification, namely that it applies to the species of plant you sow, not to other qualities it may have. When a conclusion is drawn from the premise while disregarding this qualification, the result is a fallacious inference. This type of error we shall call *the fallacy of ignoring qualifications. Its classical name is a dicto secundum quid ad dictum simpliciter,* which is usually shortened to *secundum quid. This fallacy consists in the inference that a proposition that is true given certain circumstances is also true in a situation in which these qualifications are absent.*

A fallacy of this type may occur in three different ways: (a) The inference may move from a more general to a more restricted case; (b) from a restricted to a more general case; and (c) from a situation qualified in one way to a situation qualified in some other way. Let us consider some examples:

(a)   Some species of snakes are poisonous.
      Hence, some species of snakes native to Borneo are poisonous.

(b)   Drinking a sufficient amount of alcohol will kill any human being.
      Therefore, alcohol is a poison and should be avoided.

(c)   Boxers physically assault other boxers and their actions are not regarded as a crime.

      Therefore, the action of a man who attacks another in a barroom brawl should not be regarded as a crime.

In example (a), the tacit qualification that is neglected in drawing the conclusion is that the premise refers to the total class of snakes, not those in a specific area. In this argument the inference moves from a general case to a restricted one.

In example (b), the qualification that is ignored is that alcohol kills only when a large amount of it is consumed. The premise is not true if amounts smaller than the lethal dose are taken into consideration. In this argument, the inference moves from a restricted case to a more general case.

In example (c), the neglected qualification is that boxers attack each other with previous mutual agreement in a game of skill and strength that follows established rules. The circumstances in a barroom are quite different. In this case, the movement is neither from the general to the particular nor the opposite, but rather from one particular situation to another.

In many cases, it is not possible to tell whether the inference moves from a restricted to a more general case or vice versa. This happens because we cannot determine whether it is the premise that is intended as a general statement and the conclusion as a more restricted one, or the opposite. Consider the following argument:

> (d)　A person who thrusts a knife into another person's body is guilty of a crime and should be punished.
> Surgeons thrust knives into other people's bodies.
> Hence, surgeons are criminals and should be punished.

This argument can be interpreted in two ways. We may consider the first premise as a general rule and the conclusion as a particular case (thrusting a knife with the intention of curing). Under this interpretation, the tacit qualification that applies to the premise (thrusting a knife without any specific intention of curing) is different from the more restricted one that applies to the conclusion, and the argument is therefore fallacious.

We can also interpret the premise as a qualified statement that refers to thrusting a knife with the intention of harming a person, and the conclusion as the more general case of thrusting a knife without any further qualification. Thus, the movement of meaning in the argument depends on which proposition is regarded as the more restricted one. However, it is irrelevant whether the argument moves from the general to the particular, or vice versa. The essential point is that the tacit qualification that makes the premise true does not apply to the conclusion, and this makes the inference fallacious. Hence, to analyze a case of this fallacy, we need not determine whether it moves from a general to a particular case or the other way around. It is sufficient that a tacit qualification that applies to the premise has been neglected in drawing the conclusion.

To summarize: If we use as a premise a proposition whose truth depends on a tacit qualification, and in drawing a conclusion we disregard that qualification, we commit the fallacy of ignoring qualifications. An argument of this type may move from a general to a particular case, from a particular to a general case, or from one particular case to another.

The Fallacy of False Attribution of Cause (or 'False Cause'). This fallacy consists in inferring that an event is the cause of another when in fact it is not. This mistake can take place in two ways.

In one, the fact that an event follows another in time may be mistakenly taken as conclusive evidence that the first causes the second, as in this argument:

> There was a depression in the thirties and then came the War. The depression therefore caused the War.

This type of fallacy has the classical name of *post hoc ergo propter hoc* ('after this, therefore, because of this').

A second way in which the 'false cause' fallacy occurs is that something that is in fact an effect or an unrelated circumstance is taken without further investigation for the cause, as in this argument:

> Most successful lawyers spend their vacations in Europe. So, if you want to be a successful lawyer, you should spend your vacations in Europe.

These arguments are invalid if regarded as deductive arguments. However, as in the case of some other fallacies we have studied, the same kinds of information may constitute good inductive evidence under certain specific circumstances. We learn about causal connections in nature by observing that two events occur simultaneously or in close succession. However, much more extensive reasoning is required than the knowledge that the two events occur consecutively or simultaneously. We shall discuss these more extensive requirements in the next two chapters, which deal with scientific reasoning. For now, we should be aware that the fact that two events have occurred together or consecutively is not by itself enough to establish that one is necessarily the cause of the other, as the above examples clearly show.

Begging the Question (Petitio Principii). This fallacy occurs when one assumes as a premise the conclusion one wishes to prove. The simplest instance would be a case in which the premise and the conclusion have identical wording, as in:

> John is crazy.
> Therefore, John is crazy.

Obviously, such an argument would be pointless because it produces no new knowledge. Technically, however, it is valid. Any argument which has the form

$$\frac{p}{\therefore \ p}$$

is technically valid, since if the premise is true, then the conclusion must also be true. The problem is that an argument of this kind can hardly be called an argument since it provides no reasons for accepting its conclusion, but merely asserts it.

Of course, no one would be tricked by the simple example just mentioned. To be effective as a deceptive strategy, an argument that begs the question must have the premise and the conclusion worded differently, even though they contain the same information. Thus they appear to be two different propositions, even though they are not, as in:

> Opium puts people to sleep because it is a narcotic.

Since the word "narcotic" means "sleep-inducing," the conclusion is merely a restatement of the premise. In his *Elements of Logic* (1826), Richard Whately gives a classic example of begging the question:

> To allow every man an unbounded freedom of speech must always be, on the whole, advantageous to the state; for it is highly conducive to the interests of the community that each individual should enjoy a liberty, perfectly unlimited, of expressing his sentiments.[1]

This wordy and seemingly thoughtful argument provides no reasons for believing that its conclusion is true because its initial assumption is merely restated in different words with no justification. Thus it begs the question.

The Fallacy of Circular Argument (Circulus in Probando). This fallacy is similar to begging the question. Some logicians regard the two as varieties of the same fallacy, but they are sufficiently different to deserve separate treatment. A circular argument occurs when a premise of an argument cannot be known to be true unless the conclusion is already known to be true. In other words, *the premise is used to prove the conclusion, and the conclusion is in turn used to prove the premise.* It is clear that a circular argument proves nothing, since the premise cannot be true unless the conclusion is true. Sometimes there is a series of arguments in which the conclusion of the last argument is also the premise of the first argument. A typical pattern would be: '**p**, therefore **q**; **q**, therefore **r**; **r**, therefore **s**; **s**, therefore **t**; **t**, therefore **p**.' The series forms a closed circle, hence the name.

This type of argument is strictly invalid, whereas begging the question is not invalid, but simply fails to provide a real argument.

The following example is a typical case of a circular argument.

> Mr. Smith is a good man, because he belongs to the Liberal Party. And we know that the Liberal Party is made up of good men, because worthy people like Mr. Smith belong to it.

And another example:

> I know that John is a very intelligent person, because he is smart enough to recognize *my* intelligence. And I know it is true that I am very intelligent because John, who is intelligent, says I am.

Ignoring the Issue (Ignoratio Elenchi). Ignoring the issue is a debating fallacy. It occurs when a debater, through carelessness or ignorance, or with the intent to deceive, ignores the thesis he is supposed to be defending and gives evidence that leads to a different thesis. It is a very common device. Suppose a congressman, speaking in support of a bill to cut army appropriations, argues that we should strive to achieve peace and that war is a great evil. His statements, although true, are not relevant to the thesis he is defending, namely that army

---

[1]Richard Whately, *Elements of Logic* (London: 1826). American ed. (New York: Harper and Brothers, nd), 157.

appropriations should be cut. Or suppose a prosecutor, seeking to convict a man accused of theft, argues that theft is a dangerous crime and, if permitted to go unpunished, nobody's property will be safe. What he says, although true, is not relevant to the thesis he is supposed to be defending, namely that the defendant is guilty of a particular theft.

This fallacy can be effective as a deceptively persuasive device when used in long speeches, since people tend to forget the thesis, and the emotional impact of the speech (which may contain many true statements) can influence the opponent and the audience to accept the speaker's thesis without having heard any evidence for it.

Ad Populum. The *ad populum* argument is a debating fallacy. It consists of appealing to people's passions and prejudices, rather than giving evidence to support the thesis. This fallacy is not a form of argument; it has nothing to do with reasoning because no evidence is given. It is a favorite device of propagandists, advertisers, and demagogues. It is frequently used, not to obtain intellectual assent, but to persuade people *to act* in a certain manner. This fallacy is also called *argumentum ad passiones.* The following are typical examples.

(a)   My fellow congressmen, this bill should be passed; the idea behind it is 100 percent American.

(b)   If you drink McDonald's whiskey, you will be among those who have good taste.

(c)   Read *Now* magazine, the magazine for the sophisticated.

In each of these cases, the speaker appeals to some popular sentiment, and then tries to link his or her conclusion to that sentiment as a way of persuading people to accept it. But since the speaker provides no rational evidence either for this linkage or for the popular sentiment itself, the argument is fallacious.

Complex Question. The device known as 'complex question' (or *'many questions'*) is a debating fallacy. It consists of asking a question that contains two different questions. The classical example is, "Have you stopped beating your wife?" This question cannot be answered with "yes" or "no" without tacitly admitting that one has beaten one's wife in the past. The complex question is a device to catch one's opponent off guard and trick him into admitting something he does not want to admit; it is not an argument at all. Other examples of complex question are:

(a)   Are you a mindless conservative?

(b)   Are you a screaming radical?

And a more complex example:

(c)   We must carry out a very careful investigation to determine what caused the Democratic Party to shoot itself in the foot in the 1990s by electing a president who pushed the party into supporting programs much too liberal for the average voter to accept.

There is no way to answer the question except by accepting all the assumptions it makes; thus, if we even attempt to answer it, we have fallen into the trap of endorsing those assumptions. The correct answer to a complex question is to point out that more than one question has been asked and that these different questions must be considered separately. In some cases, for example in (c), one of the questions can be significantly asked only if the other has been answered in the affirmative.

A classic example of this device is the (probably apocryphal) question King Charles II of England proposed to the Royal Society, "Why is it that a vessel of water receives no addition of weight from a live fish being put in it, though it does if the fish be dead?" It is related that, after much discussion, one of the scientists of the Royal Society found the right answer: the fact assumed in the question is not a fact at all.

Appeal to Pity (Argumentum ad Misericordiam). The appeal to pity is a debating device that does not involve giving evidence. It arises when a debater seeks to arouse the pity of the opponent to cause him or her to assent to a thesis or to act in a certain way, as in the case of an employee who tells his boss that he deserves a raise because he needs the extra money.

Appeal to Force (Argumentum ad Baculum). The appeal to force is another debating device that has nothing to do with rational persuasion. It can hardly be called a fallacy. It consists of trying to obtain assent from an opponent by an explicit or implicit threat of violence. Consider this example: "Mr. Jones, I think you will agree that a merger between your company and mine is a good idea; otherwise, you will find yourself in a price war."

The Fallacy of Extension. The fallacy of 'extension' consists of making an opponent's argument sound more extreme than it really is to make it easier to attack. For example, the conservative opponents of a moderate politician will accuse the moderate of being 'liberal' and even 'radical,' to make his views seem more extreme, and therefore, vulnerable. Extension is often used in domestic arguments, in which one spouse tries to get the other to defend a more extreme position than he or she initially wanted to. For example, if a husband says that he does not want to cut the grass because he is too tired from working all day, his wife may respond, "Oh, so since you work full time and I don't, then I should do all the housework!"

Notice that the person whose position is 'extended' in this way may be tempted to defend the more extreme position into which his opponent has pushed him. The husband in this example may become angry and respond, "Well, you've got that right! I do work full time, and you don't, so you *should* do the housework!" Of course, as soon as he allows himself to be forced into this extreme position, he has no hope of winning the argument. In the same way, the moderate politician in our other example may become angry and respond to his critics, "Yes, by God, we do need radical policies to deal with the serious problem our nation faces!" But, as soon as he allows himself to be forced into this extreme position, it will be more difficult for him to justify his position.

'*Extension*' is often thought of as a member of a more general class of arguments called '*straw man*' *arguments*. As the name suggests, a straw man argument, instead of attacking its real opponent, first misconstrues what the opponent has said in such a way as to make it easy to attack, and then attacks this 'straw man,' pretending that in this way what the opponent *really* said has been refuted. For example, an atheist may attack a 'straw man' version of an argument for the existence for God by saying "Theists base their beliefs on the existence of miracles. But every miracle that has ever been studied scientifically has turned out either to have a rational explanation, or to depend on the statements of unreliable witnesses." The main problem with this argument is simply that most theists *do not* base their belief in God mainly or primarily on the existence of miracles. Those who believe in miracles usually do so based on a prior belief in God, not the other way around. So by arguing as though the belief in God were based exclusively on the existence of miracles, the speaker merely attacks a 'straw man' version of his opponent's beliefs, and does not address their real reasons at all.

A variation on the fallacy of extension is often called the '*slippery slope*' fallacy. In this type of argument, the speaker suggests that, if we begin with the opponent's moderate position, this will eventually move us toward a more and more extreme position. He then attacks the extreme position, thinking that he has refuted the opponent's more moderate position. For example,

> The Social Security Advisory Council has recommended shifting the cost of Medicare to the general fund. This would begin the process of transforming Social Security into out-and-out welfare. Once we start in that direction, where do we stop?

The speaker implies that the moderate thesis, that we should shift the cost of Medicare to the general fund, will somehow lead to a more extreme thesis—converting the entire Social Security program into a welfare program. Yet no evidence is offered to show that the more moderate position will lead to this extreme outcome.

False Limitation of Alternatives. A very devious debating strategy tacitly assumes that only two alternative positions can be taken with regard to some issue, when in reality there are other alternative positions not mentioned. The speaker then refutes one of the two positions, concluding that the other one must therefore be the correct one. For example, an opponent of welfare policies might argue:

> Some people believe in the Marxist notion of "to each according to his needs"— that is, completely equal distribution of incomes. Others, like myself, believe that no one should receive any benefits for which he or she has not done an honest day's work. Now, the Marxist notion of complete equality of income is absurd, because if everyone were guaranteed exactly the same income, then no one would have an incentive to work productively, and the entire economic system would collapse. The only reasonable position, then, is that no one should receive any benefits for which he or she does not work.

Here is another typical example:

> A person can either believe that Jesus Christ is the son of an all-good and all-powerful personal deity, or that life is completely meaningless. Obviously, no one believes that life is completely meaningless, or else they would kill themselves. Therefore, the only reasonable position is to believe that Jesus Christ is the son of an all-good and all-powerful personal deity.

A more subtle example, often used against controversial political protest movements is:

> Those who criticize America should leave and move to another country.

The tacit assumption is that one must either think that America is beyond criticism, or else not want to live in America at all. Of course, these are not the only two alternatives. In all three of the examples, the speaker assumes that only two alternative positions can be taken on the issue under discussion, when in reality many other positions could be taken. The reason such arguments tend to be persuasive is that they correctly follow the form of *disjunctive syllogism:*

$$
\begin{array}{c}
p \lor q \\
\underline{\sim p} \\
\therefore \quad q
\end{array}
$$

The problem, of course, is that in each of the above examples the assumption '**p ∨ q**' is *false;* **p** and **q** are *not* the only two alternatives. Hence, an argument based on a false limitation of alternatives is typically valid, but not sound.

2.   Fallacies of Ambiguity

An expression is said to be ambiguous if it has two or more meanings. The word 'mad,' for example, is ambiguous: It means both 'crazy' and 'angry.' Ambiguity is different from vagueness. An expression is vague if the class of objects it denotes is not clearly defined. The expression 'tall man' is vague. It is not possible to specify, in the absence of a context, what height a man must have in order to be 'tall.' Similarly, the word 'old' is vague. It is not possible to establish a clear boundary between people who are old and those who are not. An ambiguous term or statement is different from a merely vague one in that it has two different possible interpretations.

A number of fallacies arise from the use of ambiguous expressions in reasoning and debate. Let's examine them.

Equivocation. The fallacy of equivocation can arise both as a reasoning mistake and a deceptive debating device. It occurs when an expression that has two different meanings is used in two places in an argument, and a conclusion is derived under the assumption that the expression in question has *the same* meaning in both places.

Consider this example:

Every departure from law should be punished.
What happens by chance is a departure from law.
Therefore, what happens by chance should be punished.

In this argument, the expression 'departure from law' is employed with two different meanings. In the first premise it means 'violation by a person of a criminal law'; in the second it refers to an exception to a natural law, a chance event. When the two premises are used to derive a conclusion, the result is a fallacy. A similar example would be:

Democracy is government by the crowd.
All crowds are cruel, irresponsible, and unintelligent.
Therefore, democracy is government by the cruel, irresponsible, and unintelligent.

Obviously, 'crowd' has different meanings in the first and second premises. Thus the word does not stand for the same concept in both instances. So, even though the argument sounds as if it followed the familiar pattern of *chain argument,* in reality it does not. *Chain argument* requires that the middle term be the same concept both times it occurs. In this case, the word 'crowd' is the same, but the concept is not.

Logicians often distinguish a special type of equivocation, which is called an *amphiboly.* Amphiboly begins with a premise that has, because of its grammatical construction, two different meanings, one true and the other false. If, under these conditions, a conclusion is drawn from the false interpretation of the premise, the result is the fallacy of amphiboly. The argument appears to be sound, because the premise has one meaning that is true, but in reality it is not sound. The term 'amphiboly' is derived from a term meaning 'double arrangement.' Consider a typical example:

Diamonds are seldom found in this country. So, if you misplace your diamond ring, you will probably never find it again.

The premise has two different meanings. One, that there are few diamond mines in this country, is true. The other, that diamonds somehow disappear, is obviously false. The absurd conclusion is derived from the false interpretation, but has the appearance of being derived from the true one.

Most classification systems today regard serious arguments that play on the ambiguity of a statement as *equivocations* rather than amphibolies. It is hard to imagine anybody being misled by the preceding argument; it is at best a joke. The examples of amphiboly cited in logic textbooks usually tend to be nothing more than jokes or humorous anecdotes. For practical purposes, an amphiboly can be regarded as a type of equivocation.

Composition. This fallacy consists in inferring that a property of all the parts of a whole is also a property of the whole, as in the argument:

This machine is made up of small parts; hence, it must be small.

The fallacy of composition also arises when we infer that a quality of all the members of a given class is also a property of the class taken as a whole. Properties that apply to the individuals of a class are said to be *distributive,* while those that apply to the class as a whole are called *collective.* The statement 'Horses have four legs' is true distributively, but is false if taken collectively. That is, each horse has four legs, but the class of horses itself does not have four legs. The proposition 'Human beings drink tons of water every day' is collectively true, but distributively false. Human beings may indeed collectively drink tons of water every day, but each individual human being does not. The fallacy of composition occurs when a property that applies distributively is taken to apply collectively, as in the argument:

> The janitor's union is made up of poor workers. Hence, it must be a union without very extensive financial resources.

Division. The fallacy of division is the converse of composition. It arises in two ways: When we assume that a property of a whole is also a property of its parts, as in 'This machine is complicated; so, each of its parts must also be complicated'; or when we infer that a collective property of a group is also a distributive property of its members, as in the argument 'Men have many professions; hence, any man has many professions.'

3.   The Art of Definition

There are many situations in which a deliberate and conscious attempt to explain the meanings of words is necessary. First, definitions play an important role in the process of learning that all human beings undergo as they learn their mother tongue. Moreover, all fields of human activity contain technical terms that are usually taught by means of definitions. Also, it often happens that when we communicate with another person, we are not sure that we understand, or that we are understood. In such cases the difficulty must be dealt with by explaining the meanings of some of the words we use.

The Structure of Definitions. Every definition consists of two parts: the word to be defined and the expression that defines it. For example, in the definition

> A triangle is a three-sided polygon

the word to be defined is "triangle," and the defining expression is "a three-sided polygon." It is useful to have terms to refer to the two parts of a definition. The term being defined is usually called the *definiendum,* and the defining expression the *definiens.* These terms are the Latin words that mean, "that which is to be defined" and "that which defines," respectively.

The Relativity of Definitions. Defining a word is a social act; a definition is made by a person for the benefit of some other person or persons. Thus, a definition is good in the measure that it helps enlighten the person to whom it is addressed. And, of course, different people and different situations require different definitions. *The adequacy of a definition is relative to the person to whom it is addressed.* If a four-year-old child asks her father what gold is, it would be useless for him to explain to her the atomic structure of that metal. On the other hand, the definition of gold as "a hard, shiny, yellow thing that is used to make rings and jewelry," though probably quite adequate for the child, is not sufficient for the jeweler or the chemist.

The Two Fundamental Types of Definitions. A definition may be of a concept already in use, or a new concept introduced by the definition itself. A definition of a concept that is already in use is called a *lexical* or *reported definition.* The definition of the word "triangle" given above is a lexical definition. It reports the concept English speakers refer to when they use the word "triangle."

It is often necessary to introduce new concepts and new terms to refer to them. A definition in which a new concept is introduced is called a *stipulative definition.* A definition of this kind has the form "by **W** I shall mean such and such," or "by **W** let us mean such and such." As we can see, a stipulative definition is a proposal or command and thus *it cannot be true or false.* A lexical definition, on the other hand, is a proposition, and thus can be true or false. It can also be adequate to a greater or lesser degree.

It is obvious that anybody is free to stipulate any meaning whatsoever for any expression. However, if a word that is already in use is given by stipulation a new meaning that is very different from the established one, the result may be a great deal of unnecessary confusion. Suppose, for example, that a sociologist proposes to use the term "comet" to mean "a retired employee over 65." Although, strictly speaking, he is free to do so, the stipulation is likely to create confusion. Thus, in practice, our freedom to stipulate is limited to by the established meanings of the words we use. In general, the looser the established meaning of a word is, the greater our freedom to stipulate a new meaning for it without introducing confusion. For example, the word "poor" has a vague meaning in everyday language, and in some sociological studies, it is given a more precise meaning by the stipulation that for the purposes of these studies the word "poor" will mean any person whose yearly income is less than a certain specified amount. Stipulative definitions that make the meaning of a word more precise are common in the language of the law because of the need for clear criteria to decide to what specific cases a particular law applies. For example, in the laws concerning drunken driving, the meaning of "drunkenness" is made more precise than in common usage by defining it in terms of a minimum percentage of alcohol in a person's blood stream. Definitions that perform this function are sometimes called *precising definitions.*

Another task a stipulative definition can perform is to explain the meaning of a concept that is a part of a theory. In such a case, the definition is a part of an attempt to explain something. It can be a scientific or a philosophical theory, or an attempt to explain some everyday matter. Definitions that are part of such an explanatory framework are called *theoretical definitions.* A good example of a theoretical definition is the definition of force in Newton's mechanics. A force is that which produces a change in the velocity of a body (i.e., it produces an acceleration). A theoretical definition is a part of a scheme of explanation and its adequacy depends on the adequacy of the theory itself.

The Extension and the Intension of General Terms. Disregarading proper names, we can divide English words into two kinds. The first kind is made up of the words (and phrases) that stand for the things that we talk about; words and phrases that can be the subject or the predicate of a sentence. In grammar, they are called nouns and adjectives (and phrases that perform the function of nouns and adjectives). In logic, they are called *general terms*, or simply terms. Words of the second kind are those that modify and connect words of the first kind; words like 'and,' 'if,' 'but,' 'or,' 'some,' etc. They are called *connectives* or *relational words*. They do not have an independent meaning, but become meaningful when attached to terms.

If we examine how general terms are used, we can distinguish two different aspects of their meaning. First, a term can be used to indicate or designate certain objects in order to make assertions about them. Thus, the term 'cat' is used in sentences to designate all cats or some cats or some specific cat. In the sentence "Cats are mammals" the term designates all cats, in "Many cats are blue-eyed" it designates a subset of cats, and in "The cat that just passed by is brown" it designates (with some modifiers) a specific cat. Thus, the term is used to denote or designate any cats. We express this fact by stating that the class of cats is the *extension* of the term 'cat.'

The second aspect of the meaning of a general term is the content or information it conveys about the objects it denotes. The term 'cat' conveys a number of qualities like "animal," "four-legged," "furry," "carnivorous," "predatory," etc. The qualities that a term conveys make up its *intension*.

In brief, the extension of a general term is the class of objects it denotes or refers to; its intension is the set of properties it conveys. These concepts will be useful in our discussion of the techniques of definition. We shall see that some definitions utilize information regarding the extension of the definiendum, and others utilize the intension. Definitions based on the intension of the definiendum usually provide more adequate information than those utilizing the extension of only.

TECHNIQUES OF DEFINITION

Definition by Examples. Perhaps the simplest kind of definition is the *definition by examples*. This technique consists in mentioning *by their proper name* some of the objects the definiendum refers to. The following definitions are typical instances.

President: Washington, Lincoln, Roosevelt, etc.
General: Hannibal, Napoleon, Caesar, etc.

The definition by example has some serious shortcomings. First, there are a great many things for which we do not have proper names. This fact severely limits the use of this technique. Secondly, definitions by examples tend to be very ambiguous. Consider, for example, the definition of "president" given above. Washington, Lincoln, Roosevelt can be examples of many different concepts, such as "man," "American," "statesman," etc. The list of names does not tell us which of the concepts is intended. It gives us some information about the *extension* of the term 'president' but not about its content or intension. Because of these shortcomings, the definition by examples is often a very inadequate technique Nevertheless, it is quite adequate in many situations.

Definition by Sub-Classes. Another common technique of definition is the *definition by sub-classes*. It consists in listing some classes of objects that are contained in the class to be defined, as in the following examples.

Tree: oak, elm, maple, poplar, etc.
Person: man, woman, child

The definition by sub-classes, although based on extension, is more adequate than the definition by examples, because the classes mentioned are not mere names, but general terms from which it is possible to make a generalization. Nevertheless, this kind of definition tends to be ambiguous, for the sub-classes given may be belonging to many different larger classes. Thus, the classes given in the definition of "tree" are also sub-classes of "plant," "living being," and "broad-leaf tree." A definition by sub-classes is most adequate when all the existing sub-classes are mentioned.

Definition by Synonym. Another common technique of definition is the definition by synonym. Consider the following examples:

"Insane" means crazy.
"Stupid" means dumb.
"Swift" means fast.

In this type of definition, the definiens is an expression that is a synonym of the definiendum. This technique has two shortcomings. First, synonymous expressions very rarely have exactly the same meaning. Secondly, it is not possible to use this kind of definition unless the person to whom it is addressed already knows a concept that is very close to the one being defined. Thus, a definition by synonym cannot be used to introduce a concept that is completely new to a person. Nevertheless, this type of definition is very useful. It is one of the most frequently used techniques used in language dictionaries. In fact, a bilingual dictionary is for the most part a collection of definitions by synonym.

Ostensive Definition. Sometimes it is convenient to define an expression, not by describing it but by pointing to an object that it refers to. Suppose a child asks his mother, "What is a box?" and she answers by pointing to a box and saying, "This." This procedure is called an *ostensive definition*. This type of definition is commonly used, particularly in teaching new words to children. It has the shortcoming of being ambiguous, because all things have innumerable features one can point to. Suppose someone points to a box. What is he trying to point out? The box itself, its color, its shape, its texture, its sides, the fact that it is hollow, or some other quality? It is impossible to decide, unless we already know at least something about the meaning of 'box.' Some of the ambiguity can, however, be eliminated by making several ostensive definitions of the same word. If someone, trying to teach me the meaning of the word "crimson," points to a rose, a book, a piece of cloth, and an insect, I can eliminate many incorrect interpretations of the meaning of the word. I know, for instance, that it does not mean "book," that it is not a kind of flower, or a kind of insect, and so on. In spite of its shortcomings, the technique of ostensive definition is very useful in many situations.

Classification by Division and Definition by Genus and Difference. One important way in which we can acquire knowledge of a given field is by carefully observing the objects in it and attempting to find general types (in other words, establishing some logical classes within it). Often the classes we discover have a sufficient degree of variety to allow us to establish subclasses. When this process of subdivision can be repeated, many times a systematic *classification* (notice the etymological meaning of the word: making classes) can be established. Each of the steps in this procedure is called a *division* and the result a *classification by division.*

Examples of classification by division are extremely common. Libraries use systems of classification of this type. (The Dewey Decimal and the Library of Congress Systems are the most common.) In zoology, animals are classified according to a system that contains six levels: phylum, class, order, family, genus, and species. This classification was created by the Swedish naturalist Carolus Linnaeus (1707–1778).

A classification by division can be used to systematize our knowledge of the patterns of order that are found in a given realm of phenomena. In particular, it can be used to formulate very accurate definitions of a class of objects. For instance, we can give a definition of an animal by stating to what phylum, class, order, family, and genus it belongs, and giving in addition the characteristics of the species. Thus, the species lion (called *felis leo*) can be defined as a species that belongs to the phylum chordata, class vertebrata, order carnivora, family felidae, genus felis, and has in addition certain specific characteristics. Since each of the terms of classification is defined by certain characteristics, anyone who knows the classification will immediately know all the fundamental characteristics of the species *felis leo.* A definition of this type is called a *definition by division.*

A particularly important type of definition by division is that in which only one division is made. For a definition of this type, a convenient class that contains the class to be defined is chosen. Then a definition can be made by stating that the definiendum belongs to the larger class, and has some characteristic that differentiates it from the rest of that larger class. For example, a bus can be defined as a motor vehicle used for public transportation. "Motor vehicle" is the larger class, and "used for public transportation" is the characteristic that differentiates buses from other motor vehicles. In this type of definition, the larger class is traditionally called the *genus* and the sub-class to be defined the *species.* The distinguishing characteristic of the species is termed the *difference*, or more accurately, the specific difference. It should be noted that these terms were originally developed in the field of logic. Linnaeus borrowed them when he created his botanical and zoological classification system. It is important to note that these three terms are relative to individual definitions. We talk about the genus, the species, or the difference in a particular definition, but the terms have no fixed meanings apart from particular definitions.

This technique of definition is called *definition by genus and difference*. It is, in general, one of the most adequate techniques of definition. Let us consider some examples.

A father is a male parent. (Here the genus is "parent"' the difference is "male." The species is of course the definiendum, "father.")

A proposition is a verbal message that is capable of being true or false. (The genus is "verbal message"; the difference is "capable of being true or false.")

An evergreen oak is an oak that is not deciduous. (Genus: oak; difference: not deciduous.)

A mule is the offspring of a male ass and a mare. (Genus: offspring; difference: of a male ass and a mare.)

It should be noted that, given a particular classification by division, the largest genus (sometimes called the summum genus) cannot be defined by genus and difference, because there is no larger class to refer to. Thus, for example, "animal" cannot be defined by genus and difference by means of the categories of zoological classification.

RULES FOR DEFINITION BY GENUS AND DIFFERENCE

There are five traditional rules (developed by Aristotle) that are useful in constructing and evaluating definitions by genus and difference.

Rule I. The definition should state the essential attributes of the species.

This rule means that a definition is adequate to the extent that it states the properties which constitute the meaning of the species, rather than attributes that the species happens to have, but which are not those that are conveyed when we use the term. Thus, for example, the definition "the governor of a state is a person who lives in the governor's mansion" states an attribute that governors in fact do have. However, the attribute is not what we normally mean by "governor." A governor is the chief executive officer of a state. Thus, the definition does not state what is usually meant by the word "governor."

The "essential attributes" of the definiendum are the attributes normally conveyed when we use that word. It should be noted that the essential attributes need not be objective characteristics of the objects in question; they may refer to the origin of the objects, or to their relations to other things, or the use the objects can be put to. Thus, a chair cannot be defined only in terms of shape or the material it is made of; its definition must include reference to the use it is put to. Again, "senator" cannot be defined in terms of physical or psychological characteristics of individuals. It rather refers to a relationship of certain individuals to their fellow citizens. They are elected by citizens to perform certain functions.

Rule II. A definition must not be circular.

If the definiens contains the definiendum, or a synonym of it, or a term whose meaning cannot be understood independently from that of the definiendum, the definition is said to be *circular*. The definition "A neurotic is a person who suffers from a neurosis," is circular, because "suffering from a neurosis" is just another way of saying, "being a neurotic person." A circular definition is in fact a definition by synonym; it gives a different way of expressing the definiendum, but it does not analyze that concept. A definition by genus and difference analyzes the concept by relating it to a larger class and stating its specific difference. Thus, a definition that is circular is a definition by synonym masquerading as a definition as a definition by genus and difference. The former type of definition is of course not useless, but it does not perform the same function as the more complex definition by genus and difference. The former gives us a new term to name a concept we already know; the latter gives us the most important characteristics of the concept.

Sometimes correlative concepts are defined in terms of each other. Suppose someone defines "north" as "the direction opposite to south" and then goes on to define "south" as "the direction opposite to north." It is obvious that this *circular pair* of definitions, as we shall call this mistake, clarifies neither concept. A circular pair is very easy to spot when the two definitions are close together. However, in a long discourse, such as a book, the two definitions may appear in different places, and the circularity may be very difficult to detect.

Rule III. A definition should be neither too broad nor too narrow.

If the definiens refers to a class of objects larger than the definiendum, it is said to be broader. If the group is smaller, the definiens is said to be narrower. In the definition "A square is a plane figure enclosed by four equal segments of straight lines," the definiens is too broad, for it includes squares and rhombs. In order to correct the definition, it would be necessary to add to the definiens the condition that all the internal angles are right angles.

In the definition "A triangle is a plane figure enclosed by three equal segments of straight lines," the definiens includes only equilateral triangles. Thus, this definition is too narrow. It can be corrected by deleting the word "equal" from the definiens.

Rule IV. The definiens should not be expressed in metaphorical, symbolic, or obscure language.

The purpose of a definition is to explain as clearly as possible the meaning of the definiendum. A definition that is stated in metaphorical language cannot perform this function. Consider, for example, the statement "architecture is frozen music." It conveys an interesting insight about the relationship between architecture and music, but it does not *define* architecture. In fact, in order to understand that insight one must already know what architecture is. Thus, metaphorical and symbolic expressions are not appropriate tools for definition.

Definitions stated in difficult, obscure language are usually inadequate, because it is likely that the person who knows the difficult words in the definiens already knows the meaning of the definiendum. A classical example of obscure definition is found in Samuel Johnson's famous dictionary: "A net is a reticulated texture with small interstices."

Rule V. A definition should not be negative if it can be affirmative.

The reason for this rule is simple. The function of a definition is to explain what the definiendum means, not what it does not mean. A definition's negative characterization can often be ambiguous. Consider, for example, the definition "animal" as something that is not vegetable and not mineral. We can infer from this definition that a triangle and the *Odyssey* of Homer are animals, since neither of these things is vegetable or mineral. One is a concept, the other a poem. Thus, the definition is very inadequate.

There are, however, concepts that by their nature are negative. For example, an odd number is a number that is not divisible by two without a remainder, and "blind" is the state of being deprived of vision. It is correct to define such concepts in negative terms.

EXERCISES I

Identify and explain the following fallacies. Exercises I contain only fallacies of irrelevance. Exercises II, III, and IV cover other types of fallacies with increasing degrees of difficulty.

1. Dialogue in a car:
   Son: Mother, you took that curve too fast.
   Mother: Nonsense, I wasn't driving too fast. You don't know anything about driving, anyway; you don't even know how to drive.

2. I do not have to be consistent. As Oscar Wilde said, "Consistency is the last refuge of the unimaginative."

3. LSD is not harmful. Plenty of people have taken it and have experienced no harmful effects.

4. The law says that a citizen has a right to possess a gun. Therefore, the authorities should not forbid Mr. Jones to own a gun just because he has been hospitalized for mental illness twice.

5. I have no evidence that Smith is going to pay his bills at the end of the month. So, it is clear that he is not going to pay them.

6. Dialogue in a department store:
   Customer: I would like to take a look at this TV set.
   Clerk: Do you want to pay for it in cash, or shall I charge it to your account?

7. The reason why Albert is such a good businessman is that he has a lot of business talent.

8. A man is on trial for the murder of a child. The prosecutor, asking the jury for a conviction, says: "This man must be punished. The murder of a child is the most hideous of all crimes."

9. The rise in the cost of living that we are now experiencing is inevitable in a growing economy. Hence, it is good for our economy.

10.   There is no such thing as telepathy. There is no reliable evidence that it exists.

11.   God exists, for the Bible says so. And what the Bible says must be true, because it is the word of God.

12.   Dialogue:
Mr. A: I give the orders here.
Mr. B: Why?
Mr. A: Because I am the most intelligent man in the group.
Mr. B: How do I know that?
Mr. A: Because I am the one giving the orders.

13.   The soul is immortal because it is simple; it does not have parts that can separate from each other. And we know that the soul is simple because it is imperishable; a thing that cannot be destroyed must be simple.

14.   Having an organized government is a blessing, for anarchy is a great evil. A cruel despotism is organized government. Therefore, a cruel despotism is a blessing.

15.   This pamphlet is full of lies. It is just a pile of cheap anti-American propaganda.

EXERCISES II

*The following exercises are slightly more advanced, but include only fallacies of **ambiguity**. Identify in each case which fallacy of ambiguity is being used.*

1.   Man is a rational animal. Tom is a man. So, I can expect him to be rational when I tell him that I wrecked his car.

2.   If a double dose of medicine is harmful, a single one cannot be good.

3.   The end of a thing is its perfection. Death is the end of life. Hence, death is the perfection of life.

4.   A flea is an animal. Therefore, a large flea is a large animal.

5.   All men are mortal. Therefore, mankind will one day die out.

6.   Peter was an Apostle. The Apostles were twelve. Hence, Peter was twelve.

7.   The government bureaucracy is known to be very inefficient. So, we cannot expect Jones, who works for the government, to do an efficient job for us.

8.   The dinner I am fixing tonight is going to be excellent. I am using only excellent ingredients.

9.   Everything that glitters is not gold. Gold glitters. Therefore, gold is not gold.

10. Things are made up of atoms. Atoms do not have colors. So things do not have colors.

11. A person who never has enough money is poor. Misers never have enough money. Hence, all misers are poor.

12. Joe, Jim, Margaret, Susan, and Tony are quite a crowd. So, Jim is quite a crowd.

13. Every soldier in the 25th Regiment is a good fighter. So, you can be sure that regiment will fight well.

14. All metals are chemical elements, and bronze is a metal. Therefore, bronze is a chemical element.

15. Feathers are light. Light dissipates darkness. Therefore, feathers dissipate darkness.

EXERCISES III

The eight arguments in this exercise contain only the following fallacies.

> **Extension** (three examples)
> **False limitation of alternatives** (two examples)
> **Begging the question** (two examples)
> ***Ad hominem* argument** *(one example)*

Determine which arguments contain which fallacies.

1. Distributive justice theorists argue that fairness has value for its own sake, even if it does not increase the average welfare of people in general, and sometimes even if it leads to a decrease in the happiness of a majority of people. But to suggest that fairness is the only value, and that maximizing the general welfare has no value whatever, is ridiculous.

2. I advocate a retributive approach to criminal justice. Offenders should not be allowed to make out-of-court deals with prosecutors or be released early to avoid prison overcrowding, but each individual should receive what he or she morally deserves. My reason for this belief is that there should be an exact proportion between the rewards or punishments a person receives and the goodness or badness of that person's behavior; this principle is too important to be sacrificed for any other reason, no matter how important.

3. Moral theories can be divided into two types: absolutistic and relativistic approaches. Absolutist theories suggest that moral truths are absolute in the sense that they can be known with absolute certainty, either because they are revealed by the word of God, or because they are known innately by the human mind. This view is mistaken for the following reason: If these "moral truths" were innate, then we would all know them without question, and there would be no disagreement about them. But in reality what we

find is that, for almost any given moral belief, there is someone somewhere who believes just the opposite. Thus such "truths" cannot be innate in the human mind. As for the word of God, it can be interpreted in so many diametrically opposed ways that there is no proof that one person's interpretation is any more valid than the next person's. Since absolutism is such an obviously mistaken approach to moral theory, we must conclude that moral relativism is the correct approach.

4. The Free Trade Agreement proposed by President Clinton advocates imposing tariffs on imports from certain countries, such as Japan, who refuse to buy U.S. products. But to suggest that the problems of the American economy can be solved simply by slapping an import fee on foreign goods whenever U.S. industry cannot compete fairly on the open market is ridiculous. No matter how many tariffs we impose on foreign goods, such methods will never eliminate our problems of unemployment, inflation, low worker productivity, homelessness, and the many other problems facing the poor in this country. Therefore the Free Trade Agreement is an unrealistic, misguided economic policy and should not be adopted.

5. I believe in a deterrence approach to criminal justice. The reason for this is that the purpose of the criminal justice system is not to make moral judgments of people, nor to rehabilitate them, but simply to discourage potential offenders from committing crimes. Any other purpose of punishment is irrelevant because the system's function should be to minimize the amount of crime by making people fear punishment when they think of committing crimes.

6. Some philosophers argue that human behavior is completely predetermined by environmental factors in childhood that interact with the person's innate predispositions. They would argue, for example, that criminal behavior is the result of growing up with such problems as poverty, gang-ridden neighborhoods, abusive or negligent parents, or poor educational opportunities. But we know that this view is wrong because it is possible to find individuals who suffered from all these disadvantages, yet became positive, productive, and well-adjusted members of society. Since complete determinism can be shown to be false, this means that human behavior is completely attributable to free will: That is, personality characteristics are not at all the result of environmental factors beyond the person's control, but are only the result of the individual's choices. In this view, an individual will become what he or she chooses regardless of economic and psychological disadvantages, and therefore such factors ultimately have no effect on the person's character. Since we have shown that complete determinism cannot be true, any reasonable person must therefore agree that a belief in complete free will is the only remaining option.

7. Senator Dodd has argued that the proposed investment-incentive tax deduction is unfair because it would give tax deductions to the wealthy to stimulate the economy. But Dodd's own position is self-contradictory because in the 1980s, when investment-incentive deductions were available, he took a deduction for his own investments.

8. The NAACP has been on a campaign to register black voters for the next election. This misguided notion that the problems of housing, unemployment, inner-city crime, lack of medical care, and the many other problems facing blacks can be solved simply by having blacks vote shows how naive and out of touch with contemporary reality the NAACP has become.

EXERCISES IV

These exercises include examples drawn from all the types of fallacies studied. Identify and explain the following fallacies.

1. Whatever is immaterial is unimportant. Whatever is spiritual is immaterial. Therefore, whatever is spiritual is unimportant.

2. The plan being considered by the House is economically bad because it goes against sound economic principles.

3. No news is good news because the absence of information presupposes satisfactory developments.

4. A: The most characteristic thing about modern composers is that they tend to eschew melody.
   B: But many modern composers use lots of melody.
   A: Yes, but those who use a lot of melody are not *truly* modern.
   B: Who are the truly modern ones, then?
   A: Those who avoid melody.

5. Bricklayers know their trade because they have been perfecting their techniques for hundreds of years. So, the bricklayers you hired will know how to do a good job.

6. A: Hunting is an evil and uncivilized activity.
   B: You cannot argue against hunting. You eat meat, don't you?

7. Explain this to me: Why is it that the people who defend socialism are always power-mad fanatics?

8. Smith: Don't ask for beer at a cocktail party!
   Jones: Why shouldn't I?
   Smith: It is not done in the best circles.

9. You should not try to do anything to remedy poverty. Jesus said that there will always be poor people among us.

10. A person who harms another should be punished. A person who communicates an infectious disease to another harms him. Therefore, a person who communicates an infectious disease to another should be punished.

11. Members of the jury, the defendant is guilty. He has admitted it. When I asked him: "Did you voluntarily kill the victim?" He answered "No." As you can see, he himself confessed that he is guilty of involuntary homicide.

12. You cannot read the plays of Shakespeare in one day. Therefore, you are not going to be able to read *Hamlet,* which is one of his plays, in one day.

13. All the angles of a triangle are equal to two right angles. Angle A is an angle of a triangle. Hence, angle A is equal to two right angles.

14. Mr. Smith's action is morally wrong because it is opposed to sound ethical principles of conduct.

15. "Councilman Smith says that I have lied to this Council about my finances. I am going to show that I am innocent. As a matter of fact, there are persistent rumors that Councilman Smith has been accepting money from some wealthy people in exchange for political favors."

16. All criminal actions ought to be punished by law. Prosecutions for theft are criminal actions. Hence, prosecutions for theft ought to be punished by law.

17. Everybody is allowed to express his or her opinion freely. Therefore, a person should be allowed to shout "Fire!" in a crowded theater.

18. Nothing is better than virtue. Stale bread is better than nothing. Therefore, stale bread is better than virtue.

19. What you bought yesterday, you eat today. You bought raw meat yesterday, therefore you eat raw meat today.
   (from the 12th century Munich *Dialectica)*

20. My thesis is that there is only one universal mind of which individual minds are only parts or manifestations. A human consciousness is a unity; it is not separable into parts. Hence, there can exist only *one* mind.

21. One should pay one's debts. Therefore, you should pay what you owe to the man who built your fence, even if it collapsed a week after it was built.

22. This is a black cat. So, its teeth must be black.

23. Joe is a man. Tony is different from Joe. Hence, Tony is different from a man.

24. All the players in our football team are strong. Hence, we have a strong team.

25. I know Coriscus. I do not know that man who is approaching me with his face covered by a mask. The man approaching me with his face covered by a mask is Coriscus. Therefore, it appears that I both know and do not know Coriscus.
   (from Aristotle's *Sophistical Refutations)*

26. A wind that passes through a grove of trees makes an audible noise. Now, the noise is created by a very large number of molecules hitting tree leaves and trunks. Hence, it must be true that a single molecule hitting a leaf makes an audible noise.

27. Because the poor who have cows are the most industrious, the way to make them industrious is to give them cows.

28. If Tellus winged be,
The earth a motion round;
Then much deceived they are
Who ne'er before it found.
Solomon was the wisest,
His wit ne'er this attained;
Cease, then, Copernicus,
Thy hypothesis vain!
                    (Sylvanus Morgan, 1652)

29. Strychnine is a deadly poison. Therefore, those who attempt to use it as an ingredient in medicine are doomed to fail.

30. A crime is a violation of the law. If there is no law, there cannot be any violation of it. Therefore, if we do away with all laws, there will be no crime.

31. This woman is pleasant, for she is riding a horse, and riding a horse is pleasant.

32. Anyone who does something or fails to do something *by necessity* is not a free agent. At the present moment you will by necessity either stay where you are or not stay where you are. Therefore, you are not a free agent.

EXERCISES V

Identify and analyze each of the following fallacies.

1. Since each organ of the human body has one function, the human body as a whole must also have one function.

2. If you ingest alcohol continuously, at a certain point it will kill you. This shows that alcohol is a poison and should not be drunk by anyone.

3. No citizen has the right to determine how his neighbors should live their lives. Hence, if your neighbor makes a dump in his backyard, you do not have the right to protest.

4. Every pane of glass in a geodesic dome is triangular: hence geodesic domes must be triangular.

5. Lieutenant Smith will be inefficient as an executive in our company. He just retired from the army, a notoriously inefficient institution.

6. I think rapists should be castrated to punish them. My sister was raped and she suffered a nervous breakdown.

7. All those who sell heroin should be put in jail. Hence, the undercover police agent who sold heroin while trying to break a drug ring should be put in jail.

8. Salt is not poisonous. Therefore its component elements, sodium and chlorine, are not poisonous.

9. The Swedish people are 90% protestant. Gustav is a Swede. Therefore, Gustav is 90% protestant.

10. The energy crisis was the fault of the Democrats. It happened during a Democratic administration, didn't it?

11. The price of whiskey in Atlanta has increased about 20% in the last six years. During the same period, the average salary of Baptist ministers has increased about 22%. The ministers seem to be connected with the whiskey trade.

12. Diabetics should avoid things containing large amounts of sugar. Sugar maples are things containing large amounts of sugar. Therefore, diabetics should avoid sugar maples.

13. A young man is on trial for rape. The prosecutor argues as follows: "I say this man is guilty. Think of the trauma that unfortunate young woman has suffered. Think of her bleak future. Think of the brutal disregard for the privacy of a human being. Think of the callous contempt a rapist has for women. Rape is a most heinous and repulsive crime."

14. The joke is funny. Therefore, every word in the joke is funny.

15. Prosecutor to jury: "If you don't convict this murderer, one of you may be his next victim."

16. No rumor of scandal has ever touched the senator. Therefore he must be totally honest.

17. In reply to Mr. Jones' argument, I will only say that last year he supported the very measure he now opposes.

18. It must be true that dreams represent repressed desires. I read it in our psychology textbook.

19. There is no point in listening to what you have to say. Everybody knows you are an extremist.

20. It is the old time religion, and it is good enough for me.

21. I don't care how sick she is. When the supervisor sends for someone, the employee is expected to show up.

22. All loyal Americans will welcome the passage of this bill.

23. There are laws of nature. Laws imply a lawgiver. Therefore, there is a cosmic lawgiver.

24. According to biologists, you can run a mile on a slice of bread. They must be talking about a gigantic slice of bread that is miles long.

25. A mob is no worse than the individuals that make it up.

26. If a human can think, then a cell in his organism can think too.

27. You think communal living is such a great idea. But I see you don't live in a commune.

28. Capital punishment is justified for murder and kidnapping because it is quite legitimate and proper that someone be put to death for having committed such acts.

29. No one has been able to give convincing evidence of extrasensory perception. So, there is no such thing as extrasensory perception.

30. Any law can be repealed by congressional action or constitutional amendment. The law of gravity is a law. Hence, it can be repealed by congressional action or constitutional amendment.

31. The Royal Society is ninety years old. Professor Smith belongs to the Royal Society. Hence, Professor Smith is 90 years old.

32. Dentist to his patient: "You need to have two teeth extracted." Patient: "I don't believe what you say, because you are going to make a lot of money if it is true."

33. Defense attorney to witness under cross-examination: "Why did you lie yesterday on the witness stand?"

34. New York City has more crime than any other city in the country. It also has more churches than any other city. Clearly the churches are at least partially responsible for the crime rate.

35. Every sentence in this paragraph is well written. Hence, the paragraph is well written.

EXERCISES VI

Identify the technique of definition used in each of the following examples. Discuss the possible shortcomings and judge the adequacy of each.

1. "Ornate" means adorned.

2. Mammoth: Any extinct elephant distinguished by molars having cment filling the spaces between the ridges of enamel.

3. Mansard roof: A roof having on all sides two slopes, the lower one being steeper that the higher one.

4. Phony: fake.

5. Graf: A German, Austrian, and Swedish title of nobility, equivalent to *earl* in English.

6. Salt: Any of a class of compounds formed when the hydrogen of an acid is partly or wholly replaced by a metal or a metallike radical.

7. Chemin (French): road.

8. Hypotenuse is the side of a right-angled triangle that is opposite the right angle.

9. Literature: poems, novels, stories, dramas.

10. Charisma: Clark Gable, Ella Fitzgerald, Marlene Dietrich, and Edith Piaf had it.

11. Inductance: property of an electric circuit by virtue of which a varying current induces an electromotive force in that circuit or in a neighboring circuit.

12. A young boy and his mother are watching a military parade. The boy asks his mother what a soldier is. She points to one soldier after another and says, "This, and this, and this . . ."

EXERCISES VII

Construct a definition by genus and difference of each of the following words, using in each case the genus given. You have to determine the difference and then construct the definition.

	Definiendum	**genus**
1.	bachelor	man
2.	proposition	verbal message
3.	triangle	polygon
4.	vixen	fox
5.	doe	deer
6.	ostensive definition	definition
7.	lexical definition	definition
8.	logic	branch of philosophy
9.	child	human being
10.	giant	man
11.	snack	meal
12.	banquet	meal

13.   colt   horse

14.   girl   woman

15.   freshman   college student

EXERCISES VIII

Criticize the following definitions by genus and difference. Determine which rules are violated and why.

1. Aluminum is a metal used to make kitchen pots.

2. Bread is the staff of life.

3. A horse is a quadruped that has hooves.

4. A loyalty is the flame of the lamp of friendship.

5. Man is a featherless biped.

6. A spinster is an unmarried woman.

7. Knowledge is an opinion that is true.

8. A car is a motor vehicle that is not a truck.

9. A lie is a proposition deliberately antithetical to a verity apprehended by the intellect.

10. A polygon is a plane figure enclosed by four or more segments of straight lines.

11. A psychotic is a person who suffers from psychosis.

12. A student is a person who is in the process of learning something systematically.

13. An ornament is an object that is not necessary for practical use.

14. Economics is the science that deals with the phenomena arising from the economic activity of human beings in society.

15. Man is a mammal that wears clothes.

16. A bachelor is an old man who is not married.

17. Fox hunting is the pursuit of the uneatable by the unspeakable.

18. A kleptomaniac is a rich thief.

19. Prejudice is a biased state of mind.

20. Peace is the absence of war, and war is any breach of a state of peace.

CHAPTER 9

The Use and Abuse of Scientific Reasoning

Decisions that involve scientific and technological data require reliable interpretation of the relevant empirical facts, including their verifiable cause-and-effect relationships. But scientific reasoning is inductive rather than deductive. In contrast to the deductive methods studied earlier, it is therefore probabilistic rather than certain. It lends itself to dissenting interpretations of the causal implications of known facts and therefore does not always prove beyond doubt whether the probability of a causal relationship is strong enough to warrant acting on the basis of the given information. For example, in court cases, the burden may be on the plaintiff in a lawsuit to prove that a toxic chemical caused harmful consequences, but in most such cases, only modest evidence can be given as to the probability that the toxic chemical was involved in producing those consequences. And that is the way scientific reasoning works in practical contexts. Because it is inductive, its conclusions cannot be absolutely proven to be true.

We know that poverty correlates strongly with crime rates,[1] but we are less sure how much this correlation results from a *causal* relationship between poverty and crime, and how much from the fact that poverty and crime tend to occur in the same areas for other reasons. We know that crime is aggravated by crowded living conditions, and that poverty is often concentrated in inner cities, where population density is high.[2] Thus poverty and crime could be concentrated in the same areas even if the one does not cause the other (as, for example, Vold suggests).[3] It is therefore necessary to carry out more extensive research before concluding that poverty is a cause of crime. How such a conclusion *can* be adequately supported will be discussed later.

Another more disturbing problem is this: The probabilistic nature of scientific reasoning lends itself to the possibility that people who are strongly motivated to deceive either themselves or others about an issue may use forms of reasoning that appear to have scientific

[1]This is demonstrated statistically by James Short, *An Investigation of the Relation Between Crime and Business Cycles* (New York: Arno, 1980), and by Richard Freeman, "Crime and Unemployment," in James Q. Wilson, ed., *Crime and Public Policy* (San Francisco: Institute for Contemporary Studies, 1983), 89–106.

[2]Edwin Sutherland and Donald Cressey, *Criminology* (Philadelphia: J.B. Lippencott, 1972), 95ff; Charles McCaghy, *Crime in American Society* (New York: Macmillan, 1980), 97–99.

[3]George Vold, *Theoretical Criminology* (New York: Oxford University Press, 1967).

precision, yet contain hidden fallacies of reasoning. These fallacies may be so well disguised that only someone who is fairly sophisticated in the interpretation of scientific reasoning can detect them. We seem to have reached a time in human history when the results of scientific reasoning are so widespread, and often crucial to the process of social decision making, that it is necessary for everyone to become sophisticated about the process of scientific reasoning.

Generally, four main types of errors occur in scientific reasoning corresponding to the four most important requirements for good scientific reasoning accepted by scientists and by philosophers. These four requirements have been emphasized not only by traditional philosophers of science, but also by more radical, contemporary thinkers who stress the social and historical relativity of scientific theory and research.[4] The differences between these approaches do not involve fundamental disagreement about good or 'ideal' scientific reasoning. The controversy hinges on how feasible it is for researchers to achieve the ideal, given the difficulty of overcoming tacit presuppositions of which we are unaware, yet which distort our conceptual categories, selective biases in the gathering and interpreting of data, and theoretical prejudices. But to the extent that reliable empirical knowledge is achievable, four essential requirements to verify this knowledge are:

(1) A scientific hypothesis must not be accepted until it can make genuine predictions of clearly observable and previously unknown empirical information or statistical relationships.

(2) The empirical relationships predicted by a scientific explanation must be quantitatively measurable in a precise enough way to determine whether the relationship in question is statistically significant. A statistically significant relationship simply means a stronger mathematical correlation between data than would be expected by chance or coincidence.

(3) To facilitate mathematical precision, and to prevent misinterpretations of the results, researchers must use *operational definitions* of the concepts they are studying. They must define their concepts in such a way that they can be empirically observed and measured, or at least understood indirectly by empirically observable and measurable phenomena.

(4) Even a statistically significant relationship must not be taken as supporting a causal hypothesis unless all plausible alternative explanations for the observed statistical relationship have been eliminated. Methods for eliminating alternative explanations are called *experimental controls*.

If we want to be prepared to spot misuses of scientific reasoning when they occur, and to choose wisely among alternative interpretations of the implications of scientific data, we must reflect carefully on the meaning and consequences of each of these four aspects of scientific method.

---

[4]An excellent and readable contrast between these approaches can be found in Thomas Kuhn, *The Structure of Scientific Revolutions* (Chicago: University of Chicago Press, 1962), and in Larry Laudan, *Science and Relativism* (Minneapolis: University of Minnesota Press, 1990).

1.   The Ability of Predictions to Falsify Hypotheses

Usually a hypothesis is expected to predict previously unknown information or statistical relationships. It is not enough that the hypothesis agrees with or explains information we already know. Given any collection of facts, one can think of different explanations which, if true, would explain the known facts; but there still would be no way to decide which of these possible explanations would be the true explanation. On the other hand, suppose some hypothesis predicts a previously unknown fact (i.e., a fact we would not have known is true until the hypothesis led us to it): Then if the prediction does come true, we are warranted in concluding that the hypothesis is unlikely to be false, and therefore likely to be true.[5]

For example, Einstein's theory of relativity predicted that light from a distant star would be "bent" as it passed through the gravitational field of the sun, and also predicted (based on mathematical equations) the exact extent to which the light would be bent.[6] There was no other reason to believe that the light would be bent to this exact extent, and all other systems of physics predicted (based on their mathematical equations) that the light would *not* be bent at all. However, Einstein's prediction was accurate. Common sense tells us that it would be extremely unlikely that Einstein's theory could have predicted this previously unknown information so accurately unless the theory was *true* (or at least very close to the truth on the issues relevant to the prediction).

At the same time, common sense also tells us that, if we had somehow known in advance that the light was going to be bent to this extent whether Einstein's theory was true or not, then the accuracy of Einstein's prediction would not be enough to convince us that his theory was true. For example, suppose Einstein's theory had predicted that the next appearance of Halley's comet was going to be in 1986 (as everyone believed). This would not confirm Einstein's theory, because good reasons already existed for belief that the comet would appear at this time, whether Einstein's theory was true or not. If scientists are to be convinced that a theory or hypothesis is true, they demand not only that it be able to make predictions, but that it be able to make predictions that probably would not have come true unless the theory or hypothesis that enabled us to make the prediction was also true. The prediction is then 'genuinely capable of falsifying the hypothesis' because it is the kind of prediction that is expected to turn out to be false if the theory or hypothesis from which it is deduced is false. For example, if an astrologer predicts that I am going to receive some money in the future, and indeed I do receive some money, this prediction should not convince anyone that astrology is a true scientific theory because it was already obvious that I would probably receive some money sooner or later. The astrologer's prediction therefore is not a genuine prediction at all; in scientific terms, it is not a *falsifiable* prediction.

---

[5]Carl Hempel makes this point central in his conceptualization of scientific method in *Philosophy of Natural Science* (Englewood Cliffs: Prentice-Hall, 1963).

[6]For a very readable account of this episode in scientific verification, see Percy Bridgman, *The Sophisticate's Primer of Relativity* (Middletown, Conn.: Wesleyan University Press, 1962).

A concise way to state this principle (which philosophers of science usually call the 'principle of falsifiability') is that a theory or hypothesis must make a prediction that is capable of falsifying the hypothesis. That is, it must make a prediction that we have no other reason to believe will come true except that the theory or hypothesis predicts it. Then if the prediction does come true, we conclude that the theory or hypothesis is probably true. However, we do not automatically regard the theory or hypothesis as certainly true, because there is still some chance that it may be a mere coincidence that the prediction came true, and that the scientist happened to "luck up" on an accurate prediction even though his or her theory was not true.

A prediction can fail to be capable of falsifying the hypothesis in two ways. The simpler type of case occurs when someone appears to be making a prediction, but there is really no way the prediction could possibly be false. For example, suppose an astrologer predicts that someone is going to have good luck at some unspecified time; we could never show that the prediction is false. It is not, therefore, a true test of the hypothesis that astrology is a legitimate science.

The more subtle type of case, but also the more common, is when someone makes a prediction that could *possibly* turn out to be false, but would be very *unlikely* to in fact prove false, *even if* the hypothesis is false. For example, suppose again that the astrologer predicts someone is going to come into some money within the next year. This prediction could *possibly* falsify the hypothesis that astrology is a genuine science, since it is possible that the person could fail to come into any money within the next year; but the hypothesis that astrology is a legitimate science is not 'genuinely falsifiable' in the sense we are using here, because it is too likely that the prediction could turn out to be true even if the hypothesis (that astrology is a legitimate science) is false.

A common reason for remaining somewhat skeptical about a causal theory even when it can make accurate predictions is that, in many instances, a theory may be close enough to the truth in certain respects to generate some accurate predictions, yet still may fall short of the exact truth in crucial respects. For example, in spite of the remarkable accuracy of many predictions from Einstein's theory of relativity, a few of its predictions do not seem to be true. Einstein's theory predicts that nothing can travel faster than light, but recent experiments in quantum theory show that the transmission of energy between subatomic particles in some instances *is* faster than light.[7]

Earlier we considered a similar problem with the poverty-crime hypothesis. Many of the most impoverished areas (i.e., rural areas) have the lowest crime rates. But, in urban areas, the prediction that crime rates would correlate with poverty is a reliable one—and it becomes more reliable still when adjusted for the effects of welfare programs in the impoverished areas.[8]

It seems reasonable to conclude, then, that the ability of a causal hypothesis to make accurate and genuinely falsifiable predictions does increase the probability that the hypothesis is true, although predictive power alone does not conclusively establish the truth of a causal explanation.

---

[7] Shown in a technical paper by Alain Aspect, J. Dalibard, and G. Roger in *Physical Review Letters* 39 (1982):1804.

[8] These statistical relationships are documented in Ralph Ellis and Carol S. Ellis, *Theories of Criminal Justice: A Critical Reappraisal* (Wolfeboro, N.H.: Longwood Academic/Hollowbrook Publishing, 1989), see also Ralph Ellis, "General Assistance and Crime Rates in the U.S.," *Policy Studies Review* 7 (1987): 291–303; James DeFronzo, "Economic Assistance to Impoverished Americans," *Criminology* 21 (1983):119–36.

2.   Statistical Significance

The second requirement for good scientific reasoning is that observed relationships must be quantitatively measurable and statistically significant. Scientists recognize that it is impossible in principle for the conclusion of any inductive argument—no matter how scientific—to be absolutely certain, even if we grant the truth of the evidence on which it is based. Instead, inductive reasoning can only lead to a degree of probability that the theory or hypothesis is true. The results of scientific reasoning can never be absolutely certain. But the brighter side of this unfortunate fact is that we can at least come very close to measuring the precise extent to which the theory or hypothesis is probable. In this respect, scientists have become increasingly sophisticated over the years, and many highly specialized courses teach the mathematical techniques for this kind of probability assessment.[9]

The next chapter discusses the problems of statistical reasoning and of demonstrating causal relationships in more detail. For now, it is enough to realize that all of the mathematical techniques needed for this purpose are based on a few simple, intuitive principles that most people can readily understand. If someone predicts that the first card to be pulled from a deck of cards will be the ace of spades, anyone should realize that the probability that this prediction will turn out to be true just by luck or coincidence is one out of fifty-two, or 1/52. Similarly, if a theory correctly predicts that an experiment will have a specific outcome when there are 100 equally possible outcomes, then the probability that the prediction will turn out to be true just by luck or coincidence (even though the theory may be wrong) is 1 percent. This means, all else being equal (and at the risk of oversimplification because of the many sources of error in scientific experiments we shall not discuss here), there is a 99 percent probability of at least some truth or resemblance to the truth in the theory that enabled it to predict the outcome this accurately. In this case, the probability of error, or 'level of certainty' with which the theory has been verified, is considered to be 1 percent.

For many purposes, a 1 percent level of certainty may be considered sufficient evidence to accept a theory or explanation. For example, if we have confirmed that there is a 99 percent probability that increasing welfare benefits would dramatically reduce crime rates, then we would probably want to go ahead and increase welfare benefits, since there will then be only a 1 percent chance of failure to achieve the desired effect.

For some purposes, however, a 1 percent probability of error may be considered too high. For example, we would not want to take a 1 percent risk that a nuclear power plant will melt down. The consequences of error would be too severe. In the physical sciences, therefore, scientists generally demand more rigorous standards of verification than in the social sciences. The insistence that scientific hypotheses must predict previously unknown information or statistical relationships is one way of insuring that rigorous verification standards are met. By adhering to strict verification standards, modern science hopes to err on the side of rejecting

---

[9]For example, G. C. Helmstadter, *Research Concepts in Human Behavior* (Englewood Cliffs: Prentice-Hall, 1970); Daniel Lordahl, *Modern Statistics for Behavioral Sciences* (New York: Ronald Press, 1967).

theories that *may* be true but cannot be sufficiently verified, rather than accepting theories that may be false. For example, the U.S. Food and Drug Administration may often delay approving treatments that may be beneficial because their safety or effectiveness is still in doubt. If doubtful "facts" were allowed into the general body of science, then they would be used as premises from which still more doubtful "facts" would be inferred, until science eventually would be undermined with unreliable information. Scientists therefore insist on keeping the standards for acceptable statistical relationships quite strict.

3.   Operational Definitions

Abuse of the third requirement for scientific verification, the need for operational definitions, is a major source of misrepresentation of research results and implications. Operational definition means defining the phenomena under investigation in such a way that they can be observed and measured, at least indirectly, in terms of other phenomena that can also be observed and measured. Suppose, for example, that a social scientist wants to study the relationship between the presence of multinational corporations in third world countries and economic growth in those countries. This means that 'economic growth,' 'third world country,' and 'presence of multinational corporations' must all be defined in such a way that they can be unambiguously observed and measured.

Now suppose that a social scientist defines third world countries to include countries like Saudi Arabia and Taiwan, and defines economic growth as growth in the gross national product of a country. Then it may appear that there is a positive statistical correlation between economic growth and presence of multinational corporations. Someone may then interpret this to mean that the presence of multinational corporations in third world countries is economically beneficial to those countries. This thesis was popularized by the German Chancellor Willy Brandt during the 1970s and 1980s, and has strongly influenced the foreign policies of the United States and many other developed nations. However, this interpretation would be far from the truth.

The problem is that, if we define 'economic growth' as growth in the average real income of the people in a country, and define 'third world countries' as countries whose average income in 1980 was under $400 per year, then we find that the correlation between economic growth and the presence of multinational corporations not only is not positive, but in fact is negative.[10] That is, the presence of the multinational corporations seems to retard economic growth when measured in this way.

It seems that economic growth can mean very different things, depending on whether we define it as growth in gross national product or growth in average real income of the people of the country. And what is true for one meaning of economic growth may not be true for the other. Multinational corporations may indeed improve the gross national product of third world

---

[10]Volker Bornschier, "Multinational Corporations, Economic Policy and National Development in the World System," *International Social Science Journal* 32 (1980): 158–72.

countries, yet the benefit of this increased production may end up in the pockets of foreign investors and not benefit the people in the host country at all. To give the results of a study that operationally defines economic growth as growth in gross national product, as if this indicated an unquestionable economic benefit for the people of the countries involved, is misleading.

We must guard, then, against misleading presentations of research findings that do not clearly state how the concepts under investigation were operationally defined. Consider the study by the Centers for Disease Control (CDC) to determine whether the elevated cancer rates of Vietnam veterans might have been caused by Agent Orange, a highly toxic defoliant sprayed over large areas of dense jungle during the Vietnam war. When the CDC found no significant correlation between exposure of Vietnam veterans to Agent Orange and the veterans' subsequent cancer rates, almost every newspaper in the country reported this finding in large headlines, but failed to mention that the operational definition of Agent Orange exposure was based on the amount of dioxin detected in the blood twenty years later.[11] But it is well-known by dioxin specialists that Agent Orange tends to be eliminated from the blood over a twenty-year period, so that no correlation between blood dioxin levels and cancer rates should be expected even if Agent Orange did cause elevated cancer rates.[12] The operational definition in this case was simply inadequate.

But what about those of us who are not dioxin specialists? How can we tell when an inadequate operational definition has been used when the media do not report it? We can become sophisticated enough as educated people to insist on the professional competence of scientific journalists who report such studies (see, for example, Herbert Schiller's excellent study of this problem[13]). An important part of genuine competence in scientific reporting consists of inquiry into operational definitions. If operational definitions are inadequate or misleading, the scientific journalist should know enough about scientific reasoning to not mislead the public in the process of reporting.

4.   Controls

Abuse of the fourth requirement for good scientific reasoning—the requirement that scientific studies must adequately control for alternative explanations of observed data—perhaps causes the most misinterpretation and misrepresentation of research findings. For example, returning to whether poverty is a cause of crime, we saw that the mere fact that poverty and crime significantly correlate does not necessarily show that poverty is a cause of crime. Other possible explanations may exist for the correlation between them. The increased opportunity to commit crimes in densely populated areas may account for the increased crime rates in poor

[11]Andrew Purvis, "Clean Bill for Agent Orange," *Time,* 9 April 1989.

[12]Michael Weisskopf, "Scientists Say Vietnam Troops Heavily Exposed to Defoliant: Study Disputes CDC Finding," *Washington Post,* 25 January 1989, A-2.

[13]Herbert Schiller, *The Mind Managers* (Boston: Beacon Press, 1973).

(and crowded) inner-city neighborhoods.[14] Just as much crime may occur in crowded conditions regardless of economics—for example, in the locker room of a well-to-do, suburban high school, or in the cramped living spaces aboard a Navy ship. How do we know whether it is the poverty that is causing the increased crime in inner-city neighborhoods, or whether it is the crowded conditions and thus increased opportunities to commit crimes that explain the elevated crime rates?

To find out, we must control for the effects of population density when we examine the relationship between poverty and crime. One simple way is to collect a sample of geographical areas with approximately the same population density and, within this sample, see if poverty correlates significantly with crime rates. If it does, we can eliminate the possibility that population density accounts for the correlation between poverty and crime, since we held population density constant while measuring poverty and crime rates.

A more sophisticated way to accomplish the same result, one that researchers frequently use, is to measure the relationship of population density to both poverty and crime, and then check the correlation between poverty and crime in cities of all sizes after the effect of population density has been compensated for by using statistical methods.

Many sophisticated statistical methods can be used to control for the effect of population density on the correlation between poverty and crime rates, even when comparing areas with various levels of population density, but we shall not discuss these statistical methods here. For our purposes the important point is to control for the effects of extraneous variables that could have served as other explanations for the statistical relationship observed. For any extraneous variable that could conceivably be used as another possible explanation for the statistical relationship we are studying, we simply measure that variable and statistically compensate for its effects on the other variables. If we have not done this, then we cannot claim adequate evidence for a cause-and-effect relationship.

As another example, consider a study reported by a research team at the Harvard Medical School on the relationship between coffee drinking and colon cancer. No controls were reported in the study. Yet anyone who has ever read the label on a package of nondairy creamer or artificial sweetener can easily imagine how these and other variables could have caused the coffee drinkers to be more likely to develop colon cancer, even if it were not the coffee that caused the cancer. For a team of medical doctors to conduct such a study without controlling for such obvious alternative explanations is scientifically inexcusable. Luckily, another study was done a few years later in which adequate controls were used. Interestingly, this study failed to confirm any significant correlation between coffee drinking and colon cancer once the other variables had been controlled for.

It is imperative, therefore, whenever we interpret the implications of a scientific study, to ask whether we can imagine alternative explanations for the findings, and whether these alternative explanations were controlled for in the study.

---

[14]Charles McCaghy, *Crime in Amercia* (New York: Macmillan, 1980), 97–99.

5. Scientific Uncertainties and Value Judgments Affecting Empirical Research and Its Interpretation

When evaluating the results of scientific reasoning or presentations of research conclusions, we should be vigilant in looking for abuses of any of the four main aspects of empirical verification.

(1)   We should be on guard against apparent predictions that are not genuinely falsifiable; for example, when an economist arbitrarily selects well-known facts that happen to be consistent with a preferred theory, and then presents these facts as "evidence."

(2)   We should insist that enough data be included in a study to allow for a dependable assessment of the statistical significance (or insignificance) of the relationships between different variables, and try to find what level of certainty was used in the study.

(3)   We should demand to know how the variables were operationally defined, and think carefully about whether these definitions might yield misleading results.

(4)   Most important, we should use our imaginations to think of possible alternative explanations for the observed relationships between variables— explanations that might rival the one being proposed. And we should ensure that important rival explanations were controlled for in the design of the study, or can be controlled for in follow-up studies.

But no matter how much precision has been used in the design of scientific research and the interpretation of its conclusions, the fact remains that empirical research is inherently probabilistic and in principle can never attain complete certainty. This fact has important implications as it interrelates with the value judgments that also enter into policy decisions. Often, the design aspects of scientific studies and their interpretations are value-driven. The level of certainty demanded, the completeness of controls, operational definitions, and the amount of time and money devoted to accuracy of measurements—all these choices depend on the purposes for which the information is to be used. Similarly, a decision to accept a cause-and-effect conclusion, even though supported with data at a fairly high level of uncertainty—or conversely, to reject conclusions, even though based on a fairly low level of uncertainty—may depend on the results to be achieved, as well as concern for acting on a cause-and-effect interpretation that later proves to be wrong. Also, many of the background assumptions used in any scientific study are partly grounded in similar value judgments made at some earlier time for similar kinds of pragmatic reasons. Consequently, there is need for a certain degree of skepticism about scientific conclusions, and the political agendas of anyone involved in acting on those conclusions.

In political contexts, an important distinction must be drawn between cases in which acting on a scientific assumption is appropriate, even though it involves risk of error, and cases in which this would be inappropriate. An obvious and extreme example is offered by murder trials. Prosecutors refrain from asking for the death penalty when there is much uncertainty in the evidence to prove the defendant's guilt. They know that jurors will refuse to render a guilty verdict if the consequences of being wrong are irrevocable. Similarly, in cases of protecting guaranteed rights, courts and other political agencies tend to demand a stricter criterion of verification than in cases where the only issue is to increase the general welfare without any infringement of anyone's "inalienable rights." But, since every political action either directly or indirectly affects someone's freedom to act in one way or another, this distinction is less clear-cut than one might initially suppose. The consequences of the hidden agendas and inevitable uncertainties in scientific research become increasingly important as societies become more complex and technology-dependent.

To summarize, the four main abuses in scientific reasoning that result in inadequate empirical studies are:

(1) Failure to make predictions that genuinely test the hypothesis: The researcher makes predictions that would be likely or even certain to come true, regardless of whether the hypothesis under investigation is true or not. In this case, even if the predictions do come true, they cannot be regarded as having substantiated the hypothesis.

(2) Inadequate controls: The researcher fails to eliminate alternative explanations for the data. Any extraneous variable that could provide an alternative explanation for the observed statistical relationships should be accounted for to show that none of these alternative explanations are the real explanation for the findings.

(3) Misleading or inappropriate operational definitions: The researcher's method of objectively observing and measuring the phenomenon under investigation is either not clear, or is done in a misleading way. For example, if the research deals with the variables "anxiety" and "introversion," have adequate ways to objectively measure these variables been chosen?

(4) Invalid reasoning regarding statistical significance: No way is provided for determining whether the relationships found are significant (more than just a coincidence) based on the information given. In this case, further information would be needed to show that the relationships are significant. For example, if someone reaches the conclusion that vitamin C cures cancer, based on three cases in which this apparently occurred, these data are not enough to establish statistical significance. Much more data would be needed to establish that there is any reason at all to think that this hypothesis might be true.

EXERCISES

*The following exercises cover the three most common mistakes in designing scientific research studies—mistakes involving **statistical significance**, **controls**, and **operational definitions**. State whether each of the following research designs contains (a) invalid reasoning with regard to statistical significance; (b) inadequate controls, and/or (c) misleading or inappropriate operational definitions. In each case, briefly state specifically why significance cannot be demonstrated, why the controls are inadequate, and/or why the operational definitions are misleading or inappropriate.*

Example: *Hypothesis:* Material prosperity has increased in the United States over the past twenty years.

Research design: The median family income in the United States is now $24,000 and 14 percent of the families live below the poverty level (under $14,000 for a family of four and proportional amounts for other family sizes as specified by the U.S. Department of Health and Welfare). If twenty years ago the median family income was significantly under $24,000 and significantly more than 14 percent of the families earned less than the above-mentioned poverty-level incomes, then the hypothesis will be confirmed.

Solution: *(a) Significance. There is no problem in determining whether the figures mentioned constitute a significant difference between now and twenty years ago. The percentage of families below the $14,000 income indicated can be mathematically compared to the 14 percent presently below that, and the same can be done with the median income. It can then be determined mathematically whether the difference is statistically significant.*

(b) Controls. There are serious control problems with this study. An especially important uncontrolled variable in this design is the effect of inflation on the real value of $14,000 and $24,000 over a twenty-year period. A family of four living on $14,000 twenty years ago would not have been nearly as impoverished in real terms as a family of four living on that amount now. Inflation would cause the percentage of families below $14,000 to decrease, and would also cause the number above $24,000 to increase, regardless of whether this researcher's hypothesis is true or not. That is, even if people are not *more prosperous in real terms, the amount of money they earn would be greater, simply because of inflation. Thus the effect of inflation* must *be controlled for in any adequate study of this issue.*

(c) Operational definitions. The operational definitions chosen in this study are seriously misleading. Not only is there the problem of inflation, but also the number of individuals per household who are working should be accounted for. It is misleading to represent a family of four in which two or three members are working to earn $24,000 as more "prosperous" than one in which only one member works to earn that amount. It would be more appropriate to use individual earnings as the criterion; if that were done, the findings would go against the hypothesis of this study. Individual earnings have actually declined over the past twenty years.

Consequently, we see that this study is inadequate in two of the three respects discussed. Now consider each of the following research designs and determine (a) whether statistical significance could be determined; (b) whether controls are adequate; and (c) whether operational definitions are appropriate and not misleading.

1. *Hypothesis:* TV violence causes crime.

    Research design: One hundred convicted juvenile delinquents will be interviewed about their TV viewing habits. If over 60 percent of them report having spent substantial amounts of time viewing violent programming (over four hours per day average), the hypothesis will be confirmed.

2. *Hypothesis:* Coffee drinking causes cancer.

   Research design: One thousand hospital patients will be interviewed regarding their coffee-drinking habits. If there is a significant correlation between the number of cups of coffee drunk per day and the incidence of cancer, the hypothesis will be accepted. As a control, patients will also be asked how much tea they drink. If cancer correlates with coffee but not tea, the hypothesis will further be confirmed.

3. *Hypothesis:* Pornography causes rape.

   Research design: Data will be gathered from the past twenty years. If, during the entire period, there is a significant overall increase in both pornography as defined by the U.S. Supreme Court and the incidence of rape as reported in the U.S. Uniform Crime Reports, then the hypothesis will be accepted. If not, it will be rejected.

4. *Hypothesis:* An increase in interest rates causes an increase in unemployment.

   Research design: This hypothesis would predict that, following an increase in interest rates, unemployment would rise. Based on information provided by the Federal Reserve Board covering the past twenty years, we observe that in May 1968, the interest rate increased by 3 percent and the following month unemployment increased from 4 percent to 4.2 percent. Again in 1971, interest rates increased in March and unemployment skyrocketed from 4.2 percent to 5 percent during the remainder of that year. Similar patterns can be observed in 1973, 1976, 1980, and the second half of 1984. These observations confirm the hypothesis.

5. *Hypothesis:* The presence of United States corporations in Third World countries stimulates their economic development.

   Research design: The Council on Foreign Affairs lists thirty-nine countries in Africa and Asia with substantial United States corporate presence in them. If the majority of these countries have experienced increases in their gross national products during the period when United States corporations were present, the hypothesis will be supported.

CHAPTER 10

The Structure of Scientific Knowledge: A Closer Look

1. Scientific Explanation

Scientific knowledge is primarily concerned with the determination of causal connections. Newton's theory of gravitation offered a unified explanation of the *causes* of various phenomena such as the fall of objects toward the earth, the motion of planets around the sun, the trajectory of comets, and the ebb and flow of tides. Physicians, who are applied scientists, use the results of the sciences of anatomy, physiology, pathology, etc., concerning the *causes* of diseases and the *effects* of the medications they administer.

The fundamental assumption of all the sciences is that events do not happen by chance, but that every event is the result of antecedent causes. Nature is assumed to be, not a succession of unconnected, random events, but an orderly system. It is further assumed that the patterns of this orderly system, or at least some of them, are accessible to human reason and can be expressed in human symbols (such as the natural languages or the artificial language of mathematics). These patterns of causal connection can be used for a vital purpose: the prediction of future events. One of the most important functions of scientific knowledge (perhaps the most important) is *prediction*. The astonishing ability of causal patterns or laws of the sciences to predict future events with great precision constitutes not only a persuasive reason for believing that these scientific theories and explanations are true (or at least somewhat close to the truth), but also the most important practical contribution of science to humankind. The predictive ability of scientific laws can also be used to *control* phenomena. The power to predict and control given by our scientific knowledge has caused enormous changes in human life in the last three centuries.

2. Qualitative and Quantitative Causal Laws

We often find that a phenomenon of a certain kind is, under certain conditions, always accompanied or followed by a phenomenon of another kind. Fire burns wood; striking a match ignites it; aspirin alleviates certain kinds of pain; penicillin cures staph infections; soap dissolves fats; the attraction of the sun causes the planets to revolve around it; and so on. In each such case, it is asserted that the presence of a certain phenomenon, **A**, is connected with the presence of another, **B**. In these statements, only the presence of the two phenomena is considered. No quantitative or variable characteristics of the phenomena, such as duration, intensity, or location, are mentioned. A statement of this type we shall call a *qualitative causal law*. More accurately, when we acquire knowledge that allows us to make a statement of this type, we say that we have made a *qualitative determination of a causal connection*.

In many situations, a phenomenon varies quantitatively in a certain manner, and this variation is accompanied by a variation in some other phenomenon. Examples of this type of connection are found everywhere.

(a)   The more a driver pushes the accelerator of a car, the faster it will move.

(b)   A person who drinks alcohol will become intoxicated in proportion to the amount of alcohol present in the bloodstream.

(c)   A free-falling object in a vacuum will travel a distance that is proportional to the square of the time it takes to fall.

(d)   If a mass of gas is put in a container and the volume of the container is increased or reduced, the pressure produced by the gas (other things being equal) will vary in inverse proportion to the variation of the volume.

(e)   If the supply of a commodity diminishes, its price will tend to increase.

(f)   If a beam of light is reflected by a plane surface, the angle formed by the incident ray with the perpendicular to the surface is equal to the angle formed by the reflected ray with the same perpendicular.

In the preceding statements, we do not deal with the mere presence of two phenomena, but rather with assertions about ranges of quantitative variation of phenomena. Such variations can usually be measured and such phenomena are usually called *variables*. The statement of a quantitative relationship between two or more variables we shall call a *quantitative causal law*. Since a correlation between two or more variables in mathematics is called a function, quantitative causal laws are also called *functional laws*. Whenever we are able to establish a functional relationship between two variables, we say that we have made a *quantitative determination of a causal connection*.

A quantitative determination of a causal connection constitutes a more adequate knowledge of the causal connection than a merely qualitative one. When studying a particular phenomenon, if we succeed in making a quantitative determination of a causal connection, we can apply the analytical apparatus of mathematics to the investigation of that phenomenon. It frequently happens in scientific research that a qualitative determination of a causal connection is established first, and then further investigation leads to a more precise quantitative determination.

In summation, we can analyze a causal connection in two ways. Sometimes we are able to establish that the presence of a certain phenomenon is always connected with the presence of another. A statement that asserts a connection of this type is called a qualitative determination of a causal connection. If we investigate the variations of quantity in two phenomena, and are able to establish that a certain kind of variation in one phenomenon is connected with a variation in the other, we have made a quantitative determination of a causal connection. Quantitative determinations are more accurate and scientifically useful than qualitative ones.

3.   The Concept of Causal Connection

The idea of causal connection is one of the most fundamental notions in our understanding of physical reality, together with the concepts of space, time, substance, and quality. What is involved in this concept? When we are dealing with a *qualitative* determination of a causal connection, and we state that a phenomenon of the type **A** is causally connected with a phenomenon of the type **B**, part of what we mean is that in every situation in which we find the phenomenon **A**, we will also necessarily find **B**. In other words, we assert that the phenomena **A** and **B** always occur together. Another part of what we mean is that **A** is independent of **B** in a way that **B** is not independent of **A**. In other words, if **A** is the cause of **B**, the removal of **A** from the situation will prevent **B** from occurring (unless, of course, some other cause sufficient to produce **B** is then added to the situation), whereas the removal of **B** from the situation will not necessarily prevent **A** from occurring. This is how we know that **A** is the cause of **B** and not the other way around. This uniform connection between the two phenomena, in which one is dependent on the other, distinguishes a causal connection from a mere coincidence.

When we are dealing with a *quantitative* determination of a causal connection, the assertion that two variables are causally connected simply means that the quantitative relationship between the variables is always the same (with one variable, here again, being dependent on the other, and not vice versa). Whenever the independent variable experiences a variation, the dependent one will also experience a variation in such a way that the relation between them remains constant. For example, if we change the volume of a mass of gas at a constant temperature, the pressure will vary in inverse proportion to the variation of the volume.

4.   Our Knowledge of Causal Connections at the Commonsense Level

Our knowledge of nature may be divided into three types: descriptive knowledge, classification, and knowledge based on causal connections. Of these, the most important is the third. One of the most important characteristics of the human species is its ability to discern repeating patterns in nature and to learn to describe them and utilize them. Every human society we know has accumulated a great store of knowledge of causal connections. Of course, some beliefs about causal connections prove to be mistaken.

Our idea of causal connection seems to be derived from the common observation of two different phenomena that always appear together or in close succession: for example, fire and smoke, or a person touching fire and being burned. Human beings appear to have a tendency to expect the repetition of the patterns they have encountered repeatedly in the past. Children learn, after a few experiences with fire, that it burns. Animals also appear to form habits of expectation. We see from the behavior of cats, dogs, horses, etc., that they expect a repetition of a routine to which they have grown accustomed.

The psychological process through which we infer the existence of a causal connection seems to be simply that we register that two different phenomena are found to occur together in many instances. The process may be described as follows:

> One instance of the phenomenon **A** is accompanied by an instance of **B**.
> Another instance of **A** is accompanied by an instance of **B**.
> This happens over and over again.
> Hence, all instances of **A** are accompanied by instances of **B**.

Or, if our insight into the causal connection is quantitative:

> A specific pattern of variation is observed to hold between two phenomena.
> The same pattern is observed over and over again.
> Hence, this pattern holds whenever the two phenomena occur.

This psychological process is sometimes called *induction by simple enumeration*. Obviously, it is a weak kind of inference because mistakes can easily be made. The most common sources of mistakes in inferring causal connections consist of (a) disregarding exceptions, (b) making an inference from a small number of instances, and (c) failing to consider that **A** and **B** may consistently occur together, not because **A** is the cause of **B**, but because something else (usually a more complex process) consistently causes both **A** and **B** to occur. For example, someone may think that an increase in unemployment causes a downturn in the stock market (or vice versa), simply because the two trends tend to occur together, when in reality the relationship between them may be much more complex than a simple instance of one causing the other. Both may be caused by a more complex process.

When we make hasty inductions by simple enumeration, we are likely to commit the fallacy of false cause (see Chapter 8, section 1).

5.   Mill's Methods for the Determination of Causal Connections

In a sense, we can say that there has been science ever since the human species has existed. One characteristic of human beings is their curiosity about causal connections and their use of this knowledge for prediction and control of phenomena. In Europe in the seventeenth century, a systematic method was created for the investigation of natural phenomena, in particular for physical and astronomical laws, which led to the development of what is called modern science. Since the seventeenth century, there have been several attempts by thinkers to analyze the fundamental methods used in determining causal connections.

Outstanding among these are the works of Francis Bacon (1561–1626) and William Whewell (1794–1866). John Stuart Mill (1806–1873) carried out, in his *System of Logic* of 1843, a still more systematic and adequate analysis of scientific methodology. In this work, Mill analyzed the methods used in scientific practice and everyday life and found five different patterns of inference. Three of them are used to determine causal connections in a qualitative manner. They are called '*the method of agreement*,' '*the method of difference*,' and '*the joint method of agreement and difference*.' The other two are employed to determine quantitative causal laws. They are termed '*the method of residues*' and '*the method of concomitant variation*.'

6. The Qualitative Methods

In using the three qualitative methods to investigate a phenomenon, we take into consideration a number of particular facts. In some cases we consider only facts that exhibit the phenomenon in question, but in others we also take into account situations in which this phenomenon is absent. The particular facts considered we shall call the *instances* that are observed. Our concern is to analyze the instances to find out whether some of their properties or components are causally connected with the phenomenon under investigation. These properties or components we shall call the *factors* of the case.

An example will clarify these concepts. Suppose a hospital physician is investigating a rash that suddenly appears among the patients in the hospital, and examines five patients who have the disease. Suppose further that he suspects three possible causes: (1) the soap the patients bathe with, (2) the food they ate the night before, or (3) a medication they are taking. In this example, the rash is the phenomenon whose cause the physician wants to determine; the five patients are the *instances* observed; and the three things suspected as possible causes are the *factors* under investigation.

The Method of Agreement. The first qualitative pattern of inference is called *the method of agreement*. It states that if there is one, and only one, factor present in all the observed instances of a phenomenon, then we can infer that this factor is probably causally connected with the phenomenon. The expression 'causally connected' covers four possibilities: the factor may be (1) the cause, (2) the effect, (3) a part of the cause, or (4) a part of the effect of the phenomenon.

Consider an example. Suppose four students, who live in the same dormitory, Smith, Jones, Cartwright, and Chen, developed symptoms of food poisoning on the same day. The school physician who treats them decides to find the cause of their symptoms. After examining a list of what the students ate the previous day, the doctor narrows down the possible causes of the food poisoning to three canned foods served in the dining hall the previous evening. They were green beans, hash, and tomato soup. To determine the cause, the doctor asks which of these foods the students ate. He finds out that Smith ate tomato soup and hash, Jones tomato soup and beans, Cartwright only tomato soup, and Chen tomato soup, hash, and beans. From this evidence the doctor concludes that the cause of the food poisoning was the tomato soup.

The phenomenon under investigation is the food poisoning; the students are the instances of the phenomenon observed; the green beans, hash, and tomato soup are the factors under investigation. Examining the list of foods eaten by the four students, it is obvious that tomato soup is the only factor that is present in all the instances, hence the method of agreement would imply that tomato soup is probably the cause of the food poisoning.

It is important to notice that if there is no factor that is present in all the instances, we cannot infer anything by the method of agreement. And if there are several factors that are present in all instances, we cannot decide by the method of agreement which one is the cause (or whether perhaps some combination of them is required to cause the phenomenon). It may be any one of them, or a combination of them.

The method of agreement is stronger than simple enumeration. When we use the method of agreement, we list not only one factor, but a number of factors we suspect to be causally connected with the phenomenon under investigation. The conclusion drawn from a successful case of agreement is that one factor is present in every instance. But there is more. We have also shown that the other factors are absent in some of the instances. Thus, we have eliminated the rest of the factors as possible causes.

Moreover, one aim of the method is to examine instances that are as different as possible from each other to make it less probable that the factor-phenomenon agreement is due to other factors not considered. It is easy enough to find instances to confirm any correlation, if that is what one is looking for. However, if an agreement is found in very different instances, then the conclusion constitutes strong evidence of a causal connection. Indeed, the strength of a conclusion reached by the method of agreement increases in proportion to the degree of difference between the instances used.

Suppose that a biologist testing a new drug finds that administering it to rats who suffer from a certain disease apparently causes them to recover. He then runs two experiments with a group of ten rats. The result of this experiment, though suggestive, is subject to the possibility that other relevant factors present have not been considered. For instance, the rats may have experienced a spontaneous remission; the conditions in the laboratory (temperature, humidity, etc.) may have some effect; there may be chemicals in the laboratory environment that could cause the cure; the drug in question may have impurities that actually cause the cure; the investigator may have observed the experiments inadequately, perhaps because he was already inclined to accept his hypothesis; and so on.

What can be done to decrease the probability of such neglected factors? The investigator should perform more observations under various conditions: in different laboratories, under different climatic conditions, by different investigators, with different supplies of the drug, with different species of animals, etc. If the new experiments also yield evidence of a causal connection, then the evidence for that connection is much stronger than initially. The only way to diminish the probability of neglected factors is to choose instances that differ from each other as much as possible.

The successful use of the method of agreement depends on the ingenuity of the investigator in finding relevant factors. If the real cause has not been taken into consideration because the investigator has not considered the possibility that it might be relevant, then the method will lead to a mistaken conclusion. Unfortunately, no rule can be given about the choice of relevant factors. Investigators must rely on their previous knowledge, their good judgment, or their intuition. Only one practical rule of thumb can be given: We should base our choice of relevant factors on a pool of instances in which the conditions vary as much as possible.

The primary limitation of the method of agreement is that, in most situations, the instances have more than one factor in common with each other, or some of them lack the common factor because of interference from extraneous factors that cannot be controlled. For example, suppose a group of students decided to investigate the effects of consumption of different kinds of alcohol by drinking a different type each night. One night, they drank scotch and water, and suffered from hangovers. The second night, they drank bourbon and water, and again suffered from hangovers. The third night, they drank Irish whiskey and water, and again suffered from hangovers. Using Mill's method of agreement, they concluded that their hangovers must have been caused by the water, since it was the only factor which all of the instances shared in common with each other. The fallacy in their reasoning, of course, was that water was not the *only* thing all the instances had in common with each other; alcohol, of course, was another. But sometimes it is truly difficult to realize how many possible factors may in reality be shared in common by a number of instances.

The Method of Difference. The second qualitative method is called the method of difference. In this method, we use only two observations: one in which the phenomenon under investigation is present, and one in which it is absent. We call the first form the *positive instance,* and the latter the *negative instance.* The method of difference states that *if there is one and only one factor that is present in the positive instance and absent in the negative instance, then that factor is probably causally connected with the phenomenon.* In other words, the factor that is present when the effect is present, and absent when the effect is absent, other things being equal, is the probable cause.

An excellent illustration of the method of difference is provided by two epoch-making experiments performed by Louis Pasteur in 1861 to refute the theory of spontaneous generation. This theory asserted that lower animals, such as bacteria, come to life in decomposing organic matter without having living progenitors. In the first experiment Pasteur boiled meat broth in a flask with a long narrow neck until all the bacteria in it were killed. Under these conditions, he could keep the flask for an indefinite period of time and broth did not show signs of decay. Then Pasteur broke the neck, thus letting the contents come into contact with the air. In a few hours, the liquid decomposed and bacteria were found.

This experiment showed that the presence of bacteria in the flask was causally connected with the presence of air. Reflecting on Pasteur's procedure, we can easily see that the only factor that was present in the positive instance and absent in the negative instance was air. It is important to notice that Pasteur's conclusion was that the presence of air was *causally connected* with decomposition and bacteria, not that the air was itself *the cause*. The latter conclusion would have supported the theory of spontaneous generation.

Pasteur then performed the preceding experiment in conjunction with another designed to give positive evidence for his theory that the bacteria must be the offspring of other bacteria. The coordination of these two experiments was a stroke of genius. In the second, Pasteur filtered a stream of air through two sterilized filters in succession. Then he placed each of the filters in a flask filled with boiled (and thus sterilized) broth. The first filter caused decay, and the second did not. This result showed, by the method of difference, that there was something in the air that could be filtered out and that it was this "something" that caused the bacteria to be present. Pasteur pointed out that an invisible sediment had accumulated on the first filter and later showed, by placing the sediment under a microscope, that it contained bacteria. This sediment was the *only* factor present in the positive instance and absent in the negative instance; from this, Pasteur deduced its causal connection with the presence of bacteria and decay.

The use of the method of difference is subject to some important limitations. To use it successfully, we have to assume that all factors but one are present in both instances. We have to assume furthermore that, as one factor is withdrawn, other things remain equal. If a factor we have not recorded is present in the positive instance and absent in the negative one, then it may be the cause, but we will not discover that. This method presents the same difficulty we have examined in the method of agreement. *There is no way to be completely sure that all the relevant factors have been taken into consideration.* The only way to diminish this danger is by making repeated applications of the method, observing the factors as carefully as possible in each case.

The Joint Method of Agreement and Difference. The third method is the joint method of agreement and difference. This type of inference can be used when we have several positive and several negative instances related to a phenomenon. The method states that *if there is one and only one factor that is present in* all *the positive instances, and absent in* all *the negative ones, then we can infer that this factor is probably causally connected with the phenomenon under investigation.*

Let's return to the original example of food poisoning in the dorm. Suppose the college doctor decides to do some additional research by considering some students who also live in the dorm and did *not* get sick. Suppose he finds three: Olson, Davis, and Carlyle. Olson reports that he had beans and hash, Davis ate just beans, and Carlyle had only hash. If we add this information to the information previously available when we used the method of agreement, we can use the joint method. We have four positive instances of the sickness (Smith, Jones, Cartwright, Chen), and three negative ones (Olson, Davis, Carlyle). The following chart indicates with a "+" sign those factors which are present in each instance, and a "−" sign those factors which are absent in a given instance.

Instances	Tomato Soup	Hash	Beans	Phenomenon under investigation (food poisoning)
Smith	+	+	−	+
Jones	+	−	+	+
Cartwright	+	−	−	+
Chen	+	+	+	+
Olson	−	+	+	−
Davis	−	−	+	−
Carlyle	−	+	−	−

The chart shows that there is one factor that is *present in all the positive instances* and *absent in all the negative instances:* tomato soup. This result strengthens the conclusion that had been reached earlier by the method of agreement.

The method of agreement in combination with the method of difference constitutes an extremely powerful tool for the investigation of causal connections. Often the method of agreement is used first to guess at the possible cause of a phenomenon; then evidence is gathered to use the method of difference to find out whether the guess is corroborated or was simply the result of coincidence. Thus, incorrect guesses can be eliminated. The joint method performs the same function as the successive application of the methods of agreement and difference.

A considerable amount of research in the sciences consists in alternative applications of the methods of agreement and difference. The first provides a hypothesis, the second tests the hypothesis. It should be clear that the joint method is nonetheless still subject to the dangers and limitations we discussed in relation to the first two methods. The odds of success are improved still further if the method is combined with a genuinely falsifiable prediction from the causal hypothesis, and with a conscientious attempt to control for all possible alternative explanations as to why the phenomenon correlates with the explanatory factor, but not with the other factors, in the positive instances.

7.   The Quantitative Methods

The Method of Residues. The first quantitative method is the method of residues. It can be used when we observe a variable phenomenon accompanied by several factors. It states that *if we subtract from a phenomenon the part of it that is known to be the result of a certain factor, then the remainder of the phenomenon must be the result of the remaining factors.* A simple, everyday example of this method is often used to determine the weight of the contents of a container, for example a preserve can, without opening it. If we know the weight of the empty can, we simply subtract from the total weight the part of it that represents the can, and the remainder is the weight of the contents.

A classic example of the method of residues is the investigation that led Pierre and Marie Curie to the discovery of radium. Studying radioactivity, they carefully measured the radiation emitted by samples of pitchblende. It was already known that this mineral contains uranium, and it was believed that its radioactivity was derived from its uranium content. But the Curies found that the level of radioactivity was slightly higher than that predicted by the law based on the uranium content of the mineral. This discrepancy led the Curies to suspect that pitchblende might contain some other radioactive substance. After long research, they discovered the element radium. The search was very difficult because the amount of radium in the mineral is minute. It took about eight tons of pitchblende to get one gram of radium salts. In 1903 they received the Nobel Prize for their research.

The Method of Concomitant Variation. The method of concomitant variation states that *if a variation of degree in the phenomenon under investigation is accompanied by a variation of degree in one of the accompanying factors, then that factor is probably causally connected with the phenomenon.* In brief, two phenomena that vary at the same time are probably causally connected. The correlation may in some cases be rough, in some cases very precise. For example, the economic law that the price of a commodity tends to go up if the supply goes down is relatively rough; the law that the angle of the reflected ray is equal to the angle of incidence when light is reflected off a surface is much more precise.

The method of concomitant variation presents some of the same difficulty as the other methods. Since there is a large number of phenomena varying at any given time, the investigator must select those that might be relevant. No precise rule can be given to do this. An investigator must simply imagine all possible causes that might conceivably be involved in the situation under study, and use the kinds of methodological controls discussed in this and the previous chapter to eliminate the irrelevant ones.

8.   Statistical Generalizations

The type of conclusion that can be derived from the use of Mill's methods (section 5) arises when there is a total correlation between a phenomenon and a certain factor; in other words, situations in which we can assert that, provided certain conditions exist, every time a certain phenomenon (or a variation of the phenomenon) is present, a certain factor (or variation of the factor) will also be present.

In many situations, however, only a partial or approximate connection between a phenomenon and a factor can be established. Such situations are common in everyday life as well as in scientific research. We know that aspirin cures most headaches; a man goes to a bar because he usually finds some of his friends there; a gambler knows that if he tosses a coin a number of times it will fall heads up about half of the time. In cases such as these, we say that aspirin will *probably* cure a headache, that the man will *probably* find some of his friends at the bar, and so on. We use the terms 'probable' and 'probability' when we can predict that there is a partial correlation between two phenomena. Statements of probability are useful because many situations exist in which we cannot establish a total correlation, but can ascertain a partial one. In such cases, assessment of probabilities can help predict the corresponding phenomena.

Let us now introduce two useful terms. A generalization that asserts that every instance of a phenomenon **A** will also be an instance of the factor **B** can be called a *total generalization*. A generalization asserting that such-and-such a proportion of the cases of **A** are also cases of **B** can be called a *statistical generalization.*

How is a statistical generalization supported? Suppose I wish to know the number of people in my city who drink coffee with their breakfast. The obvious thing to do is to find out the proportion of people who drink coffee with their breakfast in some sample groups of people who live in the city. A little thought will give rise to a second consideration. The sample groups should be chosen so that they reflect as closely as possible the proportion of coffee drinkers in the total population, otherwise, they will be *biased* samples. This means that the individuals that make up the samples should be selected *at random.* In the example, choosing groups of people from different sections of the telephone directory might be a good solution. Suppose that in six samples of one hundred individuals the percentages of coffee drinkers are 78, 74, 76, 80, 72, and 79; and that the percentage in the total sample is 77. Since the procedure assures a fair degree of random selection, the generalization that approximately 77 percent of the people in the city drink coffee with their breakfast is fairly good. This is, of course, a somewhat simplified case, but it illustrates the fundamental features of the process of supporting a statistical generalization.

In making a statistical generalization, we proceed as in the method of agreement. We have a population of instances of a certain phenomenon (in the example, the inhabitants of the city). We also have a factor (in the example, the factor is 'drinking coffee with breakfast'). Our purpose is to predict the ratio of instances in which the factor is present to the totality of the population. The evidence consists in collections of instances, usually called samples. (In the example, the samples are groups of one hundred persons each). The inference is as follows: If every fair sample of the population shows a certain ratio of incidence of the factor, then the incidence of the factor in the total population has approximately the same ratio.

This type of generalization is subject to limitations similar to those we examined in the case of Mill's methods. Unknown factors may cause the samples to be biased in a certain direction so that they fail to be representative of the total population. The only way to diminish the probability of a biased sampling is to determine all possible factors that may bias the samples and devise sampling methods that neutralize them. (In the example, if we know that some ethnic groups consume coffee much more than others, we should choose our samples so that they contain a random selection of the existing ethnic groups.) The correct interpretation of data obtained by sampling can be a very complex problem; it requires the use of statistical theories that are outside the scope of this book.

The prediction we can make through statistical generalization is an approximation. None of the samples in our example showed a ratio of exactly 77 percent. The prediction is stated as 77 percent because this figure is the average or arithmetic mean of the figures. We can say that the samples show a tendency toward this figure, or, more accurately, show a tendency to vary about equally in both directions around this figure.

As indicated earlier, the study of statistical correlation gives rise to complex problems that are treated in the science of statistics and cannot be considered in the present work. But even those who do not have a theoretical background in statistics can obtain computer programs that will perform the necessary operations to yield the correlation, controlling for variables chosen by the user, simply by entering the data into the program. Nowadays, only minimal computer skills are needed to perform a well-controlled statistical analysis.

9.   Uses and Limitations of Mill's Methods

It should be noted that Mill's methods result from the careful analysis of a simple idea that human beings have used through the centuries more or less intuitively: If two things are causally connected, then they always occur together; and from the presence of one, we can infer the presence of the other, and from the absence of one, the absence of the other. Mill worked out the different ways in which this fundamental relation allows us to make inferences about causal connections.

The methods are a splendid achievement of philosophical analysis and constitute a fundamental tool of scientific investigation. However, as we have seen, their successful use is subject, to some conditions, and has some important limitations. Consider again the example of food poisoning in the dorm. To use the method of agreement and the joint method, the physician had to start with a guess about the possible causes. He used his previous knowledge about the kinds of things that cause food poisoning to limit the causes to three. If the doctor had no knowledge about the causes of food poisoning, then he might have to consider almost anything that happened at the time the students became ill as a possible cause. Then the list of factors would become enormously large, and the methods would become useless. *The methods can only be useful when we can limit the factors to a small number.* Hence, the methods are normally used together with a hypothesis or an informed guess. The hypothesis may be used at the beginning, in order to determine what factors should be considered, or it may be suggested by the results of the use of the method.

As the next chapter shows, scientists have extended the same basic reasoning used in Mill's methods, combined with sophisticated statistical techniques, to handle much more complicated causal relationships. This more sophisticated application of the reasoning emphasizes the use of theories and models whose predictions serve either to confirm or to disconfirm causal hypotheses, in the continuing quest for reliable, probabilistic knowledge of nature.

EXERCISES

Identify and analyze the following examples of the use of the inductive methods.

1. A certain chemical (we shall call it X) is used as an insecticide. One day, a chemist working at the insecticide factory finds a dead rat next to a bag of X. He guesses that the rat has eaten some X. Perhaps, he thinks, X may turn out to be a good rat poison also. So, he decides to run an experiment. He gets two groups of ten rats each. He gives the

first group food mixed with a little X. The second group receives food from the same bag, but without X. The next day the scientist finds that all the rats in group I are dead and those in group II are alive and well. From this result our chemist concludes that X will be an effective rat poison. What method has the chemist used? Explain the procedure.

2. The natives of the New Hebrides Islands were in earlier times convinced that body lice were a contributing factor to good health. For centuries they had observed that healthy people normally had lice on them, whereas people who were sick with a fever did not have any (they jumped off when the skin got too hot). This led them to their belief. Explain which of Mill's methods they actually applied. Discuss the inference involved.

3. "I have eaten chitterlings four times in my life. Every time I ate some, I had a stomach ache the following night. Since the flavorings used in chitterlings do not cause me to get sick, I concluded that it is the meat itself that gives me stomach aches." What method has been used here?

4. "When I put on my shirt this morning my chest and back started itching. Then I took off my shirt and the itch stopped immediately. I concluded that the shirt had something on it that caused me to itch." Which method has been applied here? Explain the reasoning.

5. "I tried a cup of tea with with 'Sweeto' and it had a bitter aftertaste that I didn't like. Then I tried a cup of tea from the same pot without 'Sweeto' and it didn't have a bitter aftertaste. Hence, I am fairly sure that 'Sweeto' produces a bitter aftertaste because I know this taste cannot be caused by the water I use, or by the pot, because I used the pot and the same water supply for both cups." What method has been used here? Identify the instances and factors. Make a plus-minus chart.

6. "A recent experiment shows that the presence of bacteria is connected with tooth decay. Ten monkeys were raised in a normal environment for two years. Dental examination at the beginning and at the end of this period showed that each monkey developed an average of four cavities. A second group of ten monkeys were raised in germ-free glass boxes. They were fed the same kind of food, but sterilized. The monkeys of the second group did not develop any cavities." Identify the method used. What are the phenomena, the instances, and the factors? Explaining the reasoning.

7. "John has dated Mary five times. On three of those dates, he brought her a bunch of daisies. On those three dates she developed hay fever symptoms, but not on the other two dates. So they thought Mary must be allergic either to the daisies or to John. But after examining the evidence they concluded that she is allergic to daisies, but not to John." Explain the inductive method used here. Identify the phenomenon, instances, and factors.

8. Louis Pasteur discovered that certain types of bacteria live without air. According to Pasteur's account, he had once placed under the microscope a drop of sugar solution. The drop contained bacteria, which were at first moving very rapidly. Then he observed that, whereas the bacteria in the center of the drop continued to move, those at the periphery

soon came to a standstill. He realized that these bacteria were dying as they approached the surface of the drop. From this experiment Pasteur hypothesized that these bacteria normally lived without air and were killed when they came into contact with air.

9. For about a hundred years before 1894 it was supposed that the composition of atmospheric air was accurately known. It was assumed to consist mainly of nitrogen and oxygen, plus a variable amount of water vapor, and traces of hydrogen and ammonia. It was thought that, if the oxygen of a given mass of air was removed, the remainder was practically pure nitrogen. In the course of investigations aiming at a more accurate measurement of the density of the principal gases, Lord Rayleigh noticed in 1894 that nitrogen obtained from air was somewhat heavier than nitrogen obtained from ammonia. Repeated experiments led to the same results. The weight difference led Lord Rayleigh to surmise that there must be another gas present in the atmosphere that is heavier than nitrogen. With his coworker Sir William Ramsay, Lord Rayleigh obtained from the nitrogen mixture a gas which received the name of argon.

10. The naturalist Alfred Russell Wallace (1823–1913) observed that in the North African desert, where there are no trees or brush or irregularities on the surface that offer protection to animals from their natural enemies, the upper plumage of every bird, and the fur of all smaller mammals, as well as the skin of all snakes and lizards, have the color of sand. He inferred that the color is a sort of camouflage that protects the animals from their enemies.

11. In the course of his investigations designed to refute the theory of spontaneous generation, Pasteur became more and more convinced that bacteria and their spores are found almost everywhere because they adhere to particles of dust and are blown about by the slightest breeze. To test this hypothesis he designed a dramatic experiment. He filled several dozen sterilized long-necked bottles with yeast infusion and, after boiling the liquid, sealed them by melting the tips of the necks.

    Taking them to the cellar of the Paris Observatory, where he knew the air should be still, he broke the necks of ten of the bottles, which sucked in some air. He then resealed them by again melting their tips. He repeated the same operation with another ten bottles in the yard of the observatory, where he expected some wind and more dust in the air. All the bottles were then placed in the incubation oven. The result was that nine of the ten bottles opened in the cellar were clear; no germs had grown in them. Every one of the bottles opened in the yard were cloudy—they were swarming with bacteria.

    Next, Pasteur started the most dramatic phase of the experiment. He went to Switzerland and climbed the slopes of Mont Blanc, where he opened and resealed twenty bottles at different altitudes. He found that the higher he climbed, the fewer were the bottles that became cloudy with microbes. He concluded that where the air is clearer, because there is less dust, there are fewer germs. This confirmed his theory that germs are carried by atmospheric dust.

CHAPTER **11**

Scientific Discovery

1. The Process of Scientific Reasoning

We learned in the last chapter that the methods for the determination of causal connections are devices for testing hypotheses and they cannot be used without hypotheses. They are only a part of the process of scientific discovery. In this chapter we shall examine the process as a whole.

The process of scientific discovery begins when a question (or a set of related questions) about something in nature occurs to someone. The question may be inspired by different things. It may be raised by the perception of a pattern of order through one of the methods of induction; it may come to the scientist's mind as a result of extended reflection on a particular problem; or it may result from an accidental event. A question demands an answer. The answer (if the scientist has the good fortune of finding one) takes the form of a hypothesis or theory. A hypothesis is a guess, an invention, or the result of an act of creation. The diagram on the following page illustrates the resulting process schematically.

Once the scientist has a possible answer to the question, he or she has to find out if the answer really works. To bring the hypothesis into relation to the real world, the scientist asks the question, *what would happen if the hypothesis were true*? In other words: What follows logically from the hypothesis? The scientist must try to find out the logical implications of the hypothesis. This is done by *constructing valid deductive arguments with the hypothesis as the premise*, and as many arguments as possible. If the hypothesis is formulated in mathematical terms, these arguments will involve mathematical deduction. The hypothesis is used as the main premise, but it cannot be separated from the background of accepted knowledge because in formulating a hypothesis a scientist has to make many assumptions based on generally accepted scientific knowledge in addition to the hypothesis itself.

It should be noted that all the steps described so far, except the initial observations that led to the question, occur in someone's mind. The right hand part of the diagram describes what happens in the mind; the left hand part indicates what occurs in the external world. Some of the implications of the hypothesis may be statements about specific states of affairs within the reach of the scientist to observe. Such statements are usually called *predictions*. As discussed

THE STRUCTURE OF SCIENTIFIC REASONING

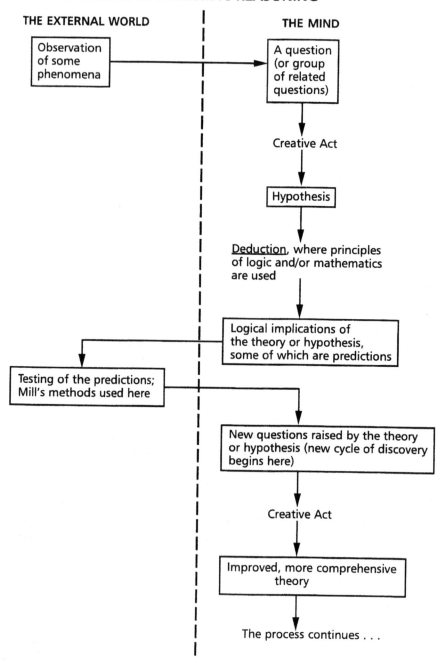

in Chapter 9, a prediction is a proposition that states that, if the hypothesis is true, a given thing should happen in a given way. Equipped with some predictions, our scientist can now turn to the external world and submit the hypothesis to a test. The test consists in discovering whether or not the predictions are true (see again the schematic diagram). It is in this phase of the scientific method that Mill's inductive methods have their place. They are the techniques by which hypotheses are tested. The result of the test allows the scientist to make a preliminary evaluation of the hypothesis. If all predictions turn out to be false, the hypothesis will probably be discarded, or at least modified. If a considerable number of predictions are true, even if some are false, the hypothesis is regarded as promising. This situation is the most common one; a successful hypothesis usually leads to true predictions for certain types of phenomena and fails with some others. The greater the number of different phenomena the hypothesis can predict, the better it is.

Once the hypothesis is shown to be more than a mere speculative guess, i.e., that it can consistently predict certain types of phenomena, it is usually called a *theory*. A theory that correctly predicts a certain range of phenomena becomes the accepted explanation of that range of phenomena, *provided that there is no theory that also explains those phenomena and is more comprehensive.*

One of the aims of scientific explanation is to achieve a coherent and unified system of explaining phenomena. The next step in the scientific method is to make the successful theory more comprehensive, i.e., to increase the range of diverse phenomena that it is capable of predicting. This may happen in three ways. (1) Sometimes the theory can be modified to make it more comprehensive. (2) Sometimes it is integrated into the framework of a very comprehensive theory already in existence. In this manner, the new theory becomes a particular case of the more comprehensive, established one. (3) The opposite can also happen. A new, more comprehensive theory can absorb an old theory, so that the latter becomes a particular case of the former. This happened in the first half of the nineteenth century with the corpuscular theory of light proposed by Newton. The wave theory of light, proposed by Christian Huygens, gained ground over the former because it was shown that a number of phenomena could be *accurately predicted by the wave theory* (for example, double refraction, polarization, diffraction, interference) which *could not be predicted by Newton's theory.*

Having examined the essential steps of the scientific method, we can see at this point, as in the diagram, that the cycle begins again. Creating a more comprehensive theory, or integrating a new theory into the accepted body of knowledge in its field, is also a creative act. When a scientist succeeds in creating a more comprehensive theory (which is a new hypothesis), a new cycle of scientific discovery begins.

Let's summarize our description of the scientific method.

1. A question (or group of related questions) arises in someone's mind.

2. By an act of imagination, a scientist creates a hypothesis, which may have been suggested by some generalization, or may be a totally new idea.

3. The scientist elaborates the implications of the hypothesis by constructing valid deductive arguments based on the hypothesis (i.e., inferences drawn from the hypothesis), using also the background of generally accepted knowledge to draw these inferences. Some of these inferences are specific predictions of previously unknown facts or relationships between facts.

4. Some predictions of the theory are tested by comparing them with the observable facts. In this step, Mill's inductive methods are used. If the hypothesis meets with some success, it comes to be called a theory.

5. The theory raises questions—either because there are phenomena that it cannot account for (i.e., it cannot predict them correctly), or because it may not be consistent with generally accepted knowledge.

6. By an act of imagination, a scientist may produce a more comprehensive theory. This may happen in three different ways. Either the new theory is assimilated into the accepted body of knowledge in the field; or the new theory proves to be more comprehensive than the older theories, thus replacing them, and incorporating them as particular cases of the new, better theory; or the theory stands alone in the field and is improved by being made more comprehensive. With this step, a new cycle of scientific discovery begins.

2. Examples of Scientific Discovery

It will be helpful now to discuss some interesting historical examples of scientific discovery.

Doctor Auenbrugger and Pulmonary Percussion. Our first example is not of the discovery of a law of nature, but rather of a diagnostic technique in medicine. It is nevertheless an excellent example of the essential features of scientific discovery. The Austrian physician Leopold Auenbrugger (1722-1809) worked at a hospital in Vienna. On one occasion, he dissected the body of a patient who had died in the hospital, and found that the lungs were partially filled with mucus. He wondered how it might have been possible for a doctor to know that this condition existed when the patient was alive. Reflecting on this one day, he suddenly remembered something from his childhood that was apparently totally unrelated to his research. His father was an innkeeper, and as a child Auenbrugger had worked at the inn. He often had to go to the cellar to get wine from barrels. He remembered a trick he had learned to find out whether a barrel had any wine in it. He would tap it; a dull thud indicated a full barrel; a hollow, resounding sound, an empty one. If the barrel was not quite full, one could find out how much wine there was in it by tapping on it with a descending motion until the sound changed—that was the surface of the wine. In a flash, Auenbrugger realized a connection: "A lung," he thought, "in a way is like a barrel." A normal lung is like an empty barrel; a lung partially full of mucus is similar to a barrel with wine in it. It occurred to him that if one tapped a patient's chest cavity and listened to the sounds produced, one might be able to tell whether there was mucus in the lungs or not. This would be a method to diagnose several illnesses of the lungs.

Auenbrugger tested his theory in several ways. He injected a liquid and also air into the lungs of a corpse and listened to the sounds produced by tapping the chest. He also identified, described, and classified the different sounds produced by percussion in live persons, and found correlations to a number of ailments of the lungs. This method, called "pulmonary percussion," is in general use today as a diagnostic tool.

The birth of percussion.
Illustration by W. C. Shepard and Dale Beronius, copyright 1927, 1930, 1937, 1945 by Alfred A. Knopf, Inc. and renewed 1955, 1965 by Mrs. Alfred B. Clark, from *The Human Body, 4th Edition, Revised* by Logan Clendening. Used by permission of Alfred A. Knopf, a division of Random House, Inc.

This discovery illustrates the different stages of scientific discovery we have described. The question that elicited the investigation is, "How could the presence of mucus in a person's lungs be diagnosed?" The hypothesis is first formulated as a vague hunch, "A lung is like a barrel." A particularly interesting feature of this discovery is that the hypothesis was suggested by an apparently irrelevant memory from childhood. This seeming irrelevance is a characteristic often found in creative thought—a relationship or connection is perceived where none seemed to exist. This illustrates the creative nature of the invention of theories. It is not the result of a logical inference, but rather a new organization of what was known, a seeing in a new perspective.

Auenbrugger made some predictions based on his hypothesis. He predicted that it should be possible to determine whether a lung has mucus by tapping the patient's chest cavity and listening to the sounds produced. This prediction turned out to be correct. Eventually, a more comprehensive technique was produced by generalizing the method to the diagnosis of tumors and many other conditions.

Newton and Gravitation. Sir Isaac Newton's theory of gravitation is one of the greatest discoveries in the history of science. An earlier German astronomer, Johannes Kepler, had discovered that the orbits of the planets around the sun were elliptical, not circles or combinations of circles, as had formerly had been thought. Kepler had established that the motion of the planets obeyed three laws: (1) The planets have elliptical orbits, with the sun at one of the foci. (2) As a planet revolves around the sun, its radius sweeps equal areas in equal times. (3) The square of the time of revolution for each planet is proportional to the cube of its mean distance to the sun.

As usually happens, this new theoretical achievement raised new questions. Why did the planets revolve around the sun in elliptical orbits? Why that particular shape? Why were the speeds not constant? What kind of force or agency could cause a motion in the shape of an ellipse? Newton, like many other people in his time, was interested in these questions.

In 1665, shortly after Newton graduated from Cambridge University, an outbreak of bubonic plague forced him to leave Cambridge and return to his mother's farm in his hometown, Woolsthorpe. He was twenty-four. There he had plenty of time to think about the questions that interested him. One day, while in the orchard by his house, he saw an apple fall at his feet. (This famous anecdote, which was assumed for generations to be a legend, has been shown to be, in all probability, true.)[1] Something happened in Newton's mind. Thoughts connected in a flash: Things "naturally" fall down. The earth appears to pull things toward it. Then he wondered, how far does this "pull" go? It seems to reach to the tops of mountains, to birds flying high in the air, to the clouds. Could it reach as far as the

---

[1] See J. Pelsener, "La Pomme de Newton," *Ciel et Terre* 531 (1987), 190–93; I. B. Cohen, "Authenticity of Scientific Anecdotes," *Nature* 157 (1948): 196–97; D. McKie and G. R. deBeer, "Newton's Apple," *Notes and Records of the Royal Society* 8 (1951–52): 48–54.

moon? But if this were so, then the moon must be falling toward the earth. Could this "falling" toward the earth be what keeps the moon in its orbit? He knew the intensity of this "pull" of the surface of the earth. A half century earlier Galileo had analyzed its effects; it causes an object to fall sixteen feet in the first second of its fall. He had also deduced from Kepler's third law and his own study of rotation, that the Earth's pull would be inversely proportional to the square of the distance to the moon. With this guess, and using some approximations, Newton calculated on the spot the force it would take to pull the moon away from a straight trajectory and keep it on a circular orbit around the earth (assuming a circular orbit as an approximation), and the value that the earth's pull would have at the distance of the moon, and he found them to be roughly equal. This was the beginning of one of the greatest discoveries in physics.

Newton did not communicate his finding to anybody, and did not develop it for a long time. He did not return to a consideration of the question of gravity until around 1684. There were formidable mathematical problems in the elaboration of the theory. Eventually, he was able to show that, assuming a gravitational force between the sun and each of the planets that is proportional to their masses and inversely proportional to their distances, the fundamental features of the motions of the planets could be mathematically deduced. Also, other phenomena such as the trajectories of comets, tides, and the law of the fall of bodies could be deduced from the principle of gravitation. Thus, the law of the fall of bodies and Kepler's three laws ceased to be the ultimate explanations of these phenomena; they became particular cases, logical implications of the more comprehensive law of gravitation. The old laws did not become false, of course; they simply ceased to be the most comprehensive principles in their respective areas. In the history of science, a similar process has occurred repeatedly and continues to do so.

Kekulé and the Composition of Organic Compounds. In the 1850s and 1860s, the German chemist Friedrich August Kekulé made two fundamental contributions to the understanding of the nature of organic compounds. In fact, his discoveries may be said to have made organic chemistry into a true science, as opposed to a collection of scattered insights and generalizations.

At that time, knowledge of the molecular structure of chemical compounds was not precise. It was possible only to determine the *relative* number of atoms a given substance contained. For example, it was known that ordinary alcohol is composed of carbon, oxygen, and hydrogen, and that there are twice as many atoms of carbon and six times as many of hydrogen as there are of oxygen, making the proportions 2:6:1. It was not known how many atoms in fact were in a molecule, and in what way or by what laws these atoms were structured. In particular, the relative proportions of the element carbon in different compounds were puzzling since they varied from one compound to another in a very irregular manner.

Thinking about these problems during a period of residence in London, Kekulé had a remarkable hallucinatory experience that led him to the creation of his first theory of the composition of organic substances. He relates that he was returning from a visit to a friend:

> I was returning by the last omnibus, "outside" as usual through the deserted streets of the metropolis, which are at other times so full of life. I fell into a reverie, and lo! the atoms were gambolling before my eyes. Whenever, hitherto, these diminutive beings had appeared to me, they had always been in motion; but up to that time I had never been able to discern the nature of their motion. Now, however, I saw how, frequently, two smaller atoms united to form a pair; how a larger one embraced two smaller ones; how still larger ones kept hold of three or four of the smaller ones; whilst the whole kept whirling in a giddy dance. I saw how the larger ones formed a chain. . . . I spent part of the night putting on paper at least sketches of these dream forms.[2]

This visionary experience led Kekulé to the inspired idea of the *carbon chain*. He saw that carbon atoms might unite together forming chains, and these might in turn combine with atoms of other elements. On the basis of this insight, in 1858, he proposed a theory that consists of two postulates:

1. Carbon atoms are quadrivalent, that is, they have four "places" or valences available for combination with other atoms. Each of these valences is filled up or "satisfied" by one atom of hydrogen or the equivalent thereof.

2. Carbon atoms have the capacity to combine with each other forming chains.

This theory explains the composition of a large number of organic compounds. For example, a carbon chain with two carbon atoms, in which the other "places" are occupied by hydrogen atoms, forms the compound called ethane with the composition C_2H_6. A chain with three carbon atoms combined with hydrogen produces propane (C_3H_8).

Kekulé's theory was extraordinarily successful. It made it possible for chemists to understand the composition of a very large number of organic substances as well as predict the existence of compounds not yet known.

In spite of the enormous success of Kekulé's theory, there remained a group of organic substances, the so-called *aromatic* compounds, whose composition could not be explained by the theory. These compounds are characterized by two facts: (1) They contain a relatively high proportion of carbon, and (2) they contain a minimum of six carbons in the molecule. The simplest compound of this group is the hydrocarbon benzene, which had been discovered by Faraday in 1825.

---

[2]Quoted by Alexander Findlay, *A Hundred Years of Chemistry* (London: Gerald Duckworth, 1937, reprinted 1955), 36–37.

In the year 1865, Kekulé was Professor of Chemistry at Ghent. One evening, while working on a textbook, he had another visionary experience. He related it thus:

> I turned my chair to the fire and dozed. Again the atoms were gambolling before my eyes. This time the smaller groups kept modestly in the background. My mental eye, rendered more acute by repeated visions of the kind, could now distinguish larger structures, of manifold conformation; long rows sometimes more closely fitted together; all twining and twisting in snake-like motion. But look! What was that? One of the snakes had seized hold of its own tail, and the form whirled mockingly before my eyes. As if by a flash of lightning I awoke.[3]

The image of the snake biting its own tail gave Kekulé the idea that solved the riddle of the structure of the aromatic compounds. In a flash it occurred to him that their basic pattern could be a *closed* carbon chain with six atoms. Arthur Koestler writes that Kekulé "dreamt what was probably the most important dream in history since Joseph's seven fat and seven lean cows."[4] The structure that occurred to him was something like this:

This theory presented an important difficulty. In this structure, the carbon atoms have only three valences. Thus the theory is inconsistent with the earlier one, which postulated four valences for carbon atoms, and which was moreover highly confirmed by a number of correct predictions. In order to eliminate this inconsistency, Kekulé modified his original idea. He now conceived the six-atom ring as formed by alternating single and double bonds, as shown in the following formula:

[3]Ibid., 38–39.

[4]Arthur Koestler, *The Act of Creation* (New York: Dell, 1964), 118.

This new conception eliminated the inconsistency, but introduced other difficulties. The theory predicted two different structures for the compound paradichlorobenzene where in fact only one type had been found. Thus, hypothetically, there would be two kinds of paradichlorobenzene, one with a double bond between the two chlorine atoms, and one with a single bond between them, as shown in the structural formulas below.

```
        H                          H
        |                          |
        C                          C
      // \                        / \\
 H — C    C — Cl          H — C    C — Cl
     |    ||                   ||   |
 H — C    C — Cl          H — C    C — Cl
      \  /                        \ //
        C                          C
        |                          |
        H                          H
```

Again Kekulé modified his theory to bring it into agreement with observation. He assumed that *the double and single bonds alternated continually.* This additional hypothesis would account for the fact that there is only one kind of paradichlorobenzene.

The theory of the benzene ring showed itself capable for explaining the essential features of the composition of the aromatic compounds. It led to a number of predictions that gave it ample confirmation. It was extremely fruitful, although later modified by more complex theories—as is continually the case in science.

Nicolas Fabri de Peiresc and the Rain of Blood. Nicolas Claude Fabri de Peiresc (1580–1637) was a gifted researcher in astronomy and other sciences.[5] He was born in Belgentier in southern France, the region where he spent most of his life. Peiresc lived in a period of great scientific discoveries. He carried out and organized a number of important astronomical observations, and was a patron to other investigators, including Pierre Gassendi. Peiresc was a priest, and also held several important public offices: he was a senator and a member of the Sovereign Court of Provence. During the famous trial of Galileo for heresy, Peiresc wrote a letter of protest to Cardinal Francesco Berberini on behalf of the great scientist. He pointed out that in the long run a condemnation of Galileo would benefit neither the cause of religion nor that of truth. If Galileo turned out to be right, he would become a martyr; and if he was wrong, he would be seen as a victim of a religion that professed mercy.

---

[5]On Peiresc's biography see *Dictionary of Scientific Biography,* ed. Charles Coulston Gillispie (New York, 1974). On Peiresc's investigation of the "rain of blood," see Pierre Gassendi, *The Mirror of True Nobility and Gentility, Being the Life of Nicolas Claudius Fabricius Lord of Peiresk, Senator of the Parliament at Aix,* tr., W. Rand (London: 1657).

In early July 1608 there appeared puddles of red-stained water on stone walls and trees in and around the city of Aix-en-Provence where Peiresc lived. The populace attributed these splashes to a "rain of blood." There were many folktales about rains of blood, which in some instances had been reported by historians. The common people regarded this occurrence with superstitious awe, and Peiresc became interested in studying the phenomenon. In gathering information about it, he was told that several farmers had been surprised by the rain of blood in the fields and had run terrified to the nearest houses. Upon close questioning, Peiresc found out that this story was false. Nobody actually knew the farmers in question, and nobody had actually *seen* the rain of blood. Some people thought that it was the work of devils and witches.

Shortly after these rather perplexing findings were made, an accident happened out of which Peiresc conceived an explanation of the phenomenon. For one of his many experiments, he had collected a caterpillar and put it in a box. One day he heard a buzzing in the box, and when he opened it, a beautiful butterfly flew out, leaving behind its cocoon. On the bottom of the box there was a red drop about the size of a small coin—the insect's excrement. Since at the time of the "rain of blood" an enormous multitude of such butterflies had been seen flying around the city, Peiresc surmised that these insects, resting on walls and in trees, had left their droppings there. The splashes were about the same size as the one in the box.

This conjecture led Peiresc to reexamine the supposed bloodstains on the stones, and found out that they were not found on housetops, nor upon the tops of fences, as would have happened if the "blood" had fallen from the sky. On the other hand, they were found in crevices, holes, and the undersides of stones, where small butterflies might find shelter. Moreover, the spotted walls were not in the middle of the town, but bordered on wooded areas. Finally, spots were only found at a moderate height, about the range in which butterflies usually fly.

Thus Peiresc found a satisfactory explanation for the rain of blood. Convincing as it was, it nonetheless eventually was proved wrong. Later investigations showed that the red splashes occurred without the presence of swarms of butterflies and therefore were not butterfly droppings. It is known now that the red color is caused by microscopic algae that under certain conditions reproduce at a very fast rate in droplets of water.

Although Peiresc's theory turned out to be wrong, his method of studying the phenomenon is exemplary. First, he examined the evidence and separated actual observations from unverified tales. Then he tested his conjecture by examining the actual position of the red droplets. He countered the superstitious fear that made it difficult to examine the actual facts by a careful rational examination of observations and testimonies. Finally, his discovery shows the role of a coincidence that can lead a mind that is attuned to a problem to see a connection that others miss.

3.   Deductive Logic in Scientific Reasoning

Although we have emphasized that inductive reasoning is essential to the process of scientific thought, it does not operate independently of the deductive methods of formal logic covered in earlier chapters. Indeed, empirical observation and experiment may be said to take place within a frame where deductive processes are constantly involved, though perhaps not obviously. It may be appropriate then to relate some formal logic procedures to the process of scientific reasoning.

We have seen that scientific theories are accepted or rejected on the basis of their capacity to predict specific events. A theory that is so formulated that no specific prediction can be derived from it is useless. A theory that predicts accurately in many situations is regarded as reliable. And the more comprehensive the theory, the better it is. When a prediction P, deduced from a theory T, turns out to be true, we say that the theory is *confirmed* by that finding. If a prediction P is found to be false, then we say that T is *disconfirmed* or *falsified.*

In the process of testing a theory, deduction is used to derive the predictions. The deductions, however, are not used to prove the theory, and cannot be used to prove the theory, because the theory is the premise, and the predictions are the conclusions that we derive from it. The predictions follow logically from the theory we have chosen. But the theory itself is not proven in any sense of the word, because the theory is always the premise.

We can also look at this question from another point of view. Suppose we have a theory T from which we can logically deduce the prediction P. Suppose we find this prediction to be true. Does this successful prediction *prove* that T is true? Let's consider the inference we would have to make to claim a deductive proof. We can say that

$$T \rightarrow P$$

and also, we know that P is true. Do these two premises together allow us to infer that T is true? The pattern that such an inference would take is as shown in the following formula:

$$T \rightarrow P$$
$$\frac{P}{\therefore \quad T}$$

This argument, as we learned in deductive logic earlier, is an instance of the fallacy of asserting the consequent. And whether we have one, or one thousand, or one million correct predictions, the result is the same. Correct predictions make a theory a good scientific explanation, but they do not prove its truth deductively. An important part of the confirmation of a theory, T, is that the prediction, P, is such that it is unlikely, given the background knowledge, that P would be true unless the theory T is true. So even though the inference pattern above is *deductively* invalid, T is nevertheless a good *inductive* inference, assuming that the prediction from it was confirmed in a well-controlled, operationally well-defined, and statistically significant way.

The situation is paradoxical. A successful scientific theory is a proposition (or a set of propositions) that we know we can use as a premise to obtain true predictions within a certain range of phenomena. At the same time, the only justification for the theory is that true predictions follow logically from it.

Scientific theories are the assumptions that the scientific community accepts in a given field at a given time, and from which we derive predictions. Theories are guesses or surmises about the hidden workings of nature; they allow us to explore the patterns of order in nature. When we use the scientific method, the theories we use are the assumptions, and the predictions are the conclusions we draw from the assumptions. We do not actually prove theories, and in the strict sense, we *cannot* prove theories. We use a theory so long as it continues to predict correctly. We reject or modify a theory that leads to predictions that conflict with experience.

The Importance of Disconfirming Instances. If we cannot prove a theory true, we can, with certain qualifications, prove it false. If a theory **T** implies a prediction **P**, and this prediction turns out to be false, we can make the following argument:

$$T \rightarrow P$$
$$\sim P$$
$$\therefore \quad \sim T$$

This argument is valid; it is a case of *modus tollens*. A theory that predicts incorrectly is false. It should be noted, however, that there are certain qualifications. If **T** is not a single statement, but a complex system of propositions, then the argument does not tell us what particular proposition makes **T** as a whole false. Secondly, the argument assumes that the rest of the accepted background of knowledge remains the same. It may happen that changes in the accepted background of knowledge alter our understanding of the premises. For instance, the prediction **P**, on more careful observation, may not be false. When a theory **T** can be shown to make a false prediction, we say that they theory is *disconfirmed* by that prediction. This process of disconfirmation is very important in the scientific method because only through it can we find under what conditions a promising theory fails to predict. When we find out what predictions turn out to be false, we can think backwards to the premises to see whether the premises can be modified to avoid the false predictions. *We must learn in what situations a theory fails to predict to be able to improve it.*

Prediction and Comprehensiveness. As we have seen, the central fact in the evaluation of theories is *prediction.* A theory will stand or fall on the basis of its capacity to predict future events. We have used the term *comprehensiveness* (or *predictive power*) to refer to the range of different types of phenomena that a theory is capable of predicting correctly. The more comprehensive a theory, the better it is. One of the aims of scientific explanation is to explain and predict as many phenomena as possible with as few assumptions as possible. The greater the variety of different phenomena that can be brought into a unity by a theory, the better the theory. Therefore, if a situation arises at one point in which two rival theories explain roughly the same range of phenomena, that one will be accepted which ultimately proves to have the greater comprehensiveness. Conflicts between rival theories have occurred frequently in the history of science.

Since scientific theories cannot be ultimately proven, whether a theory is *true* cannot be answered in a definitive manner. For this reason, the terms "fruitful" and "useful" are often used in discussions of the scientific method to describe a successful theory. The French physiologist and philosopher Claude Bernard repeatedly said that scientific theories are neither true nor false; they are fruitful or sterile.

As we inspect the history of any science, we find a succession of theories with increasing degrees of comprehensiveness. A theory begins by bringing in a new insight that increases our knowledge of the field. It leads to predictions and often to new factual discoveries, which are made possible by its predictions; i.e., it proves *fruitful*. Then, usually as a result of the very insights and discoveries that it has produced, the theory begins to lead to difficulties; phenomena are found that it cannot explain. Such difficulties lead a creative scientist to seek a more comprehensive theory. Paradoxically, a successful theory creates an expansion of knowledge that may eventually destroy it. However, a theory that has been superseded may live on in the form of a particular case of the theory that replaces it.

CHAPTER 12

What Is Philosophy?

In the preceding chapters we have covered a great deal of material about reasoning. We have seen how to formulate valid deductive arguments, to identify and avoid fallacies, and to utilize the scientific method to obtain rational explanations of natural phenomena. All these techniques are used to reach reliable conclusions and avoid erroneous beliefs. In brief, a knowledge of logic assists us in what is usually called "the pursuit of truth," and the pursuit of truth, in its most general sense, is the central concern of philosophy, of which logic is a branch. This concluding chapter is intended, then, to give the reader a brief overview of the general subject of philosophy.

1. The Nature of Philosophy

Philosophy, put in the simplest way, is the name of any attempt to think clearly and consistently about reality. Our English word 'philosophy' is derived from the Greek word 'philosophia', which is composed of two parts. The first is the stem common to the words *philos* (friend, lover) and *philia* (friendship). The second is the word *sophia*, which means 'wisdom'. Thus the etymology yields the meaning 'love of wisdom'.

Philosophy is not necessarily an academic discipline with a specific subject matter. It is rather the activity of thinking a person engages in when trying to clarify his or her understanding of any aspect of reality. Such a process of clarification is usually called *philosophizing*. Since this process is based on the human faculty of reason, philosophizing is also defined often as the process of criticizing fundamental beliefs and the reasons we have to hold them.

Through this process of philosophizing, a thinker may create theories about the nature of things. A statement of theories reached through this process is called a philosophy. In this sense we talk about Plato's philosophy, Kant's philosophy, and so on. Thus we see that the term 'philosophy' has two different, but closely related, meanings; (a) the activity of clarifying one's understanding of any aspect of reality through rational thinking, i.e. philosophizing; and (b) a statement of theories a thinker has reached through such a process.

We can get a clearer idea of the nature of philosophy if we consider the different attitudes people may bring to the situation in which they need to acquire knowledge. In general we can say that there are three different attitudes one can take. We shall call them the practical, the scientific, and the philosophical attitudes.

The Practical Attitude. The practical attitude is that of a person who has a problem and wants it solved. When we take this attitude, we are concerned with finding a particular solution to a particular problem. If we find a solution that works, we are satisfied. We are not concerned with finding out why the solution works. We are not interested in investigating the relationships the problem may have to other things, nor searching for general principles.

Suppose a man wants to build a new room in his house. For this he needs to find out what kind of beams and beam structure to use. If he takes the practical attitude, he will not be concerned with the theoretical reasons that make a certain kind of structure necessary. If he gets reliable, practical information, he will be satisfied. He will use techniques that are known to work, and his problem will thus be solved.

The Scientific Attitude. The scientific attitude seeks to find out the general laws that govern a particular kind of phenomenon. The science of physics, for example, investigates the general laws of matter and motion. The sciences in general investigate the laws of phenomena by means of a method called the *hypothetico-deductive* method, which we have studied in some detail in Chapters 9 and 10. The essential point is that scientists create *theories*, which are used to make *predictions*; theories that can systematically predict phenomena in a given area are accepted as good explanations. Scientists continually seek to make their theories more *comprehensive* by modifying them to encompass a greater range of true predictions. From our analysis of the scientific method we have seen that one of the most important characteristics of scientific theories is that they can be used for the *prediction* and *control* of phenomena.

Each of the sciences deals with a specific kind of phenomena. Physics deals with phenomena that can be reduced to properties of matter and motion; biology deals with phenomena that are characteristic of living beings; sociology with group behavior in human societies; astronomy with the characteristics of celestial bodies; and so on.

In brief, the purpose of a science is to find the laws of a specific type of phenomenon, and in turn whatever can be surmised about the nature of things on the basis of the laws found. Each science deals with a specific kind of phenomena and necessarily disregards the rest. This is a very important fact: Each science abstracts from the concrete reality we experience in order to isolate a specific type of phenomena. Suppose, for example, a physicist, with the help of an assistant, is studying the laws of collision of elastic bodies by hitting billiard balls on a pool table. The physicist analyzes the situation in terms of the properties of the balls and their motion: forces, masses, velocities, acceleration, momentum, etc. But the moving and colliding balls are a part of a larger situation the physicist does not consider. A ball is animated with a force *because* the assistant hit it with a cue, and while doing this (a) some contractions of the arm muscles occur. And the muscles contract because (b) an act of will, which occurs because (c) the physicist gave the command to hit the ball. The whole investigation takes place because (d) the physicist believes that the possible discovery of new theoretical truths has value and (e) the assistant wants to earn some extra money.

The physicist's investigation does not deal with the phenomena listed under (a), (b), (c), (d), and (e); they are disregarded for the purposes of the investigation. *This is not a short-coming of the science of physics; it is the business of physics to deal with phenomena that can be analyzed in terms of the properties of matter and motion.* The phenomena involved in (a) are the subject of physiology, and the factors involved in (b) concern the interaction between the mind and the body. A consideration of (c) would lead to the study of how human languages work, and dealing with (d) would raise the question of the value of theoretical truth. And there may well be many other factors in the concrete situation facing the physicist that might be considered.

Take another example. For an astronomer the earth is a large mass of matter with a quasi-spherical shape. That is all the astronomer needs to consider to study the motions of the earth in relation to other heavenly bodies. The irregularities created by mountains, oceans, etc., and the existence of living beings on its surface can be neglected. So the astronomer eliminates by abstraction many phenomena that exist on the earth (including, incidentally, his or her own existence) because such phenomena do not have, as far as we know, any perceptible influence on the phenomena concerning astronomy.

Thus, we see that each of the sciences, by its very nature, deals with a certain kind of phenomena and necessarily abstracts from the concrete reality of the world. This means that each science gives us *a partial picture of reality*. The foregoing analysis leads us to a very important question. What is the connection between the theories of the different sciences? For example, do the laws of physics have any relevance to psychology or sociology? Can the laws of physiology help us understand thought? Such questions are by no means easy to answer. Although we cannot carry out a full discussion of these questions, we can point out an important consequence: Such questions *cannot be addressed by each of the sciences separately*. In general, the nature and aims of the scientific attitude are as follows:

1. The scientific attitude looks for laws—patterns of order in nature.
2. It uses a specific method in which theories are formulated and tested according to their capacity to predict phenomena systematically.
3. It leads to knowledge that can be used to predict and sometimes control phenomena.
4. Each science deals with a specific type of phenomena; thus, each science abstracts from reality and gives us a partial picture of it.

The Philosophical Attitude. The philosophical attitude may be described as an attitude of *wonder.* It is the attitude we take when we want to know the nature and significance of something just for the sake of knowing it. Philosophy, as Aristotle put it, begins with wonder. This remarkable feeling has been insightfully described by the poet Emily Dickinson:

> Wonder is not precisely knowing
> And not precisely knowing not;
> A beautiful but bleak condition
> He has not lived who has not felt.[1]

The philosophical attitude is a desire for knowledge for its own sake. This does not mean that such knowledge does not have practical consequences; it usually does. But the motivation for thought is not to acquire practical knowledge, but to see reality more clearly.

The philosophical attitude leads people to ask questions about the *nature* of the object of their concern, and also about the *relations* of that object to other things, in order to see its proper place in the world and to understand its significance. Philosophical reflection is concerned with acquiring a *unified understanding* of reality. Philosophy, then, is not a science with a specific subject-matter, but rather the name of the activity of philosophizing, the activity of seeking to understand reality in a unified way. One can philosophize about anything.

The preceding discussion leads us to the following working definition of philosophy: *Philosophy is a human activity that is inspired by wonder and consists in the attempt to clarify one's understanding of reality by means of reason with the aim of achieving a unified view.*

We say that philosophizing is an attempt to *clarify* one's understanding of reality, because nobody starts philosophical reflection in a state of complete ignorance. By the time our rational faculties have developed to the point that we begin to raise philosophical questions, we already have a great deal of knowledge. It is the perception of an *inadequacy* in our present knowledge that leads us to philosophical reflection, in order to obtain more adequate knowledge. The experience of wonder seems to consist in the paradoxical feeling that our knowledge of something leads us to surmise that there is a deeper or more adequate knowledge to be had.

2.   The Branches of Philosophy

Philosophy is traditionally divided into six main branches: logic, metaphysics, epistemology, ethics, aesthetics, and political philosophy.

Logic is the study of the correct principles of reasoning. It is the fundamental tool of all rational thinking.

Metaphysics, or ontology, is the study of the nature of reality as a whole. It deals with the most general characteristics of reality as a whole. In philosophy, the term 'being' is often used as a collective term to refer to everything that exists. Hence, metaphysics is often defined as the *science of being* in general. It deals with questions such as: What exists? Are there one or

---

[1]Thomas H. Johnson, ed., *The Complete Poems of Emily Dickinson* (Boston: Little, Brown & Co., 1960), 577.

more ultimate substances of which everything that exists is composed? Is the universe ultimately composed of matter or is it ultimately a spiritual reality? (Or are there two distinct substances, matter and spirit?) Why does the universe have an orderly structure? Did the universe come into being or is it eternal? Why do some things cause others? What is the nature of space—is it infinite or finite? What is the nature of time? These and many such speculative questions are the domain of metaphysics.

Epistemology, or theory of knowledge, is the study of the nature and foundations of knowledge. It deals with questions such as: Is knowledge of reality possible? What are the sources of knowledge? What is the proper use of reason? Can we trust the evidence of our senses? What is the foundation of scientific knowledge?

Ethics, or moral philosophy, studies moral beliefs, i.e., conceptions of right and wrong, good and bad, virtue and vice. It deals with questions such as: Why do human beings (unlike other animals) have conceptions of right and wrong? What is the meaning of concepts like 'right,' 'wrong,' etc.? What is the significance of moral conscience in human beings? Does it indicate that mankind in general has an innate awareness of a higher spiritual reality, or are moral beliefs merely the result of social rules that were originally created because they were socially useful? Are there moral standards that can be shown to be valid for all places and all times, or on the contrary, are there no objectively valid standards of conduct?

Aesthetics, or philosophy of art, is the branch of philosophy that deals with the nature of art, beauty, and artistic creation. In contemplating natural phenomena or human creations, many people experience feelings that they value very highly. They often say that they are *moved* by the *beauty* of certain objects. What is the nature of these experiences, which are usually called aesthetic experiences? What is apprehended through them? If what is apprehended is beauty, what is beauty? Are there canons of beauty that are valid for all places and all times, or is beauty "in the eye of the beholder?" Works of art are often said to contain profound insights about reality. How are these insights conveyed? All human societies have developed a variety of forms of art, and they all cherish and preserve their great works of art. What is the nature and the foundation of the great value human beings see in works of art? Why do works of art have such a great power to move us? Do they bestow upon us glimpses of a high spiritual reality that we cannot otherwise perceive? Or does their power depend upon some psychological or physiological satisfaction they give us? Such questions typically characterize the study of aesthetics.

Political philosophy studies the institutions through which human beings are organized into a society. An essential characteristic of human beings is that they live in society, and a society, in order to function, must be to some degree orderly. A social order is achieved through structures of authority through which certain individuals (such as kings, presidents, magistrates, legislators, judges, etc.) are empowered to make decisions in the name of society. And these decisions must be generally accepted as binding by most of the members of that society and habitually obeyed. What is the nature and the origin of social order? Do human societies have a merely utilitarian function, or do they make possible the full actualization of the individual human being? What are the essential characteristics of the different types of social order (monarchy, aristocracy, direct democracy, representative democracy, tyranny)? What is a legitimate government? What is justice? Is there a form of government that is the best possible in all places and at all times?

The preceding disciplines are the fundamental branches of formal philosophy. However, as we observed earlier, it is possible to philosophize about any aspect of reality. Whenever we ask questions about the ultimate nature and significance of anything, we are philosophizing. For example, if we seek to answer questions about the nature and significance of the natural sciences, if we attempt to clarify and criticize their fundamental principles, we are doing philosophy of science. Likewise, we can do philosophy of history, philosophy of education, philosophy of religion, philosophy of economics, philosophy of mathematics, philosophy of language, philosophy of music, philosophy of literary criticism, philosophy of ritual, philosophy of sports, and so on. As we have seen, philosophy is the term for a kind of rational thinking. It consists in asking, and attempting to answer, questions about the nature and significance of something. Anybody who asks questions of this kind at any time philosophizes. This pursuit is not the exclusive property of a group of specialists; it is a fundamental human activity that almost everyone engages in—indeed, is forced by many vicissitudes of life to engage in—on many occasions.

The authors hope that the study of this book will encourage readers to engage in some further study of the philosophical tradition and to engage in rational and independent thinking about the ultimate questions that their life experience will inevitably thrust upon them.

CPSIA information can be obtained
at www.ICGtesting.com
Printed in the USA
FSHW021323031219
64683FS

9 780757 512476